Ritual Humor in Highland Chiapas

Texas Pan American Series

White Heads dance beside a Spaniard. (Photo by Frank Cancian)

Ritual Humor in Highland Chiapas

By Victoria Reifler Bricker

UNIVERSITY OF TEXAS PRESS, AUSTIN & LONDON

The Texas Pan American Series is published with the assistance of a revolving publication fund established by the Pan American Sulphur Company.

The publication of this book was assisted by a grant from the Andrew W. Mellon Foundation.

Library of Congress Cataloging in Publication Data

Bricker, Victoria Reifler, 1940–
 Ritual humor in highland Chiapas.

 (Texas pan-American series)
 Bibliography: p.
 1. Tzotzil Indians—Rites and ceremonies.
 2. Tzotzil wit and humor—History and criticism.
 3. Indians of Mexico—Dances. I. Title.
 F1221.T9B74   970.4'27   73-6501
 ISBN 0-292-77004-9

Composition and printing by The University
 of Texas Printing Division, Austin
Binding by Universal Bookbindery, Inc., San Antonio

Ta šak'be h-beh ʔelov;
　　Ta šak'be h-beh loʔil;
　　　　Ta šak'be h-beh ȼeʔeh,
Ta šoral,
　　Ta ʔamak',
Ta spasik sk'in;
　　Ta spasik spasku,
Htotik hesus,
　　Htotik lasareno.

They will offer a little entertainment;
　　They will offer a little joking;
　　　　They will evoke a little laughter,
On the roadway,
　　In the plaza.
They will celebrate the festival;
　　They will celebrate the holiday,
Of our father Jesus,
　　Of our father the Nazarene.

CONTENTS

PLATES

MAPS

FIGURES

PREFACE

It was quite by accident that I first became aware of the genre of humor which I call "ritual humor." In August 1965 I went to highland Chiapas to carry out the research for my doctoral dissertation on the humor of the Zinacanteco Indians. In early December of that year, one of my informants informed me that my knowledge of Zinacanteco humor would not be complete unless I attended the fiestas of Christmas, New Year's, and the Sixth of January (Epiphany). He said that he would try to obtain permission for me to stay in the house of his future father-in-law, who would be a religious official during the coming year and would be sworn into office on New Year's Day. He urged me to tape-record portions of these fiestas and assured me that it would be feasible to do so if I stayed in the house of his fiancée's father. Thus, according to plan, on the day before New Year's I went with my tape recorder to the house of my informant's prospective father-in-law. When I arrived, some members of his household instructed me to hang the tape recorder on a hook near the door of the house. About an hour later we began to hear music in the distance and I was told that in about ten minutes I should turn on the tape recorder. About ten minutes later a group of costumed people arrived and put on a performance in the courtyard in front of the house. There was a great deal of laughter, but there were so many conversations going on at once that I did not know what people were laughing at. The tape recorder, of course, recorded all the conversations faithfully; the data are presented in chapter 2.

It was not until several weeks later, when an informant had transcribed the tape for me, that I realized the significance of what had occurred on that occasion. Although anthropologists had been working in Zinacantan for more than five years at that time, the performance in question had remained a puzzle because no one understood the verbal behavior. Without a transcription of the utterances of the performers, the fiesta seemed like a confused jumble of figures drawn from several historical periods. The tape revealed that, although historically unrelated elements were present, these elements had been "syncretized" and organized into coherent themes. Furthermore, the tape indicated that the costumed figures were humorists with the license to make obscene and sacrilegious remarks in the context of religious ritual. I discovered from follow-up interviews that these humorists were the only people in the community permitted such license. My task during the next few months was to find out more about these humorists, whom I dubbed "ritual humorists" because their humorous performances took place only in ritual contexts.

The operational definition of humor which guided my field work was inspired by Edmonson's characterization of humor as a cultural tradition—"an assemblage of observed regularities in behavioral sequences leading to laughter" (1952:6). In terms of this definition, humorous behavior must be interaction behavior, because it is the audience's response which determines whether an action may be defined as humorous or not. I found it useful to phrase my definition of humor in terms of Goffman's dramaturgical model of interaction (1959:15–16): humor is a cultural tradition which characterizes a class of social interactions in which actors behave in ways which stimulate laughing responses from audiences.

Zinacantecos make a fundamental distinction between humor that occurs in everyday contexts and humor that takes place during fiestas (Bricker 1968:40). Fiestas are one of the contexts for religious ritual; they are therefore ritual settings. I discovered that in fiesta settings there are performers in distinctive costumes who stimulate laughing responses from audiences. Their costumes bear no resemblance to clothing worn in everyday contexts. It is the humor of these costumed performers that Zinacantecos call "fiesta" humor. I call the performers "ritual humorists" and their performances "ritual humor" because the fiesta setting in which they are found is a ritual setting.

I learned that humor of this type also occurs at the fiesta of San Sebastián, which takes place in late January. I made arrangements similar to those I had made for New Year's Day to tape-record ritual humor at that fiesta. The tapes revealed that, at this fiesta too, the ritual humor was based on a limited number of themes which developed as the fiesta ran its course. I began to wonder, then, if there were not fiestas in other Mayan communities at which ritual humorists put on dramatic performances which might be compared with those of Zinacantan.

The best opportunities to tape-record ritual humor occurred during the visits of the ritual humorists to the homes of religious officials because recording could be done less conspicuously in a house than outside in a large crowd. Furthermore, the acoustics were better in the houses than outdoors; informants transcribed tapes which had been recorded indoors with ease.

There are three fiestas in Zinacantan at which ritual humorists perform, and during all three they visit the homes of religious officials. It occurred to me that this might be true in other Mayan communities —that if I wished to make a comparative study of ritual humor, I should make arrangements to stay in the homes of religious officials during the fiestas which interested me. My hunch was confirmed by the following statement made by the Spanish priest, Fray Diego de Landa, in describing the Maya of Yucatán: "On the evening of that day they went forth with a great procession of people, and with a large number of their comedians from the house of the lord . . . The comedians went during these five days among the principal houses, playing their pieces and collected the gifts which were given to them, and they carried the whole of them to the temple where, when the five days were ended and past, they divided the gifts among the lords, priests and dancers" (Tozzer 1941:158).

Before 1969 the only communities of highland Chiapas for which ethnographies had been published were Chamula (Pozas 1959) and Chenalhó (Guiteras-Holmes 1961). Both Pozas and Guiteras-Holmes

mention performances of costumed figures during the fiesta of Carnaval. There, as in Zinacantan, the costumed figures blacken their faces:
they are called Blackmen in Zinacantan and Chenalhó and Monkeys
in Chamula. Neither Pozas nor Guiteras-Holmes indicates whether the
performances of these Blackmen or Monkeys are humorous. However,
Guiteras-Holmes does mention entertainers who "mock the serious
ceremonies, the races, and the ruling political and religious function-
aries" (1961:101). I suspected that the Blackmen of Chenalhó and the
Monkeys of Chamula were ritual humorists. Fortunately Pozas and
Guiteras-Holmes do say that these costumed figures visit the homes of
religious officials during the course of the fiesta of Carnaval (Pozas
1959:178; Guiteras-Holmes 1961:101). Armed with this knowledge,
I prepared to return to highland Chiapas to conduct an investigation of
ritual humor in Chamula and Chenalhó. I returned at the beginning
of December 1967, with the intention of staying until the end of
March 1968. I allowed myself two and one-half months (from December 1, 1967, until February 16, 1968) to obtain permission from
the authorities in Chamula and Chenalhó to perform this research and
to make arrangements to stay in the homes of religious officials during
the fiesta of Carnaval.

Due to a series of fortunate circumstances the task of obtaining permission proved to be less difficult than I had anticipated. My friend Dr.
Gary H. Gossen was at that time engaged in field work in Chamula,
and he very kindly offered to introduce me to that town's civil and religious authorities, whose assistance I needed. It was also through Dr.
Gossen that I made the acquaintance of several Chamulas who later
worked for me as informants. By the beginning of January 1968 all the
necessary arrangements had been completed for me to stay at the home
of one of the religious officials who would sponsor the fiesta of Carnaval in Chamula. In the meantime I worked with informants, learning from them what the fiesta of Carnaval was all about.

Through Dr. Gossen I also made the acquaintance of Jacinto
Arias, the son of Manuel Arias Sohóm, who had been Guiteras-
Holmes's chief source of information when she made her study of
Chenalhó. Jacinto Arias offered to introduce me to his father, who

he thought might be willing to give me some data on the fiesta of Carnaval in Chenalhó. We arranged for me to go to Chenalhó at the end of January 1968 to meet Manuel Arias and to make arrangements to stay in the house of a religious official during the fiesta. Those arrangements were made without difficulty.

I originally thought that it would be possible for me to attend the fiesta of Carnaval in both communities, since the fiesta is usually celebrated on different days in Chamula and Chenalhó. Carnaval always occurs exactly four weeks after the fiesta of San Sebastián in Chenalhó (Guiteras-Holmes 1961:101), while the dates for the same fiesta in Chamula are determined by the Easter calendar. But for the first time in many years, although they were calculated on the basis of different calendars, the dates for the fiesta of Carnaval in the two communities coincided. Thus it was not possible for me to take advantage of the arrangements I had made in one of the two communities, and I elected to forego being present at the fiesta in Chenalhó. My data on the fiesta in Chenalhó are therefore less complete than the data I obtained for Zinacantan and Chamula. The chapter on the fiesta of Carnaval in Chenalhó is based on interviews with three informants, supplemented by Guiteras-Holmes's field observations from 1944 (Guiteras-Holmes 1946). I am grateful to Gertrude Duby de Blom who took photographs for me in Chenalhó.

In all, I spent four months in Chiapas that winter, collecting data on ritual humor in Chamula and Chenalhó, in addition to the eight months I had spent in Zinacantan during the 1965–1966 field season. I also returned to Zinacantan in 1968 to retape ritual humor on the Sixth of January and during the fiesta of San Sebastián. The object of retaping the humor was to determine to what extent it changes from year to year. The results of this investigation are presented in chapter 7.

ACKNOWLEDGMENTS

My fieldwork in Chiapas was supported by NIMH Predoctoral Fellowship MH-20,345; the Harvard Chiapas Project directed by Professor Evon Z. Vogt; and a grant from the Harvard Graduate Society. I am deeply grateful to these institutions for their generous support, which has made the research possible.

There are three people to whom I wish to give my very special thanks. They are Professor Evon Z. Vogt of Harvard University, Dr. Robert M. Laughlin of the Smithsonian Institution, and Dr. Gary H. Gossen, now at the University of California at Santa Cruz.

Professor Vogt has been my friend and adviser since I entered Harvard University in 1962, and it was he who introduced me to Mexico and highland Chiapas. Under his guidance I experienced the first difficult weeks of field work, and I would here like to express my gratitude to him for his continuing interest in and encouragement of my research and his help on practical matters, both in the field and at the university.

I am grateful to Dr. Laughlin for letting me use a preliminary version of his Tzotzil-English dictionary. Without the use of that dictionary I would have been unable to translate the taped and textual materials on which this work is based. Dr. Laughlin has also been kind enough to correct the translations of many of my texts, and he has made many helpful comments and suggestions concerning my research.

I have already mentioned the immeasurable assistance provided by Dr. Gossen in securing permission for me to conduct field work in Chamula and in introducing me to informants from both Chamula and Chenalhó. I benefited greatly from his knowledge of Chamula culture, which he shared with me freely, and from the opportunity to consult his field notes and texts concerning the fiesta of Carnaval, which he very generously put at my disposal. Without his unstinting help and cooperation my research in those communities would not have been possible.

In San Cristóbal Las Casas I was especially helped by Gertrude Duby de Blom, Patricia Arca, Leopoldo Velasco Robles, and the González family at the Baños Mercedarios. Mrs. Blom's excellent library was of great assistance to me, and I am very grateful to her for "covering" the fiesta of Carnaval in Chenalhó for me with her camera while I was occupied in Chamula. Both she and Miss Arca outdid themselves in making me feel at home at Casa Blom during my last field trip.

In Zinacantan, the assistance of José Hernández Gerónimo, Do-

mingo de la Torre Pérez, Domingo Pérez Hacienda, the Vázquez family
of Nabenčauk, and José Sánchez, who was *presidente municipal* of
Zinacantan at the time, was most appreciated. All of them took a lively
interest in my work and called my attention to events which they
thought relevant to my research. I am grateful also for the cooperation
of Salvador López Calixto, Manuel López Calixto, Mariano López
Calixto, Salvador Guzmán López, Mariano Gómez Pérez, Agustín
López ʔIk'alavil, and Juan Gómez Oso of Chamula, and Manuel Arias
Sohóm, Jacinto Arias, and Miguel López ₵u of Chenalhó.

In February 1971, at the invitation of Ermilo Marín Mendoza, I
made a brief trip to the Yucatán peninsula to observe the fiesta of
Carnaval in Hocabá. Mr. Marín had previously assisted me in the instruction of his language (Yucatec Maya) at Tulane University for
several months in 1970. I am indebted to Mr. Marín not only for his
hospitality, but also for the data he gave me concerning the fiesta of
Carnaval in his village. I am grateful to the Center for Latin American
Studies at Tulane University for having made Mr. Marín available for
this work.

My stay in Mexico was made pleasant by the warm hospitality of
Professor and Mrs. Vogt, George and Jane Collier, Gary and Eleanor
Gossen, Jorge Capriata, Carol Sawyer, Janet Marren, and Marcey
Jacobson. More recently I am grateful for the kindness of Mrs. E.
Wyllys Andrews IV, who made it possible for me to see the Dance of
the Pig's Head at the fiesta of Concepción in Telchaquillo (Yucatán)
in December 1971.

I would like to express my appreciation to other fieldworkers who
have worked in highland Chiapas, whose notes and publications supplement my own observations. The notes of Professor Vogt, Dr.
Guiteras-Holmes, Dr. Laughlin, Dr. Gossen, and Professor Frank C.
Miller were particularly relevant to my research. Mrs. Vogt saved me
much time by summarizing the information about fiestas which she
found in the field notes of the Harvard Chiapas Project, especially
those of Dr. John D. Early, Dr. Laughlin, and Manuel Zabala Cubillos.

Four people read the manuscript and offered suggestions for im-
proving it. Professor and Mrs. Vogt and Dr. Laughlin brought me up
to date on highland Chiapas ethnography and offered valuable criti-

cisms of some of my interpretations. Professor Munro S. Edmonson helped to put my data into geographical perspective by drawing my attention to Yucatecan and Guatemalan parallels in ritual humor.

I would like to take this opportunity to thank the following people who have, in conversation, made helpful suggestions for the study of humor: Professor Arden R. King, Professor Richard E. Greenleaf, Professor A. Richard Diebold, Professor Alberto M. Vázquez, Dr. Peggy Golde, Dr. Jorge Capriata, Dr. George Appell, Dr. Eugene Ogan, Dr. Karl Heider, Dr. Daniel B. Silver, Dr. Louise Lamphere, Dr. George A. Collier, Dr. Jane F. Collier, Dr. Antonio Gilman, Dr. Michelle Zimbalist Rosaldo, Carter Wilson, and Nancy Chodorow. At Tulane University, Professor Edmonson, Professor Donald Robertson, and Miss Marjorie Le Doux were of great assistance in locating accounts of pre-Columbian humor in Mexico and Guatemala.

I am also deeply indebted to Sharon Maal, who made invaluable suggestions concerning the translation and interpretation of *bombas* in chapter 4. I would also like to thank her here for the painstaking care with which she typed the manuscript.

Finally, my husband, Harvey M. Bricker, has made many contributions to my research, not the least of which was putting up with my prolonged absences during field trips. I appreciate his sympathetic understanding for my love of field work and his willingness to structure our marriage around that commitment. His insistence that my translations of Tzotzil humor be colloquial rather than literal has become a guiding principle of this book. In order to put this principle into practice he has served as informant on numerous occasions when my knowledge of colloquial American obscenity was inadequate. Last, but not least, I would like to thank him for his advice and assistance with the illustrations for this book.

V. R. B.

Ritual Humor in Highland Chiapas

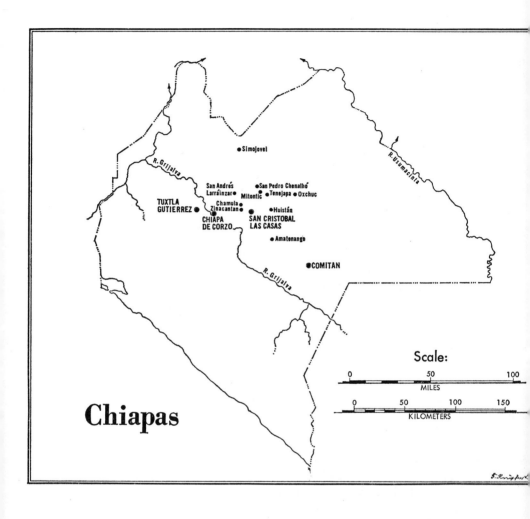

Chiapas

Scale:

MILES

KILOMETERS

1. Introduction

Zinacantan, Chamula, and Chenalhó are neighboring Mayan communities situated in highland Chiapas, Mexico, not far from the town of San Cristóbal Las Casas. The inhabitants of all three communities speak dialects of the Tzotzil language.

The population of Zinacantan in 1960 was 7,650 persons (Cancian 1965:7). By now it has increased to 11,600 inhabitants (Vogt, personal communication). Gossen estimates the population of Chamula as approximately 40,000 persons (1970:57). The population of Chenalhó in 1961 was 5,500 persons (Guiteras-Holmes 1961:8). Most Indians in the highlands of Chiapas live in widely dispersed hamlets. Chamula, Chenalhó, and Zinacantan comprise distinct political units called *municipios* by the Mexican government. Cancian suggests that they are equivalent to townships (1965:7). Each township has a cere-

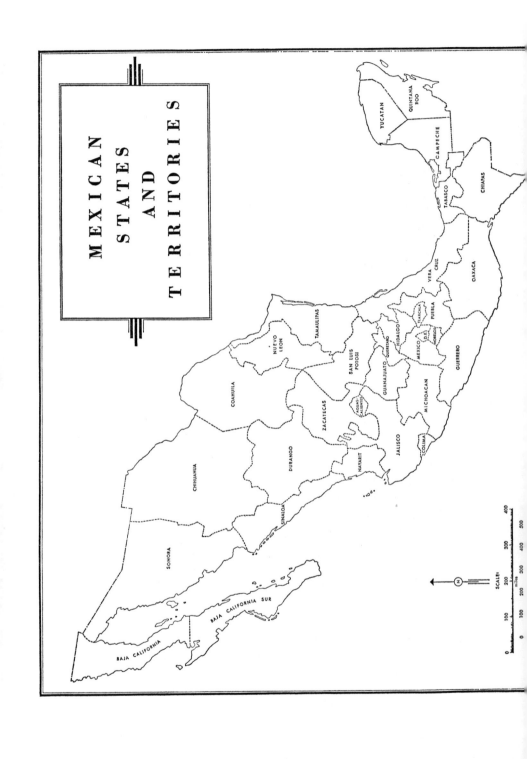

MEXICAN STATES AND TERRITORIES

monial and political center called *hteklum* where the principal churches, the town hall, a school, a medical clinic, and some small shops are located.

In Zinacantan the important political and religious units are the township and the hamlet. Chamula is divided into three wards, called barrios, each of which takes its name from its own patron saint: San Juan, San Pedro, and San Sebastián. Each barrio is represented by political officers in the town government and religious officials in the religious organization. Chenalhó was formerly divided into endogamous upper and lower sections, corresponding approximately to the southern and northern halves of the community respectively, which were equally represented in the political and religious bodies (Guiteras-Holmes 1961:64–65). There are no longer such geographically based endogamous groups in Chenalhó, nor do geographic considerations enter into the recruitment of political and religious officers.

The highlands of Chiapas are inhabited by two major ethnic groups: Ladinos and Indians. "Ladinos are persons who wear European clothes and speak Spanish as their principal language (although their ancestors may be Indians)" (Cancian 1965:7 n.). Historically, relations between the two groups have been hostile. "Ladinos in general look down on the Indians, accuse them of witchcraft and speak derisively of their customs and beliefs while trying to make the best of them in commercial transactions" (Guiteras-Holmes 1961:23). Many Ladinos view Indians as uncivilized, dirty, and uneducable. Indians, for their part, regard Ladinos as exploitative and aggressive; they associate Ladinos with the devil in their myths and dreams. Some years ago the Indian inhabitants of Chamula expelled their resident Ladino population from the township, and to this day they permit no Ladinos to live within the boundaries of the township, with the exception of some school teachers. Zinacantan and Chenalhó support small Ladino populations in their ceremonial centers. Only about fifty Ladinos lived in Zinacantan Center in 1960.

The traditional occupation for men in all three communities is maize agriculture. In Chamula the man-land ratio does not permit all men to make their living by farming. Therefore many Chamulas supplement their farm incomes by hiring themselves out to work on the land of wealthier members of the community or of Zinacantecos. Some Chamulas support themselves by engaging in the manufacture of pottery, musical instruments, ceremonial robes, and charcoal, which they sell to Indians in other communities and, in the case of pottery and charcoal, to Ladinos.

The town governments in the three communities are headed by men called *presidente* and include *síndicos, regidores, jueces,* and *mayores.* In Chamula and Chenalhó, but not Zinacantan, there are officials called *alcaldes* and *gobernadores.* The position of *mayor cabildo* exists uniquely in Chamula, and the position of *alguacil* is today peculiar to Chenalhó. In the past, however, there were *alguaciles* in Zinacantan who functioned as tax collectors (Zabala 1961:148). The *presidente* serves as the mayor of the township and is the principal link between the Mexican government and the Indian community. He also takes a leading role in mediating legal disputes. In Zinacantan the *síndico* is like a vice-mayor, who substitutes for the *presidente* when he is absent. In Chamula the ranking *alcalde* is the *presidente*'s alternate; the *síndico* takes care of collecting taxes in the market. In Chenalhó "the síndico, in actual practice, is the president's assistant and generally accompanies him" (Guiteras-Holmes 1961:80). *Gobernadores* in Chamula look after the church. The *jueces* are judges who play a role in settling disputes. *Regidores* in Zinacantan have no special responsibilities; in Chenalhó the *regidores* are in charge of the ritual aspects of political life, bearing standards in all religious ceremonies, determining which men to appoint to office, and swearing them in on New Year's Day (Guiteras-Holmes 1961:81). Those duties are assumed by the *mayor cabildo* in Chamula. In Chenalhó the *alcaldes* are in charge of social welfare. "They are spiritually and materially responsible for the respect due to life and limb" (Guiteras-Holmes 1961:80). The *alcaldes* of Chamula collect the taxes which are used to pay the salary of the Ladino secretary. *Mayores* in all three communities (together with the *alguaciles* in Chenalhó) constitute the township's police force. In addition they serve as messengers for all the other political officers, and they are the ones who are sent to fetch people who have been accused of crimes to stand trial. Some important auxiliary members of the political organization are the *escribanos*, or scribes, who are responsible for keeping records and writing official correspondence.

In Chenalhó the political and religious offices in the community are arranged in a single hierarchy of nine levels. There are two levels of religious positions (known as *cargos*) sandwiched between seven of political positions. In Zinacantan and Chamula the political and religious hierarchies do not interlace as they do in Chenalhó. Except for the position of *mayor* (policeman and messenger), service in political office in Zinacantan does not count for progression up the religious hierarchy, and vice versa (see Vogt 1969:272). Similarly, in Chamula the political hierarchy is an independent entity; moreover, religious offices in Chamula are not arranged in a hierarchy. Instead, the *cargos* are distributed among two independent cults. There is no prescribed order which Chamulas follow in taking religious *cargos*. Typically they take the most expensive *cargos* they can afford.

Religious *cargo* holders in Chamula and Chenalhó are called *alféreces* and *mayordomos*. In Zinacantan a man begins his "*cargo* career" by taking a *cargo* on the *mayordomo* level, continues with *cargos* on the *alférez* and *regidor* levels, and concludes with a *cargo* on the *alcalde* level. In all three communities *mayordomos* and *alféreces* are responsible for the care of and ceremonies in honor of the saint images in the churches. *Cargo* holders take turns sponsoring fiestas in honor of the saints.

Shamans (*hʔiloletik*) comprise the third sector of public life in the three communities. The chief means of recruitment is by dreams—shamans learn of their calling in a series of dreams in which they see native deities who live inside the mountains. Zinacanteco shamans are organized in a formal hierarchy based on length of service. A man who makes his debut at fifteen is ranked higher than one who receives the call at forty. Although this ranking of shamans is always recognized in interactions between shamans, the frequency with which a shaman is asked to perform private ceremonies depends more upon his reputation for success than upon his rank. The shamans of Chamula and Chenalhó are also ranked in terms of length of service, but their organization seems to be less formal than that in Zinacantan.

Each Zinacanteco, Chamula, and Pedrano[1] has two souls: (*a*) an inner personal soul called *č'ulel* and (*b*) an animal alter-ego called *čanul* in Zinacantan, *č'ulel* in Chamula, and *wayhel* in Chenalhó (Guiteras-Holmes 1961:139–140). The Zinacanteco acquires his "animal spirit companion" at birth; when the ancestral deities "install a *ch'ulel* [*č'ulel*] in the embryo of a Zinacanteco, they simultaneously install the same *ch'ulel* in the embryo of an animal. Similarly, the moment a Zinacanteco baby is born, a jaguar, coyote, ocelot or other animal is born. Throughout life, whatever happens of note to the Zinacanteco happens to his *chanul* [*čanul*] and *vice versa*" (Vogt 1965:34). No information is available from Chamula and Chenalhó concerning beliefs about the relationship between the personal and animal souls.

Many religious beliefs and practices in these communities are Catholic in form but Mayan in meaning. For example, Calvary Hill has lost its specific New Testament significance as the hill on which the crucifixion of Christ took place and has become the name applied to local mountain shrines on the township, barrio, or hamlet level. Each barrio in Chamula has its own Calvary Hill (*kalvaryo*). There is a large Calvary Hill in Zinacantan Center and smaller Calvary hills in the hamlets. The summits of these hills are marked by three crosses. In general, shamanistic practices have been less influenced by Catholicism than have the ceremonies of the religious *cargo* holders.

The people of Chamula, who continue to use the ancient Mayan calendar, assign to the five days of the Catholic fiesta of Carnaval the dates for the five unlucky "lost days" (*č'ay k'in*), the final days of the Mayan year. In Yucatán shortly after the conquest, this five-day period, designated as *uayeb*, was regarded as unlucky and bad (Tozzer 1941: 134). During this time people kept to their homes and did no work (Tozzer 1941:166). In the years when the color associated with this unlucky period was black, a bonfire was constructed of firewood and set ablaze. When the fire had burned down to coals, men ran barefooted through the coals in order to rid themselves of the bad omens associated with those days (Tozzer 1941:148–149). The fiesta of Carnaval in

---

[1] The term "Pedrano" is commonly used to refer to the inhabitants of San Pedro Chenalhó.

Chamula ends with a fire rite which is similar in both form and function (see chapters 5 and 9).

For the inhabitants of Chamula and Chenalhó, the five days of Carnaval are evil days when all kinds of evil spirits appear to perform their awful and obscene deeds. In Chamula it is the Monkeys who take over the earth for five days. As each new day of the fiesta dawns in Chenalhó, a new group of horrible figures "comes out" (from the earth)—Jaguars, Blackmen, and Abductors. In both communities all those who have come into contact with these figures are tainted with evil and must be purified at the end of the fiesta. In Chamula they run through fire; in Chenalhó they are whipped to purge them of their sins.

The five "lost days" of the Chamula calendar and the *uayeb* days of Yucatán are similar in other respects as well (see chapter 9). One point of difference is the seasons at which they take place. According to Landa, the five *uayeb* days preceded the first day of the Mayan New Year, which began on July 26 (Tozzer 1941:139, 151). The fiesta of Carnaval takes place in Chamula in February or March during the days before Ash Wednesday. Apparently after the conquest the ceremonies of the Mayan five-day "month" of *č'ay k'in* or *uayeb* were combined with those introduced by the Spaniards during the Carnaval season and shifted from July to February.

In Zinacantan, Chamula, and Chenalhó this period is characterized by drunkenness, license, and obscenity. For five days any man in the community may assume the identity of a Monkey, Blackman, or woman, ignore the normative code which usually guides his behavior, and release his inhibitions in an orgy of drinking and obscene behavior. It is against this background that performances of ritual humor occur. In Chamula and Chenalhó the fiesta of Carnaval provides the only setting for ritual humor.

There are three fiestas in the ritual calendar of Zinacantan which provide occasions for ritual humor: the season between Christmas and Epiphany, the fiesta of San Sebastián (January 18–22), and Carnaval. Unlike the fiesta of the same name in Chamula and Chenalhó, Carnaval in Zinacantan is predominantly a Catholic festival, commemorating both the battle between the Christians and the Moors in the reconquest

of Spain and the suffering of Christ at the hands of the Jews. Although
Carnaval is regarded as a period of license, it seems to be so more in
the European than the Mayan sense; the costumed performers in the
drama have European rather than Mayan antecedents. On the other
hand, the activities characteristic of the fiesta of San Sebastián, which
takes place approximately a month earlier (the dates of Carnaval are
dependent on when Easter falls in a given year), are much more in
the Mayan tradition. Jaguars, Blackmen, Feathered Serpents, and other
bizarre figures appear for five days to behave obscenely and torment
the spectators. The Blackmen perform a role which is analogous to
that performed by the Monkeys in Chamula and the Blackmen in
Chenalhó during Carnaval.

Thus, functionally the fiesta of San Sebastián of Zinacantan is equivalent to the fiesta of Carnaval in the other two communities. In Chamula and Chenalhó the ceremonies of the Maya five-day "month" of
č'ay k'in (the "lost days," sometimes also called the "nameless days")
were combined with those introduced by the Spaniards in honor of
Carnaval. In Zinacantan they remained distinct.

Five fiestas in three communities provide the data for this comparative study of ritual humor. In two communities (Chenalhó and Chamula) ritual humor is concentrated in the five-day period of a single
fiesta, while in the third (Zinacantan) similar themes are distributed
over three fiestas. Thus, although it may seem that undue emphasis
is given to Zinacanteco ritual humor, in fact an exhaustive comparative
study of ritual humor would be impossible if the analysis were re-
stricted to the fiesta of Carnaval in the three communities.

The humorous performances which are the subject of this study
share in common their setting—the fiesta. Fiestas are religious festivals
which are held in honor of saints. Although the Indians of highland
Chiapas do distinguish between sacred and profane acts and have a
clear sense of what is sacrilege and what is not, this distinction is not
equivalent to a distinction between the solemn and the comic, as is
often the case in our own society. Thus humor and religious ritual need
not be mutually exclusive with respect to setting. Nor, in some cases,
are their themes different, for ritual humorists are permitted to mock

curing rites, prayers, and change-of-office ceremonies. Ritual humor, like religious ritual, is conservative: performances of ritual humor vary little from one year to the next (see chapter 7).

2. A Woman's Place . . .

Mock bullfights are performed in Zinacantan during the Christmas–
New Year season, which runs from the evening of December 14
through the night of January 6. During this period occur ceremonies
in honor of the Virgin of Nativity (December 15–25) and the Christ
Child (December 24–25), as well as the celebration on New Year's
Day, which is also the day when most of the new religious officials
take office. The holiday season ends with Epiphany.

For the *cargo* holders this is a season of rejoicing, sorrow, and excitement; as the new officials take office in eager anticipation of the ex-
citing year to come when they will be directing the ritual activities of
the community, the outgoing officials reluctantly and tearfully hand
over their symbols of office and return to the dull routine of life in
their hamlets. Against this backdrop of mingled joy and sorrow, of one

year's end and another's beginning, appear the Bull (*torito*) and its owners—the Grandfathers (*mamal*) and Grandmothers (*meʔčun*)[1]— with their children—the two Angels (*ʔanhel*)—who dramatize the birth, life, and death of the Bull and, through humorous behavior, teach young girls the proper behavior of women in Zinacanteco society.

The Performers

The first event in the bullfight sequence is the construction of the Bull, which takes place on December 24 in the house of the Mayordomo of the Rosary. Present are the four *mayordomos* who will eventually dress up as Grandmothers and Grandfathers, the two young boys who will be costumed as Angels, a painter from the hamlet of Pasteʔ, and the man who will perform as a Bull.

The Bull is made of reed mats which are sewn together to cover a framework made of three-quarter–inch saplings tied with string or vines. The structure is hollow and open at the bottom so that the Bull performer can enter.

The painter paints with red, black, and white the squarish rectangles resulting from the juncture of the under-framework. A large ⌒⌒ representing the cattle brand of Zinacantan is painted on the top left rear square. The square next to the Bull's head bears in Spanish the following "bill of sale":

> Zinacantan 1° de
> Enero 1966
> Compró un toro
> de $1800 de valor
> en la Finca de
> Santa Tomas.[2]

The date first placed on it is December 24. The Bull is repainted on December 31, and the price may then be higher. The price is always ridiculously high, even at first painting.

On the top front is a small triangular bull's head with two tiny horns

---

[1] *Mamal* means "grandfather" and *meʔčun* means "grandmother" in Tzeltal. The terms do not exist in Tzotzil.

[2] "Zinacantan, the first of January, 1966. A bull was bought for 1800 pesos at the ranch of Santa Tomas."

painted green, red, and white—Mexican flag colors. At the top rear is
a tail that looks like a real bull's tail (plates 1, 2).

After the Bull has been constructed comes the dressing ceremony
for the Grandfathers and Grandmothers, which is accompanied by
three rounds of rum drinking. The roles of Grandfathers are played by
two high-ranking *mayordomos*, while their "wives," the Grandmothers, are impersonated by two lower-ranking *mayordomos*.[3] The
Grandfathers and Grandmothers, who masquerade as old people, are
the ritual humorists of this fiesta season. They change from *mayordomo*
costumes to the special costumes described below.

Each Grandfather (their names are ?Akuštin and Matyo) wears a
blue-and-white checkered kerchief tied around his head, an old
Zinacanteco hat hanging down his back, a red face mask with black
painted beard, a collarless white woolen shirt with three-quarter–
length sleeves, brown leather or chamois knee-length breeches, and
high-backed leather sandals. They also wear necklaces of small red and
yellow crab apples strung on wire (plate 3). In their left hands both
hold six-foot-long stick horses and short red leather reins. The horses'
heads, which are carved by hand, feature metallic eyes and forehead
decorations. In their right hands the Grandfathers carry gourd rattles
covered with chicken feathers and hafted to deerbone handles.

The Grandmothers (whose names are Lolen and Katal) wear outfits similar to those worn by Zinacanteco women: long dark-blue skirts
pleated in front, red sashes, white blouses hanging loose and over the
skirts (instead of being tucked inside the skirts in Zinacanteco
fashion). A large white cotton scarf or shawl with bright pink pom-
poms on the corners is worn over their heads and tied under their chins
babushka style. This head scarf is so large that the ends hang down
to their waists in front. It is similar to the headcoverings worn by the
old women who carry candles in a procession during the fourth Friday
of Lent. Female ritual sponsors of brides and grooms at weddings also
wear the white cotton shawl. The Grandmothers wear high-backed

---

[3] All the *mayordomos* of the religious hierarchy take turns playing the roles of
Grandfather and Grandmother. The first to become Grandfathers are the senior
mayordomos of Sacramento and Santo Domingo, and the Grandmother role is played
by their junior counterparts. The last to play the roles (on January 6) are the junior
and senior *mayordomos* of Santa Cruz and San Antonio.

sandals and necklaces of red and yellow crab apples like their husbands, the Grandfathers (plate 2).

The attire of the Grandmothers is the key to the humor which will follow. These men do not masquerade as women in order to make fun of the opposite sex, their characteristic attitudes, movements, appearances, and roles. Rather, they perform as Grandmothers with the sole purpose of showing how ridiculous women can be when they try to behave like men. Although costumed like women, the Grandmothers make no attempt to behave like them. Instead of mincing around, as would female impersonators in our own society, they stretch their legs wide apart until their skirts are tight against their calves and their calf muscles ripple. They jump up and down, prance around, and hoot like men. They behave like men and in so doing express most dramatically how incongruous and inappropriate masculine behavior is for those who wear women's clothing.

The Angels are the last to be dressed in their costumes. They are young boys from ten to twelve years old chosen by the school principal for their ability to read and write and because they are serious, studious, and interested in becoming future sacristans (Early 1965:313). They play the role of the sons of the Grandfathers and Grandmothers. Their outfits consist of high-backed sandals, bright pink or red knee socks, blue or green velvet knee-length breeches with small bells at the knee fastenings, white long-sleeved shirts, red vests, and red turbans surmounted by birdcage headdresses one foot high, made of two bent slim reeds or saplings whose arches cross each other at the top and whose ends are held in place (in four equidistant positions) on a sapling circlet that rests on their foreheads over their turbans. The sapling circlet and arches are painted red, yellow, or green, and paper flowers are attached to the top of the frame crown where the sapling arches cross.

The historical origins of these figures are unknown. A myth says that the bull was present when the Christ Child was born. The child was dying from the cold, but the other animals would not stay for the birth to help warm the little house with their breath. Instead they fled to the mountains. Only the bull obeyed Joseph and Mary's request to stay. That is why the Bull is honored at this time of year. The Grandfathers, with their "wives," the Grandmothers, are the "owners" of the Bull and accompany it wherever it goes. The two young boys dressed as Angels represent the angels present at the birth (Early 1965:317).

The Performance

Once all the members of the bullfight party are in costume, they are ready to perform. Each performance is made up of three episodes, and each episode is composed of five basic elements. The performances form a developmental sequence over time; any performance is related to the performances which have preceded and will succeed it. Variations in the performances are related to differences in their settings, both physical and temporal.

A feature common to every setting is a distinctive musical piece played by musicians who accompany the bullfight party on all occasions. All episodes begin with this musical accompaniment.

All three episodes follow the same basic pattern. For example, in the first episode, the first element is a "charge" or a "fight" involving the Bull and the stick horses. The Grandfathers and Grandmothers line up facing the Bull. The Grandfathers stand at the ends of a small line, next to their Grandmother "wives," holding their horses in their outside hands (left hand for the Grandfather on the left end, right hand for the Grandfather on the right side) and rattles in their inside hands. The Grandmothers lift their skirts to exhibit their genitalia and prevent the Bull from killing their husbands.

The Bull charges toward the four dancers as they "ride" their horses and run toward him and then return to their original places. The third time the Bull charges, he "wounds" or "gores" the riders, and the Grandfathers fall to the ground groaning and writhing as if in great pain (plate 4).

The second element of this episode dramatizes the pain and agony of the wounded riders, as their "spouses" rush to their side to help them. The Bull retires to his position to one side and stands quietly during what follows. The Grandmothers hover over their fallen "husbands," wailing and crying. Finally they seize the stick horses and use the bottom of the poles to help lift the men (plate 2). This is often done by pushing the poles far up the Grandfathers' groins, ostensibly to help them get up, but also with much obscene, sexual joking accompanying the prodding. The Grandfathers finally crawl and/or limp over, with the help of the Grandmothers, to the highest-ranking official seated nearby watching.

In this context the official plays the role of a curer or bonesetter. The wounded Grandfathers are brought before him by the Grandmothers, who beseech him to heal their mates' wounds. Who the person playing the role of curer is depends on the setting. It can be the *presidente* (when the performance takes place in front of the town hall), a *cargo* official or an official host (when the bullfight party visits at some of the houses), or one of the musicians (when no one of rank is present). If there are two persons of authority present (such as both the Junior and Senior Alcaldes), the one of higher rank "cures" the higher-ranking Grandfather, and the authority of lesser rank "cures" the lower-ranking Grandfather.

The fourth element is the curing ceremony. The official takes the rattles from the Grandfathers' hands and uses them to "cure" the portions of the prostrate Grandfathers' bodies that have been "gored" by the Bull. The cure consists of three passes of the rattle over each wound, accompanied by the recitation of a curer's prayer. The "curer" usually manages to strike his "patient's" genitals whether or not they have been "gored." Often, also in jest, the official who is "curing" may reach over with the rattle to touch the genitals of one of the Grandmothers (or put the rattle up her skirt) and ask the Grandfathers if the Grandmothers are really women. One Grandfather may reach over to touch the other Grandfather's "spouse" on the buttocks and be scolded or hit by the first and jealous Grandfather. The spectators respond with peals of laughter to each of these antics.

The episode ends with the dramatization of the recovery of the Grandfathers, who rise from their lying position on the ground, leap into the air three times to show that they are well again, and then jump onto their stick horses to run about energetically and noisily, indicating that they are ready to bait the Bull or fight each other again.

The first episode begins with the Grandfathers being charged by the

Bull. In the second episode the Grandfathers charge at each other and are wounded by kicks from their horses when they fall down after the third charge. The Bull does not participate in this episode. The Grandmothers are the ones who ride the horses and are gored by the Bull in the third episode. But in spite of such variations, all three episodes in a performance are composed of these five basic elements: (*a*) a charge or fight involving a Bull and/or stick horses; (*b*) the wounded riders displaying their agony and being helped by their mates; (*c*) the petitioning of an official or a musician to repair the wounds; (*d*) the curing ceremony; and (*e*) the dramatization of the effectiveness of the cure and the recovery of the riders from their wounds.

The first performance of the bullfight group takes place in the courtyard of the house of the Mayordomo of the Rosary, just after the Bull has been constructed and the other chief performers have dressed. Other performances take place inside and outside the churches of San Lorenzo and San Sebastián, during visits to the houses of other *cargo* officials, and in front of the town hall on New Year's Day and January 6. In the following pages, detailed accounts of performances in each context will be given in their approximate order of occurrence, to illustrate how the humorous verbal and nonverbal behaviors of the performers contribute to the development of the themes in the sequence of performances.

The Spinning Lesson

After performing in the courtyard of the house of the Mayordomo of the Rosary, the bullfight party moves on to the church of San Lorenzo, where they perform as usual, both inside and outside the church, as they await the birth of Jesus Christ. On the next day (December 25) two new Senior Mayordomos assume the role of Grandfather and two new Junior Mayordomos the role of Grandmother.[4] The ritual dressing again takes place in the Mayordomo of the Rosary's house, for he is the sponsor of the fiestas. The scene then shifts to the church of San Lorenzo.

---

[4] The Angel and Bull roles are performed by the same individuals throughout the fiesta period.

In the church, the same three episodes are performed. After that a new routine is added. The Grandmothers sit down on benches, where they demonstrate their "skill" at spinning and weaving to the many Zinacanteco women who are present. They use gourds, spindles, and cotton thread as props. One of the grandfather impersonators gave the following description of this episode:

> The Grandmothers show all the girls so that they will learn to spin like the Grandmothers. The Grandmothers say to the girls:
>
> "Look, girls, and look, women!
> This is how you should spin.
> You should learn how to spin well so that you can make your husbands' clothes well, so that you will not only love your husbands, but will also not deceive them [by not knowing how to spin properly].
>
> "If you don't know how to spin,
> And if you don't know how to weave,
> Then watch us!
>
> "My husband desires me, but [in addition] look how beautiful his clothing which I have woven is!
>
> "We like good clothing.
> It's not just that the man likes it, but that if we care about a man, it means that we want to know how to make his clothing well.
>
> "Look at me!
> See how well I know how to work!
> We have bought our horses because I know how to work properly with my husband.
>
> "We were able to buy a bull and horses with the money that we received from our soap root and our beans and our labor.
>
> "Now we are rich—
> That's why we learned to spin and weave well and to take good care of our husbands.
>
> "Girls!
> If you are looking for husbands, then you should be able to

make clothes for them, just as we are making clothes for our
husbands."

That's what the Grandmothers say to the girls, and the girls
are most ashamed when they are told this. The Grandmothers
teach the women well, for they are spinning in the church and
don't want to be ashamed. But there are some Junior Mayordomos who, when they act as Grandmothers, they keep breaking the thread as they demonstrate in the church, for they
don't know how to spin very well.

The Grandfathers often join in this humorous "lesson" by picking
out specific women to scold for being poor spinners and weavers. The
women who have been chosen for such special comment pull back in
real dismay and embarrassment, covering their mouths with their
hands and pulling their shawls across their faces.

When the Spinning Lesson ends, the Angels pray to the Christ
Child and then begin to sing and touch their toes and dance. The
Grandfathers answer the prayers, but make up words as they go along,
mocking the forms of words used in the ritual utterances. The Spin-
ning Lesson is repeated in the same form on the mornings of New
Year's Day and January 6.

The Visit

Following the performance in the church, the bullfight party moves
on to visit the homes of the *cargo* officials, where they are served a
sweet dark-yellow corn drink (*pahal ?ul*). On Christmas Day they visit
the homes of the *cargo* holders who will end their period of community service in a few days' time (December 31). Visits are made to
the homes of the new *cargo* officials on New Year's Day. The following is a description of such a visit to the house of the new Second
Regidor on New Year's Day, 1966. I was present during this visit and
was able to make a tape recording of the entire event.

The highest-ranking official present at the visit was the Second Regidor's father, a man who had long since passed through the four levels
of the religious hierarchy and who was serving as ritual adviser to his
son; on this occasion he was the official host. The visit took place in the

late afternoon, but the official host was an old man of over seventy, and he was napping when the bullfight party came. When his family heard the sound of music in the distance, they roused the old man, who hastily put on his black robe trimmed with red satin at the neck and tied the red bandanna striped with fine black lines around his head. When the bullfight party arrived in the courtyard, the official host went to the door of the house to chant the official greeting:

> Well, Grandfather,
>   Lord:
> How long are you waiting here for my earth?
>   Are you waiting here for my mud?
> We are gathering together;
>   We are meeting.
> I see the house of poverty;
>   I see the house of wealth
> Of His laborer,
>   His contributor;
> Holy Esquipulas, thou art my father;
>   Thou art my mother.
>
> Well, Grandfather,
>   Lord:
> Your earth is gone;
>   Your mud is gone.
> You see the house of poverty,
>   The house of wealth
> Of His laborer,
>   His contributor,
> Holy Esquipulas.

The Grandmothers responded with the greeting:

> Well, Grandfather,
>   Lord:
> How much your earth is gone;
>   Your mud is gone.
> The soul of my face
>   And heart [i.e., personality].
> You see the house of poverty,

> The house of wealth
> Of His laborer,
>   His contributor,
> Holy Esquipulas.

The onlookers laughed when they heard the words "the soul of my face and heart." This phrase is used exclusively by older men in greeting younger men, their social inferiors. It was therefore insulting for the grandmother impersonators, who were younger than the official host, to address him with these words. But in another sense the Grandmothers were only being true to their role as *old* women when they greeted the official host in this fashion.

As the bullfight party entered the house, a brother-in-law of the *regidor* walked up to a Grandfather and asked him: "Grandfather, where is the fruit?" and grabbed at a crab apple on the Grandfather's necklace. All laughed at this.

The members of the bullfight party began to dance together. Then the Grandfathers mounted their stick horses and ran toward the Bull, which charged at them. On the third charge the Bull "gored" the Grandfathers and they fell down with broken bones. The Grandmothers ran over to where their "husbands" lay and helped them remount their horses. As this went on, they "accidentally" goosed their "husbands" with the stick horses. The Grandfathers limped over to the official host.

Grandmother: Please, father,
                     Please, my patron,
                 Mend the bones of my husband,
                     My companion.

Host: Why, what happened to him?

Grandmother: A bull gored him.

Host: Well, why did you buy the bull then?

Grandmother: He thought it was a good bull and, besides, I wanted it. I thought it would be good.

Host: You shouldn't have bought it, for its goring is causing much suffering. Is anything broken?

Grandfather:	Yes, something is broken. Please mend my bones.
Host:	I'll try to mend them.
Grandmother:	Please mend them if possible.
Host:	I'll recite the [curing] formula:

Tontikil puḉul
   ʔi tontikil ḉ'aben,[5]

Find your place, bones!
   Find your place, muscles!
Don't leave your hole, muscle!
   Don't leave your hole, bone!

Good.

Try it and see if they are well;
   Try it and see if they are healed.

[Grandfather jumps into the air three
times and repeats the following formula:]

Grandfather:	Stretch out, bone!

   Stretch out, muscle!
Remember your place, bone!
   Remember your place, muscle!
Don't go to another hole, muscle!
   Don't leave your hole empty, bone!

Host:	Good. Are you all right now?
Grandfather:	I'm fine. Thank you. How much do I owe you?
Host:	I don't want any pay. I only want to sleep with your wife [the Grandmother] for a night. I don't want any money.
Grandfather:	Well, all right.

[5] According to Robert M. Laughlin, "*tontikil ḉ'aben* is rattle-box (Crotalaria pumila) ort. It is the same as the normal *ḉ'aben*, chipilin, that is eaten as greens. *Tontikil puḉul* is not a 'real' plant name. *Puḉul* is a lady slipper (Cypripedium irapeanum) Llave and Lex. It is sold in San Cristóbal as a flower. Nobody could tell me why these two plants are associated with bone-setting in the joking" (personal communication, September 12, 1972).

Host:	Entertain us some more so that the people can watch.

This time the two Grandfathers rushed at each other on their horses and fought each other. During the third charge they fell down and broke their legs. The Grandmothers rushed up to help their "spouses":

Grandmother:	You've had it! What happened this time?
Grandfather:	The horse finished me.
Grandmother:	Can't you see that our horse is very vicious?
Grandfather:	But I want to ride my horse and fight the bull.
Grandmother:	But when you ride, you fall off and break your bones.
Grandfather:	I don't hurt myself very much. I only broke my leg a little.
Grandmother:	Get up, then, and I'll take you to be healed.

The Grandfather climbed back on his horse and rode over to where the official host was sitting.

Grandmother:	Please heal my husband.
Host:	What happened to him?
Grandmother:	He fell while he was on his horse.
Host:	Is your horse pretty crazy?
Grandfather:	Well, it's new. I just bought it with Lolen.
Host:	But why did you buy your horse if you can't gentle it?
Grandfather:	But, Man, because we wanted a horse and a bull so much. But it is very vicious. And we earned the money for it with such difficulty. We sold our soap root, our beans and vegetables in order to earn the money for them. Therefore, our father, our patron, please mend my bones.
Host:	But you hurt yourself.

Grandfather:	I hurt myself.
Host:	Where are you wounded?
Grandfather:	My back is broken [but points to his genitals].
Host:	Was the blow very hard?
Grandfather:	It was very hard.
Host:	Did a piece of bone pierce the skin?
Grandfather:	Yes, here it is!
Host:	Well, we'll fix it [fixes it].

Tree that has been made green![6]
  Stone that has been made green![7]
Tontikil puçul
  ʔi tontikil čʼaben.
Heal, bone!
  Heal, muscle!

See if it's all right now.

Grandfather:	Fine.
Host:	Stand up! Jump up!
Grandfather:	Stretch out, bone! Stretch firm, muscle! Like those of the official host.
Host:	Is that all right?
Grandfather:	It seems to be all right. Thank you. How much do I owe you?
Host:	I don't want any money.
Grandfather:	What do you want then?
Host:	I want a vegetable pear.[8]

[6] Bone that is restored to youth so that it resembles a young tree.

[7] Stone that is restored to youth so that it resembles a "young" stone.

[8] A vegetable pear (*Sechium edule*) is a fruit about the size of an orange, with which a woman's genitalia are sometimes jokingly compared. It is partially furrowed like a peach or an apricot.

Grandfather: Wouldn't you rather have a dog?[9]

Host: No, I don't want that. Don't come to me to
                  mend your legs! Why do you want to give me
                  a dog?

Grandfather: Oh, it's just talk.

Host: Well, go and entertain us some more.

The Grandfathers knelt and prayed, asking the help of all the saints in calming and taming their horses: "In the name of God, Jesus Christ, our Lord, Señor Esquipulas, San Lorenzo, Santo Domingo, Virgin of Rosario . . ." (Zabala n.d.:11). They crossed themselves with the rattles as they prayed and then passed the rattles over the backs of their horses three consecutive times. Meanwhile the Grandmothers had been trying to tame the horses by placing the horses' heads under their skirts (as they had earlier tried to tame the Bull). With the Grandmothers still holding the horses, the Grandfathers attempted to mount their horses, pretending to vault onto their backs. But the Grandmothers pulled the horses away as if to suggest that the horses were still skittish and bucking. The Grandfathers prayed before they tried to mount again. On the third try they were successful and demonstrated their delight in having tamed their horses by running, jumping, and leaping around with the stick horses. The Grandmothers followed their "husbands," finding it hard to run and keep up with them because of their long skirts.

Now it was the Grandmothers who galloped around on the stick horses, attacking each other. They rushed at each other three times also. The third time they fell down and broke their backs. As they lay there moaning, their skirts flew up, revealing their buttocks. The Grandfathers rushed up to them and pulled their skirts down so that their genitals would not show. One Grandfather asked his "wife" why she fell off her horse, for her buttocks could be seen by everyone.

The Grandfather took his "wife" to the official host to have her back mended:

[9] Insinuates that the official host likes to mate with animals. The Grandfather also implies that the official host, like a dog, cannot control his sexual desires during the fiesta. See chapter 8 for explanation of this ploy.

Grandfather:	Look, father; look, mother! Please heal my wife.
Host:	What happened to her?
Grandfather:	She fell off the horse.
Host:	But why did she get on the horse in the first place?
Grandfather:	Because she wanted to mount it. She wanted to know what it was like to ride a horse.
Host:	But look, she fell off the horse and hurt herself.
Grandfather:	Yes, she's hurt herself.
Host:	On which side [is she hurt]?
Grandfather:	Here.
Host:	Oh, poor thing. Her womb is ruined.
Grandfather:	Please fix it, because I want her to recover and because I want to have many more children. For the two children that I have already [the Angels] aren't enough; that's why I want my Katal to recover. I don't know if her womb is completely destroyed as a result of falling off the horse.
Host:	We'll see if we can mend it.
Grandfather:	Fine.
Host:	[Takes rattle and hits Grandmother on genitals.] We'll recite the [curing] formula:

Green stone,
  Green vine;
Tontikil puṣul,
  Tontikil č'aben.
Tender bone,
  Tender muscle.
Mend, bone!
  Mend, muscle!
Stay rigid, flesh!

> Stay rigid, bone!
> Don't leave your stick, flesh!
>> Don't leave your stick, devilish flesh!
>
> See how it is now, if it is better!
>
> Try it!
>> Jump!
> Jump up three times and repeat this formula:
>
> Stretch out, bones!
>> Stretch out, muscles!
>
> Are you all right now?

Grandmother: I seem to be all right now.

Host: Now, don't do that again. Don't get on horses. It's not for you. It's only for men— only *they* may mount horses.

Grandmother: I think that's a good idea, my father, my patron.

Host: Good. Fine. That's all. Go and dance now, and don't mount horses. Now sing.

The Grandmothers sang:

> Your rope's earwig,
>> Hoarse Katal.
> Halalalalala,
>> Ha la la la la.

and:

> Not for his Katal.
>> Not for his Lolen.
> Halalala la.

and:

> Why are you giving me the finger?
>> Why are you stroking me?
> Halala lalalalala,
>> Halalalala lalalalala.

and:

> This is a stick, Lolen;
> This is a stick, Katal.
> Halalay, halalay,
> Halalay, halalay.
> Go away, Lolen;
> Come here, Katal.
> Halalay, halalay,
> Halalay, halalay, ho ho o.
> Throw it, bull;
> Throw it, cow.
> Halalay, halalay,
> Halalay, halalay.

Discussion of Spinning Lesson and Visit

In real life Zinacanteco men and women do not behave toward each other as the Grandfathers and Grandmothers do. Their behavior is inappropriate, and the audience recognizes it as such. The contrast between what is appropriate and what is inappropriate role behavior is expressed in various ways in the bullfight sequence. In the Spinning Lesson, the Grandmothers boast to the women in the audience of how well they know how to spin and weave, but the women observe that the Grandmothers often break their threads and that their motions are clumsy. The words of the Grandmothers remind Zinacanteco women of what kinds of role behavior are expected of them, but their actions belie their words. There is, then, a discrepancy between the verbal and nonverbal behaviors of the Grandfathers and Grandmothers. Similarly, when the fallen Grandfathers come to the "curer" and are asked where they have been injured, they say that their backs or legs are broken, but they point to their genitals. The "curers" respond in the same vein, striking their genitals with rattles or diverting themselves by thrusting a rattle up the skirt of a Grandmother while intoning a prayer for setting bones. The nonverbal behavior brings out the obscene connotative meaning of the verbal utterance. The healing formulae of the "curer" and the Grandfather who is his patient may be interpreted in these terms. The ritual host chants:

> Find your place, bones!
> Find your place, muscles!
> Don't leave your hole, muscle!
> Don't leave your hole, bone!

The denotative meaning of this utterance is as follows: Healthy bones and muscles enjoy a fixed spatial relation to other bones and muscles. Healing a wounded person involves coaxing bones and muscles to return to their proper places. But this spatial imagery only transparently veils the connotative meaning of the utterance: the bones and muscles mentioned are references to the penis, and "place" and "hole" refer to the vagina. Therefore, the "curer," while appearing to set bones, is actually talking about sexual intercourse!

The person who is healed continues in the same vein:

> Stretch out, bone!
> Stretch out, muscle!
> Remember your place, bone!
> Remember your place, muscle!
> Don't go to another hole, muscle!
> Don't leave your hole empty, bone!

If "bone" and "muscle" are again translated as "penis" and "hole" and "place" as "vagina," the sexual meaning of the chant is obvious.

When the official host "cures" the Grandmother, he says:

> Stay rigid, flesh!
> Stay rigid, bone!
> Don't leave your stick, flesh!
> Don't leave your stick, devilish flesh!

Here "flesh" and "devilish flesh" must be replaced by "vagina" and "stick" by "penis." Thus this incantation too seems to advocate sexual intercourse.

Finally there is the odd phrase in the song of the Grandmothers:

> Your rope's earwig,
> Hoarse Katal.

Zinacanteco informants point out that if one replaces "earwig" with "vagina" and "rope" with "penis" the phrase reads:

> Your penis's vagina,
> Hoarse Katal.

There is another sense in which the healing incantation of the curer impersonator highlights the contrast between appropriate and deviant behavior: it is actually a parody of the prayer which Zinacanteco bonesetters recite when mending broken bones. The full text of a bonesetter's prayer appears below to facilitate comparison with its parody.

The Bonesetter's Prayer

My God, my Lord of Calvary,
   Father of Calvary, my Lord!
Are you standing erect?
   Are you stamped down?
Will a bone be well put together?
   A muscle?

God,
   Jesus Christ, my Lord!
Will you repair for me a bone?
   Will you make me successful [in mending] a muscle?
That's what I'm saying;
   That's what I'm praying.
The holy bone,
   The holy muscle.

My Lord, will the holy bone straighten immediately?
   Will the holy muscle straighten immediately?
The shattered,
   The splintered [bone].

My Lord, will the tender bone straighten?
   The tender muscle?
The tender stalk?
   The tender piece?
The tender young bone?
   The tender young muscle?
Bone joint,
   Muscle joint,
Rise, then;
   Get up, then.

Green bone,
　　Green muscle,
Rise then;
　　Get up.
You are shattered;
　　You are falling apart.
Have the holy fathers finished shaking?
　　Have the holy mothers finished shattering?
The holy bones,
　　The holy muscles.

My God,
　　My Lord, Jesus Christ!
Heavenly Woman,
　　Heavenly Ladina!
Are you upright because of a bone?
　　Because of a muscle?

My God,
　　My Lord!
My holy mother,
　　My holy treasure!
You are shaking there,
　　You are shattering there
The little animal,
　　The little jaguar.
You are shaking there,
　　You are shattering there
The little gray coyote,
　　The little gray jaguar.
Give grace, holy elder sisters,
　　Holy mothers!
Gather the holy animals for me!
　　Gather the holy jaguars for me!

God,
　　Jesus Christ, my Lord!
Holy Saint Cecilia, my mother,
　　My holy treasured Cecilia!
May you give grace!
　　May you do the favors!

Fix the bone for me!
　Fix the muscle for me!
May you be well disposed, my father!
　May you be well disposed, my Lord!
Holy white cave, my father!
　Holy white cave, my Lord!
You are surrounded in back,
　You are surrounded on the side;
By your engendered children,
　By your born children.
Are you angry in your head?
　Are you angry in your heart?
Perhaps you won't discard once,
　Perhaps you won't throw away once
Your engendered child,
　Your born child.

My God,
　My Lord!
Holy Hearthstones,[10] my father,
　Holy Hearthstones, my Lord.
You have watched over the holy animal,
　The holy jaguar.
Will you throw him [the patient] away?
　Will you discard him?
Will you be angry in your head?
　In your heart?
Did you shake the tender bones?
　Did you shatter the tender muscles?

My Lord!
　Will you stand up for me?
The twelve little bones,
　The twelve little muscles.
May you be well disposed, San Lorenzo, my father,

[10] "Holy Hearthstones" refers to a sacred mountain by that name in which, according to Zinacanteco belief, a series of supernatural corrals, containing an animal-spirit-companion for every person in the community, are located. If a Zinacanteco's alter ego escapes from its corral, the person becomes ill. The object of the curing ritual is to force his animal-spirit-companion to return to its corral (Vogt 1969:371–372).

San Lorenzo, my Lord!
Will it be by common agreement?
    Will it be by shared words?
Will the bone be repaired?
    Will the muscle be repaired?
May you be well disposed, holy father,
    Holy mother!
Will you stand up?
    Will you stand firmly?
For one tender bone,
    For one tender muscle, my Lord?

Look, father,
    Look, my Lord!
I am not the only good person;
    I am not the only fine person.
I give it in the mouth,[11]
    In the lips,
The bone,
    The muscle.

Look, father,
    My Lord!
I shared the leftover,
    I shared the remains:[12]
The cause for fear,
    The cause for shame [rum liquor].
It is closed;
    It is unfinished,
My piece of incense,
    My bit of smoke.
Look, holy bone!
    Look, holy muscle!
Stand erect, then!
    Stand firm, then!
Get up, then, bone!
    Recover, then, muscle!
Tender little bone,

[11] Blows rum on break.
[12] Rum, after supernaturals have drunk.

Tender little muscle,
Stand erect!
    Stand firm!
Come delighted;
    Come rejoicing.
May you be well disposed, holy green bones,
    Holy green muscles!
Stand erect!
    Stand firm!
You were thrown,
    Heaved,[13]
By the holy father,
    By the holy mother.
You know, my fathers,
    You know, my Lords:
Will a bone be fixed?
    Will a muscle be fixed?
I did not bring [my knowledge],
    I did not discover it anywhere but
There at your feet,
    There beneath your hands.
There I received it;
    There I possessed it forever,
My way of repairing,
    My way of succeeding [in curing];
The bone,
    The muscle.

Look, father,
    Look, my Lord!
Holy father of Calvary,
    Holy mother of Calvary—may you be well disposed!
It was not elsewhere that the bone,
    The muscle shattered.
There perhaps at your threshhold,
    There perhaps beneath your hands.
Look, all holy fathers!
    All holy mothers!

[13] Addressing the bones.

I've finished repairing the holy bone;
  I've finished repairing the muscle.
I've finished talking;
  I've finished praying.

Look, my father!
  Look, my Lord!
There is still a little;
  There is still a bit
Of the cause for fear,
  The cause for shame [rum liquor].
The words are ended;
  The prayer is ended,
Holy fathers,
  Holy mothers.

Look, my father of Calvary,
  My Lord of Calvary!
My piece of incense,
  My bit of smoke.
May I pass in front of you;
  May I pass before your face!

First of all, the parody imitates the couplet structure of the prayer, which is the characteristic structure of Zinacanteco formal or "good" (i.e., normative) speech (Bricker n.d.*a*). It is this structure which identifies the curer impersonator's utterances as a parody rather than as some other kind of humorous speech.

Second, some of the verses in the two versions are almost identical, both in their content and in their phrasing. This is particularly true of the following passage from the bonesetter's prayer:

Green bone,
  Green muscle;
Rise, then;
  Get up. . . .
Look, holy bone!
  Look, holy muscle!
Stand erect, then!
  Stand firm, then!

> Get up, then, bone!
> > Recover, then, muscle!
> Tender little bone,
> > Tender little muscle.

which the curer impersonator parodies as:

> Green stone,
> > Green vine;
> Tender bone,
> > Tender muscle.

and:

> Stay rigid, flesh!
> > Stay rigid, bone!
> Don't leave your stick, flesh!
> > Don't leave your stick, devilish flesh!

and:

> Stretch out, bone!
> > Stretch out, muscle!
> Remember your place, bone!
> > Remember your place, muscle!
> Don't leave your cave, muscle!
> > Don't leave your cave empty, bone!

The change in wording from "Stand erect!" and "Stand firm!" to "Stretch out . . . !" and "Stay rigid . . . !" and the addition of the lines beginning with "Remember your place . . . !" and "Don't leave your stick . . . !" are sufficient to transform the sacred bonesetter's prayer into obscenity. But the mock bonesetter's prayer is still similar enough in wording to the prayer which it parodies that the audience can both recognize it as a parody and identify the prayer which is its referent.

The Angels seem to play rather passive roles in the bullfight performance. Most of the time they walk in processions or sit with the musicians, watching the antics of the Bull, the Grandfathers, and the Grandmothers with folded arms. They pass out cigarettes to officials during the many visits to the houses of *cargo* holders. Their only opportunity to participate actively in fiesta activities comes on the last day

of the fiesta season—January 6—when they are given lassoes to help
to chase and rope the Bull for its ritual killing; but by then they have
changed out of their Angel costumes.

The Grandfathers and Grandmothers often refer to the Angels as
their sons. Since they are so regarded, their passive role is not difficult
to understand. Young boys do not take an active part in ritual activities—they are onlookers (thereby learning proper adult behavior),
and they serve as errand boys (just as the main function of the Angels
is to pass out cigarettes to *cargo* officials). Apparently the passive role
of the Angels symbolizes the proper behavior of young boys, just as
the humorous antics of the Grandmothers teach the proper behavior
for women to young girls.[14]

The Angels play another role, which is symbolic of the functions of
curers and *cargo* holders in Zinacantan. After the other members of the
bullfight party have finished their performance in the church, the
Angels pray in front of the Christ Child. The Grandfathers "pray"
also, but mockingly. Just as the people of Zinacantan may go about
their daily chores secure in the knowledge that the *cargo* holders are
performing the necessary ceremonies for the saints in their stead, so the
Angels represent the bullfight group when they pray and relieve the
others of that responsibility.

The behavior of the Angels and that of the Grandmothers seem to
serve a similar function: that of showing Zinacantecos what behavior
is expected of them. But the means by which they accomplish this are
quite different. The Angels teach young boys how to behave by engaging in the ideal behavior themselves. The Grandmothers teach
women and young girls how to behave by describing their own behavior as ideal while at the same time behaving as deviants. The moral
theme of the Spinning Lesson is concerned with how women ought to
work. Because the Grandmothers are really men and are therefore not
accustomed to spin and weave (women's tasks), they cannot help but

---

[14] Vogt (personal communication) suggests that the performance of the Angels
might symbolize boys passing through the latency period, then adolescence, to adult-
hood. They begin very passively, become more active in chasing the Bull, and then
end up helping to kill it. At each stage of their development they behave appropriately
for their current status.

seem awkward and bumbling as they "demonstrate," at the same time broadcasting loudly how proficient they are. This incongruity of men dressed as women pretending to do women's work serves to ridicule women who do not perform the woman's role adequately and who thus seem as awkward as men doing women's tasks. The fact that the Grandmothers are really men serves yet another purpose. It permits men to state how they believe their wives ought to behave. The behavior of the Grandmothers is humorous and all laugh at it, but the lesson is clear.

In the Visit, correct female decorum is spelled out in the episode in which the Grandmothers ride the horses. One can easily picture the Grandmothers enviously watching their husbands ride the horses which have been purchased with their combined earnings (from her weaving and from selling his crops). Finally the Grandmothers plead to be allowed to ride the horses also; their husbands agree and help them mount the horses.

The same fate overcomes the Grandmothers as that which befell their husbands, but the reaction of the "curer" is different in their case. When the Grandfathers fall off the horses, they are berated for having bought such wild animals. But when the Grandmothers come to grief, the official host tells them that they must not try to do what their husbands do—that only men should ride horses. Women who ride horses always disgrace themselves, because they cannot keep their skirts down; they behave without demeanor. Riding horses is too dangerous for women—they risk damaging their reproductive organs beyond repair, so that they will not be able to fulfill their main function, that of procreation. This is the lesson of the bullfight performance.

The Jail Scene

On the evening of December 31, the Bull is repainted in accordance with the ancient Mayan custom of destroying ceremonial objects which were in use during the previous year and starting afresh with new objects (and new *cargo* officials) for the new year (Tozzer 1941: 139). During this painting ceremony, the price which was quoted as being paid for the Bull may be changed—usually a larger sum is substituted.

On New Year's Day, the bullfight company participates in some of the same activities as on Christmas Day. The Spinning Lesson is re-enacted in the church for the edification and amusement of the women. Visits are made to the homes of the incoming *cargo* officials. While these visits are taking place, the *presidente* receives a letter from a scribe, complaining that he has lost a bull and two horses resembling those of the Grandfathers and Grandmothers. The sacristans look into the matter and send a letter to the scribes which says that, as far as they can tell, the Grandfathers did buy the Bull, but at a suspiciously low price, and that they received no bill of sale for the horses. The letter suggests that the Grandfathers stole the horses and robbed a helpless drunk of his hat and mask.

The scribes send back another letter saying in effect: "Please summon them here to the town hall so that we can find out how much they paid for their bull and whether their livestock is branded correctly." In all, three letters are exchanged.

The bullfight party is then summoned to the town hall. Upon their arrival, the Angels loudly read off the brand of the Bull and how much was paid for it. When the *presidente* hears how little was paid (actually the price is ridiculously high), he says to the Grandfathers:

Presidente:	You know that it is wrong? You don't have the correct receipt. You stole it and the two horses.
Grandfather:	I bought it! I bought it! I didn't steal it.
Presidente:	You're lying when you say you bought it. You stole it! Seize him and take him to jail!

There follows then a lively game of chase and pursuit as the Grandfathers and Grandmothers flee down the road to escape the policemen. They are captured, then escape, to be captured again. This occurs three times. The third time, they cannot escape, and the Grandfathers are thrown into jail, leaving the Grandmothers weeping in front of the *presidente*.

Each Grandmother pulls out a bottle of rum in order to request her husband's release from jail:

Grandmothers:	Please Mr. Presidente, let our two husbands out of jail.
Presidente:	Why did they steal, then? After all, they had the wrong receipt.
Grandmothers:	Oh, our husbands are very stupid! Please let them out. Pardon us with the rum. Settle this matter for us.
Presidente:	Wait a while. They must be punished for an hour.
	[After an hour the Grandfathers are let out.]
	Well, you're out now.
Grandfather:	I'm out. Why did you imprison me?
Presidente:	Because you were guilty. Because you didn't have the correct receipt for your bull.
Grandfather:	But I didn't know that, like a fool that I am.
Presidente:	Well, don't do it again. Wait a while, and we'll fix up your receipt for you [fixes it]. Go now and entertain us!

The company then puts on its performance in front of the town hall, the *presidente* serving as "curer." Following that, the bullfight party resumes its visits.

Change of Office Ceremony

On January 6, after dressing in their costumes, all members of the bullfight party, including the Angels, join in a dance. The Senior Angel, Grandfather, and Grandmother stand on one side, facing their junior counterparts. In time with the music, they slowly raise right legs to touch toes with their opposites, then lower them to the ground. They then raise left legs and, in a similar fashion, touch left toes. This is repeated with right legs and toes, after which the pairs of senior-junior characters (Angels, Grandfathers, Grandmothers) cross over—

trading places. This small dance figure resembling a polka is done three times. Then the Angels retire to the sidelines to watch and occasionally pass out cigarettes as the regular bullfight performance begins again. The whole performance as described earlier is now performed three times before the entire bullfight company proceeds to the church.

In the church, after the regular performance, the Spinning Lesson is dramatized for the last time. In the afternoon, a large procession forms to make the circuit of the ceremonial center to collect money to pay for expenses which will be incurred in celebrating the fiesta of San Sebastián (see next chapter). The bullfight group leads the procession, followed by the *mayordomos* carrying flags, the sacristans, the musicians, the scribes, and the senior members of the hierarchy. They stop at each cross they come to and wait there while the *regidores* and scribes go from house to house asking for money. While waiting, the bullfight company sometimes goes through its routines; the spectators reach for the small apples of the performers' necklaces as often as they can.

When the procession returns to the church, it is time for the flag ceremony marking the *cargo* change of the *alféreces* of Divina Cruz and Soledad. Now present as well are the *presidente* and the other civil officials.

The bullfight group stands to one side of the *alféreces*, who are seriously performing this part of their change-of-office ceremonies. As the *alféreces* bow, kiss, and exchange each others' necklaces of coins, the Grandfathers and Grandmothers bow, kiss, and exchange their necklaces of apples, ending by eating some of the apples. When the *alféreces* cross themselves and pray, the Grandfathers and Grandmothers cross themselves with their rattles and pray long, loudly, and ludicrously. As the *alféreces* exchange flags, the Grandfathers mimic them by exchanging stick horses. The ceremony ends with a procession of the important members of the real and mimic groups.

Here again the behavior of the Grandfathers and Grandmothers is a humorous distortion of what in this case is a change-of-office ceremony. In the "curing ceremony," curing ritual was mocked through the use of verbal formulae with sexual connotations. Here a parody of the change-of-office ritual occurs simultaneously with the actual ceremony. The crab-apple necklaces are similar to the *alféreces'* rosaries in their form and the manner in which they are worn. But they are essentially different in substance and function: the Grandfathers eat the apples. The stick horses which have been used to "goose" the performers provide a ludicrous parallel to the sacred flags. And the rattles which have been used to heal wounded genitals provide the ultimate mockery of the *alféreces'* change-of-office prayers.

The Final "Killing"

The climax of the day and of the whole fiesta season comes in the evening. The excitement builds up all day long; the Bull, sensing that his end is near, moves more and more frantically. Instead of charging at the Grandfathers, he runs away and hides in the crowd. He is chased many times down the main road of the ceremonial center.

The Angels change out of their costumes and are given lassoes with which to rope the Bull, as are two sacristans. The Grandfathers remove their masks just before the Bull is "killed."

Finally the Bull comes to the house of the Mayordomo of the Rosary. At about midnight the Bull is caught and pulled to the ground. He is tied to a thick post planted in front of the house. The Grandfathers and Grandmothers get on top of the Bull with a wooden knife covered with silver foil from cigarette wrappers. They plunge this into the "neck" of the Bull, holding a clay vessel underneath with which to catch the Bull's "blood." Rum liquor is poured into this pot, to which mint leaves, chili peppers (to color it red), and onion are added. This drink is served by the Grandfathers to all present.

Men get inside the Bull and thrash about in it until the reed mats which compose its body are torn apart. Then the "dead" Bull is put aside to be dismantled the next day, and a meal is served to everyone. The "death" of the Bull is the signal for the musicians to play a new musical piece—the one they have been playing until now is considered "bad."

The ceremonial meal represents the feast after the sacrifice, accompanying the ritual drink of "blood." Only girls and young women are permitted to prepare tortillas for this meal. The women are told by the Grandfathers: "Wash the lime-soaked kernels well and take them to the mill! The girls must be accompanied by older women so that no boys will accost them on the path. Watch that the miller doesn't seize their hands! Count your change well so that he doesn't cheat you. When the corn is ground, return together. When you get home, make a lot of tortillas. People from all the hamlets are going to eat together once we have killed the Bull."

The unmarried young men watch to see which girls make the best tortillas. Those who do not know how to make good tortillas are mocked; those who make them well and have pretty faces are admired by the boys, who will then want to marry them. The passions of these young men are said to be inflamed then—and they become jealous on account of the beautiful girls who already have husbands. Their ardor and envy are assuaged when they drink the "blood" of the Bull.

This scene is the culmination of the moral theme of the bullfight sequence. It provides young women with the opportunity to show off their culinary skills—to demonstrate to the young men who are or will become their husbands that they know well how to perform that most essential of all female tasks—the work of preparing corn, the Zinacanteco's staff of life, for consumption. This time it is the girls themselves, rather than the Grandmothers, who must face the ridicule if they do not fulfill their role adequately.

And so the "life" of the Bull ends. In the short space of the thirteen days which span the end of the old year and the beginning of the new, the Bull is created, lives, and dies. The Bull is the last object left over from the old year to be destroyed; the Grandfathers and Grandmothers are the last of the first-level *cargo* officials from the preceding year to relinquish their offices. The two events occur at the same time. The life of the Bull is a microcosmic representation of the events of the ritual year—the year beginning with the new *cargo* officials donning their special garments and accepting their symbols of office, continuing with their observance of the major festivals in the ritual calendar, and ending with the handing over of the symbols of office to a new person and their own return to their previous way of life.

The life cycle of the Bull has yet another meaning. The Bull is an evil creature. Time and time again the Grandfathers are told by the

"curer" that they should not have bought the Bull, that it is a bad animal because it gores them and causes much suffering. The Bull is in-
directly associated with witchcraft. Zinacantecos believe that witches
transform themselves into cows at night and wander around the countryside in that guise, bringing illness to men. The Bull is responsible
for the Grandfathers' wounds, which must be healed by a "curer."
From the time that the Bull is constructed until its ritual slaughter, the
musicians play only one musical piece, which Zinacantecos think of as
"bad." When the Bull dies, they can play "good" music again. When
the Bull framework is not being used, it hangs outside under the roof
of the Mayordomo of the Rosary's house. Three times a day it is "purified" with incense in an apparently unsuccessful attempt to keep evil
spirits away from it. The Bull is also a scapegoat (a witch?). Perhaps
through its ritual killing and the ceremonial feast which follows the
killing, the evil in the community is exorcised every year.

3. The Entertainers

Activities in connection with the fiesta of San Sebastián begin on about January 14 and end on January 25. During this time, those *cargo* officials who did not change office on New Year's Day or January 6 do so. They are the *alféreces* of San Sebastián and the Senior Alcalde. The fiesta of San Sebastián provides the new officials inaugurated on New Year's Day with their first opportunity to celebrate a major fiesta. It is also the occasion for the outgoing *cargo* officials to perform the last duties which their *cargos* entail. Both sets of *cargo* officials appear at this fiesta, but only the new officials appear in their garb of office.

The outgoing officials are called "entertainers" (*htoyk'inetik*). They wear costumes which are quite distinct from those worn by the new *cargo* officials. There are two groups of entertainers: a senior group, composed of men who have served *cargos* of the top three levels of the religious hierarchy, and a junior group, which includes members from the three bottom levels. Only the top two levels of the hierarchy are fully represented. None of the outgoing *mayordomos* and only four of the fourteen *alféreces* are entertainers.

The senior entertainers are six officials divided into three costumed couples:

Junior and Senior Spanish Gentlemen or Spaniards (*hkašlan*)
    —two alcaldes.

Junior and Senior Spanish Ladies (*šinulan*)—*alféreces* of Santo
    Domingo and San Lorenzo.

Junior and Senior White Heads (*sak hol*)—First and Second
    Regidores.

The Spanish Gentlemen (frontispiece) wear red coats and knickers embroidered in gilt, red knee socks, and high-backed sandals. Both men suspend mirrors from their wrists and necks. The senior member of the pair carries a picture of San Sebastián in a net bag attached to a leather strap around his shoulder and a jousting target in his hand. On January 25 he gives this sacred picture and other objects which have been in his keeping to the new Senior Alcalde.

The two Spanish Ladies wear white dresses trimmed with embroidery and feathers at the hem over red skirts, knee-length red socks, and high-backed sandals. Their heads are covered by finger-tip-length purple or red veils, topped by large black felt hats banded with gold and decorated with peacock feathers on the sides. Their jewelry consists of bead necklaces, mirrors, and rings; they carry combs and small blue-and-white enamel bowls in their hands. The Spanish Ladies are also known as "Oaxaqueñas," or "women from Oaxaca."

The two White Heads (frontispiece) are dressed in white except for red turbans and knee socks. Each White Head wears a mask on his forehead in the shape of a large block tinsel **E** turned ninety degrees clockwise so that the open side of the letter faces down toward his nose. Like the Spanish Ladies, the White Heads adorn themselves with necklaces and mirrors. A small bow and arrow in one hand and a rattle in the other complete their costume.

According to several informants, the White Heads are sometimes called Montezumas or Aztecs. This implies that the senior entertainers once performed a Dance of the Conquest, variants of which are still performed in other areas of Middle America (see chapter 9). However, if the White Head role is a vestige of this drama, the behavior associated with that role no longer suggests it.

The junior entertainers are composed of five costumed groups: two Lacandons (*káʔbenal*), two Jaguars (*bolom*), two Plumed Serpents (*k'uk'ul čon*), two Spanish-Moss Wearers (*ʒon teʔ*), and five or six Blackmen (*hʔik'aletik*). The parts are taken by the following members of the religious hierarchy:

> Junior and Senior Lacandons—Third and Fourth Regidores.
>
> Junior and Senior Jaguars—*alféreces* of Trinidad and San Antonio.
>
> Junior and Senior Plumed Serpents—two *mayordomo reyes*.[1]
>
> Junior and Senior Moss Wearers—two *mesoneros*.
>
> Blackmen—six policemen.

In 1555, 1559, and 1696, the Spaniards were engaged in efforts to subdue and convert the Lacandon Indians, who were raiding Christian settlements in parts of Chiapas and Guatemala (Thompson 1970:27–38). Two hundred Zinacanteco Indians and six hundred Chiapanec Indians took part in the 1559 campaign (Remesal 1932:II, 396). Indians from Chiapas (their tribal affiliation is not specified) also participated in the 1696 operations against the Lacandon Indians (Villagutierre Soto-Mayor 1933:222). One of the Lacandon leaders in 1696 was a man named Cabnál (Villagutierre Soto-Mayor 1933:223, 241–242). According to J. Eric S. Thompson, the name Cabnál or Cabenal was assumed by Lacandon chiefs generation after generation, for Spaniards met Lacandon chiefs with that name in 1586, 1608, 1695, and 1696 (1970:29–30). This being the case, *káʔbenal* is probably derived from Cabnál or Cabenal, which it resembles closely in pronunciation; Zinacantecos refer to the impersonators with this name as

---

[1] *Mayordomo rey* and *mesonero* are two *cargos* which belong to the bottom level of the religious hierarchy (Cancian 1965:30).

Lacandons. Each Lacandon impersonator wears a purple tunic and a fuzzy green straw hat from which a long red or purple braid dangles to his waist (Lacandon men are famous for their long hair). He carries a rattle in one hand and a bow and arrow tied together in the other (plate 5). The primitive Lacandon Indians of the jungles of Chiapas still hunt with bows and arrows.

The two Jaguars wear one-piece outfits of brown or yellow painted with black circles and dots, tails, and hats of jaguar fur (plate 6). Their paraphernalia includes stuffed animals, such as squirrels, iguanas, and coati-mundis, as well as whips and sharp pointed sticks reddened at the tips. When they speak they imitate the jaguar's cry: *huh-huh-huha*.

The Feathered Serpents wear green knee-length trousers, white shirts dotted in red and green, and beaked headdresses with red dots. The beaks are held open by ears of corn (plates 5, 7). Small wings are strapped to their backs. The Feathered Serpents make the sound: *hurr-hurr*.

The Spanish-Moss Wearers are dressed in green velvet trousers, black wool robes, and black felt hats from which long bunches of Spanish moss cascade down their backs (plate 5).

Five of the Blackmen wear leather breeches and jackets; the sixth is dressed like a Ladino woman who carries her "child" (a white doll) in her arms. The Blackmen blacken their faces and arms with soot. The Blackman dressed as a woman wears a blue mask with white rings outlining the mouth and eyes (plate 9). Like the Jaguars, the Blackmen carry stuffed animals (squirrels and a spider monkey) and sharply pointed sticks (plate 10). They make the sound: *ves-ves-ves*.

Every year there are a number of *cargo* holders, usually policemen, who, instead of coming to the fiesta of San Sebastián to carry out the last of their ritual obligations by performing as entertainers, return to their homes in their hamlets after New Year's Day. The neck of each stuffed squirrel carried by the buffoons is draped with necklaces and ribbons, such as Zinacanteco women wear, for the squirrels are meant to symbolize the wives of the delinquent *cargo* holders. The genital region of each squirrel has been emphasized with red paint.

The squirrels are said to be women who have no shame. The Jaguars carry pointed sticks reddened at the tips, which they jab at the under-

sides of the squirrels. On their visits to the homes of the *cargo* officials
they lay the squirrels next to the fire and poke at their undersides. They
tell the women who are grinding corn by the fire that *they* (the women) are different—they have shame and do not perform sexual
intercourse in public.

The men who have defaulted are accused of having no time to come
to the fiesta because they are busy making love to their wives instead.
The money which they should be spending on their *cargos* they use to
buy fancy ribbons and necklaces for their wives. This is one of the
themes which is developed by the junior entertainers in the course of
the fiesta of San Sebastián.

The performances of the entertainers occur in two settings: the
churchyard of San Sebastián by day and the houses of *cargo* officials at
night. During the daytime they perform simultaneously, but usually
in different parts of the churchyard and its vicinity. At night their visits
to the houses of *cargo* officials are separated by two-hour intervals. For
example, on the morning of January 20, 1966, the junior entertainers
arrived at the house of the Second Regidor at 3:45 A.M.; the senior
entertainers did not come until two hours later, at least one hour after
the first group had left.

On the evening of January 19 the junior entertainers gather together. The group visits each junior entertainer's house. When they
arrive at a house, a Jaguar and a Blackman go to the door and stand
there like official hosts. They borrow a woman's ceremonial robe, which
one of them puts on. They joke and comb the hair of their fellow Blackmen in imitation of the performance of the senior entertainers (see
below). These visits enable the junior entertainers to find out which
outgoing officials from their ranks have decided not to appear at the
fiesta. In this way they learn the names of the delinquent officials and
their wives, whom they will mock in their subsequent performances.

Dressing the Spanish Lady

On the same night (January 19) the senior entertainers put on their
costumes for the first time. The Spaniards go to the homes of their
consorts, the Spanish Ladies, to fetch them. While the Spanish Lady
dresses, the Spaniard pretends that he is courting her. "Her" father

treats the Spaniard as though he were going to become his son-in-law, saying, "Don't beat the Spanish Lady. Be honest and kind to her." The father tries to find out more about this stranger, whose customs he suspects are so different from those of the Zinacantecos:

Father: What is your food like? I know that you drink only water. Do you eat fried foods? Do you eat a lot?

Spaniard: Ah, I only know how to eat meat.

Father: Have you already learned our language?

Spaniard: I already learned it. The Spanish Lady taught me, because of course she knows the words.

Then the girl's father inquires about her suitor's intentions:

Father: When will you marry?

Spaniard: Not until tomorrow. But it's all right if we sleep together now. We have the right to do so now because it won't be long before we marry.

Father: But don't beat your wife.

Spaniard: But she doesn't mind the blows. I beat her until I was spent but she didn't leave. "Go!" I told her yesterday, but there she was huddled. She didn't want to go.

Everyone: Hi, hi, hi.

Father: Well, I'll give you some advice. You are much older than your wife. She's still a girl.

Spaniard: So you say. But your daughter really wants me because she will eat well [i.e., I will support her well].

Father: Are you a rich man?

Spaniard: That's not important. I know how to work well at night—at least that's what some women say. Wealth isn't everything. Fruit and bread aren't everything. All that is important is that there be a man [to sleep with], for that is something that [women] can't get along without.

Everyone: Hi, hi, hi.

Father: Spaniard, how many children do you have already?

Spaniard: Only one.

Father: Will you kiss her?

Spaniard: Well, what's it to you if I kiss her?

Father: But you are an old man. My daughter is still a girl. See how pretty she is. You are old and pock-marked.

Spaniard: So, she's still a girl. What good would she be to me if she were already an old lady!

Everyone: Hi, hi, hi.

Spaniard: Now look, my father, my Lord, drink up a little. Thank you for giving me your daughter. My foot has received, my hand has received your daughter.[2]

Father: You won't suit my daughter because you are already an old man.

Spaniard: Please don't interfere. But don't criticize your daughter. You keep saying, "You are already an old man," but your daughter wants me so much that she doesn't see me as an old man. You will just offend her if you keep telling her, "He's too old." Your daughter doesn't view me as an old man, because she wants someone who is a little more mature, someone who has already worked for some time. Younger men have worked less. So, father, what you ought to tell your daughter is, "Sleep with your husband!" Teach your daughter well.

Everyone: Hi, hi, hi.

Father: You are a stupid, useless person!

Spaniard: But your daughter wants me even if I am a useless, stupid person. Even if someone cleverer were to appear, your daughter wouldn't want him.

Father: Ah, you're nothing but a *mamal*!

---

[2] Words customarily recited by a suitor when the girl's father agrees to the marriage.

In this joking interaction the "girl's" father questions the suitability of the match. His chief objection is the great discrepancy of ages. He fears that the Spaniard is too old for his daughter, that he is close to senility and therefore like the buffoon of the preceding fiesta who impersonates a foolish old man called Grandfather (*mamal*). The Spaniard counters with the argument that his age is an asset. He is financially able to support his wife in grand style. This is a common theme in joking interactions involving both old and young men. The younger man claims that women are drawn to him because of his youth, while the older man counters that he is more attractive to women because of his greater experience and wealth. Throughout the fiesta the Spaniard's right to the Spanish Lady is challenged and defended in these terms.

The Churchyard of San Sebastián

January 20, 21, and 22 are the main fiesta days. The entertainer groups spend most of the daytime in the churchyard of San Sebastián. Near the churchyard cross, two upright posts with a crossbar have been set into the ground. From the crossbar hangs a cylindrical target which

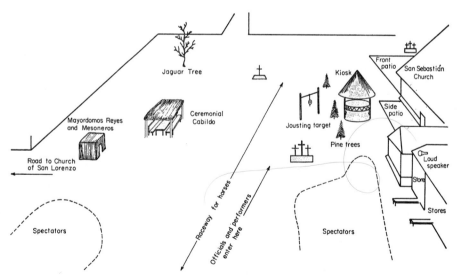

1. Churchyard of San Sebastián in Zinacantan. (From Vogt 1969:544)

the senior entertainers approach on horseback, one at a time. Behind them rides a man carrying two black and red poles which the horsemen will use to strike at the target. He is known as the pole bearer (*bč'am te'*). The Senior Alcalde rides up to the target, takes a pole from the pole bearer, prays to the sun, to San Lorenzo, and to Santo Domingo, then rides up to the target and tries to hit it with his pole. Zinacantecos say that if he misses the target, he will die soon—it is a sign from God that he will not live much longer. After striking at the target the alcalde dismounts, and the next senior entertainer goes through the test. When all have had a turn, the senior entertainers enter the church as a group in order to pray. Later in the day the junior entertainers will take turns trying to hit the target also.

After praying in the church, the senior entertainers return to the churchyard and proceed to the set of three crosses, on the cement base of which their musicians settle. The Senior Alcalde removes the picture of San Sebastián from his net bag and places it in a niche at the base of the crosses. As the musicians play, the six senior entertainers of the fiesta begin their dancing and drinking that continues at this spot for the rest of the day.

The junior entertainers perform at the west end of the churchyard, where a special cross and a tree trunk with branches from which all the leaves and twigs have been stripped have been erected. A drum is carried by one assistant and played by another, and the group dances (at times backwards)[3] to its beat as they wind their way through the crowds in the churchyard, tossing their stuffed squirrels and jabbing them with sticks. Then the drum is placed at the base of the western cross and liquor is imbibed nearby.

On January 20 and 22 a banquet is served to the civil officials and new religious officials under one of the brush shelters in the churchyard of San Sebastián. During this meal, the senior entertainers come over to the table, banter, and dig out bits of sticky jam on knives from small round wooden boxes which they hand out to the officials and boys standing nearby. The officials offer the senior entertainers eggs and pieces of chicken from their meal in exchange for the sweets.

While the senior entertainers are joking with the officials, the junior-

---

[3] The senior entertainers dance only in a forward direction.

entertainer group has divided into two smaller groups, one of which goes to the Jaguar Rock (*bolom ton*) and the other to the Sacred Water-hole (*nio?*), both places not far from the San Sebastián churchyard. Three of the Blackmen, the two Jaguars, and the Senior Lacandon, Plumed Serpent, and Spanish-Moss Wearer go to the Jaguar Rock, which is a large limestone boulder in the pasture nearby, but screened from view from the church of San Sebastián by trees. At the base of the boulder is a wooden cross, where the Lacandon, flanked by the two Jaguars, places four white candles and lights them. The others join the Lacandon and Jaguars to kneel, pray, and finally dance in front of the candles and cross. Then the Jaguars and Blackmen climb on top of the boulder, and the Jaguars light three candles in front of a cross there. The Jaguars and Blackmen subsequently set fire to a heap of corn fod-der and grass on top of the rock and shout for help as they toss the stuffed squirrels down to their fellows on the ground, who in turn toss them up again. Back and forth these stuffed animals fly, accom-panied by insults about the people whom the animals represent. As the fire blazes, powder blasts are set off by assistants on the ground, and rounds of liquor are passed as the musicians play and march around the boulder.

The grass fire on the boulder signifies the burning of the Jaguar's house (*bolom na?*) and the death of the Jaguars; the two Jaguar char-acters descend from the rock with the Blackmen and crawl into a cave-like indentation at the base of the rock to lie still, pretending to be dead. As the Jaguars lie there, the Lacandon pokes or "shoots" at them with his bow and arrow and then turns to seize two Chamula boys from the onlooking crowd. He brings them near the prone Jaguars and "shoots" the boys with his bow and arrow. Symbolically, the Jaguars are revived by the transference of the souls of the Chamula boys to their animal bodies and they leap up, "alive" again, to drink rum, dance awhile, and then cavort with the other costumed members of this subgroup of the junior entertainers as they return to the San Sebastián churchyard.

They meet the other subgroup, which meanwhile has been lighting candles, praying, and dancing at the nearby Sacred Waterhole. The re-assembled junior entertainers approach the special banquet already in progress to entertain the new religious officials during their meal. The

Blackmen capture Chamula boys time and time again and drag them to the officials to bargain for food in exchange for the boys, whom they threaten to castrate and eat:

Jaguar:	*Ves-ves-ves-huh-huh-huh.* Ladies and gentlemen, why don't you line up? I bring you something here to go with your eggs![4]
Blackman:	*Huh-huh-huh-ves-ves-ves.*
Clown:	Make way![5]
Women Spectators:	It's splitting off like uncombed hair going off in all directions![6]
A Man:	Ha, ha, ha.
Blackman:	[To men eating.] *Ves-ves-ves.* Give me the thigh, because the thigh of the chicken is delicious.
Another Blackman:	Hi, hi, hi. I'll tell you this, sir. This is Manvel Lopis who lives in the hamlet of ?Elan-vo? [pokes squirrel he carries with sharp stick].
Religious Officials:	He, he, he.
Blackman:	If my squirrel falls, I won't have any potency then.
Someone:	Yes, it's good if one has a squirrel.
Blackmen:	*Ves-ves-ves.*
Feathered Serpent:	*Hurr-hurr.*
Jaguar:	*Huh-huh-huh.*

Jaguars and Blackmen appear as evil figures in Zinacanteco folktales. Both figures are associated with caves, which are a symbol "of fear and uncertainty, symbols of special intensity. The cave is a place

---

[4] The "something" to which the Jaguar refers is one of the Chamula boys.

[5] To keep onlookers out of the way of a man wearing a bull's head of woven reeds mounted with fireworks going off in all directions.

[6] Referring to fireworks going off on bull's head.

where people are swallowed up" (Laughlin 1960:12). The indentation at the base of the Jaguar Rock represents such a cave.

According to Zinacanteco folklore, the world was once dominated by jaguars who inhabited a large cave. No one could pass by the cave safely. Finally a brave man entered the cave and slew most of the jaguars (Laughlin n.d.:T-2). The death of the jaguars is recapitulated at Jaguar Rock.

The Blackman once carried a little Chamula girl off to his cave. Soon afterward the girl gave birth to a baby Blackman. She finally died from a swollen belly because the Blackman's penis was too long (Laughlin n.d.:T-130).

When the junior entertainers return to the churchyard, the Blackmen seize the Chamula boys and offer them as a garnish for the banquet. They threaten to castrate and eat the lads, but they release them in exchange for food.

The food they receive is taken by the Blackmen to the Jaguar's Tree (plate 8), where they climb to the branches to spit and throw eggs and other food down to other junior entertainers. They also offer bits of food to their stuffed squirrels, as well as continuing to toss these animals back and forth and poking at their genitals with the sticks, shouting, "Look sir, at what Marian Peres Tanhol [policeman who did not show up at fiesta] is doing with the woman, Katal ?Ernantis Parisvan!" and, "Where are you going, Maruč [wife of policeman who did not show up]? You, who are constantly baring your ass to others." Then the Jaguars replace the Blackmen in the tree and throw the stuffed animals back and forth. When they descend from the tree they leave their stuffed spider monkey hanging by its arms from a branch of the tree as though it had been crucified. As the last Jaguar descends from the tree, his legs hanging free, a Blackman rushes up and pokes him in the crotch with a stuffed squirrel. Then they all run through the crowd, throwing their stuffed animals at spectators, poking the undersides of the squirrels with sticks, and then beating them with whips.

Visits

In the evenings, the two groups of entertainers make their rounds of the new officials' houses. At 3:45 A.M. on January 20, 1966, the first group of "visitors" arrived at the house of the Second Regidor. After reciting the prayers of greeting at the entrance to the *regidor*'s house, the junior entertainers entered and began their performance:

First Blackman:	Look, ladies and gentlemen! See how long the neck ribbons of Lol ʔUč's wife are. They just buy for themselves, but they don't pay for his *cargo*.
Second Blackman:	Look also at Marian Peres from Masan! He does nothing but fuck all the time at the foot of a mango tree.
First Blackman:	Look, my mother; look, my lady, at what Lol ʔUč is doing with Maruč [his wife]! How shameless they are, always fucking each other, even when not in their own home. [To squirrel] Now don't *you* kneel and fuck here! Ha, ha, ha. Is this your house here? Yes, you may join the musicians, but don't fuck each other by the fire.
Another Blackman:	*Huh-huh*, tricky jaguar, licentious jaguar. *Hurr-hurr-ves-ves-ves.* Look! Maruč is above and Lol ʔUč is below! Look, mother; look, my lady! See what Lol ʔUč is doing! Look at Lol caught in his wife's embrace! Look at Lol lying above his wife! He is hanging his head over there where you keep your pots [in the corner of the room].

The implications of the words of the Blackmen are clear. Both Lol ʔUč and Marian Peres are men who served as policemen during the year 1965 but did not appear to finish their terms of office during the fiesta of San Sebastián. The accusation against Marian Peres is particularly pointed:

Labal kobvaneh ta spas ta h-mek ta yolon manko.
He does nothing but fuck all the time at the foot of a mango tree.

This resembles in form, but contrasts in meaning with the ritual statement of a Zinacanteco's duty to the saints:

> . . . *spas ʔabtel ta yolon yok ti kahvaltike.*
> He does his duty at the feet of Our Lord.

"At the foot of a mango tree" refers to the settlement of Masan, the
home of Marian Peres, which specializes in growing mangoes. The
gist of the Blackman's attack on Marian Peres is that Marian ought to
be carrying out his ritual obligations "at the feet of Our Lord" in Zinacantan Center, instead of indulging in carnal pleasures "at the foot of
a mango tree" in his hamlet.

In their attacks on Lol ʔUč, the Blackmen point out some moral and
psychological flaws in his character. His wife is the center of his universe. That is why he spends all his money on elaborate neck ribbons
for her and nothing on ceremonies in honor of the saints. That is also
why he succumbs to sexual temptation at a time when *cargo* holders are
required to abstain, thereby defiling himself and his office. And what
is more, Lol is apparently not master in his own home: "Maruč is
above and Lol ʔUč is below!" implies that Lol is dominated by his
wife—that she is the more aggressive partner.

This outburst was followed by a drinking ceremony and some joking
exchanges between the Second Regidor's father, who served as official host again, and the visitors. Then the visitors prepared themselves
for the next act of their performance:

> *Jaguar*: My mother, my lady, lend me your [ceremonial]
> robe for a little while, because I am going to ex-
> tract the soul of Lol ʔUč's little son from the
> ground. The child took magical fright when his
> father became drunk while serving as policeman.
> [Puts on robe and a shawl and kneels near the fire
> with his stuffed squirrel.] *Hurr-ves-ves-ves.* Come,
> you know our house. Maruč, join your little child,
> who took fright when your husband beat you when
> he was drunk as a policeman.
>
> [Audience laughs.]

> *Hu-hu-hu* [blows on a bottle to call missing parts
> of child's soul which fled when the child took
> fright].[7]

> *Blackman*: Look! You succeeded in extracting the missing
> parts of his soul from the ground. Now that he's
> better, Maruč is kissing him.

The son of Lol ʔUč "took fright" when Lol became drunk and beat
up the child's mother. In spite of the heavy drinking which is expected
of them, *cargo* officials are expected to remain sober at all times. Cancian (1965:118) cites the case of a man who was removed from his
alférez post in midterm for drinking excessively. Thus Lol ʔUč's list of
"misdemeanors" increases—not only did he fail to finish his term of
office, but he also behaved intemperately while in office.

The Jaguar performed a mock curing ceremony. First of all he borrowed a woman's ceremonial robe (used by women curers) and put it
on. Then he tied a man's kerchief around the neck of his stuffed squirrel to represent the son of Lol ʔUč and went through the motions of
curing it. Instead of the small gourd whistle customarily used by curers
to call the missing parts of the soul, he blew on a bottle partly filled
with rum. He held a small pine bough behind the squirrel to symbolize
the curing cross. The "ceremony" ended with the Blackman beating
the squirrel (once again representing the wife of Lol) with whips and
jabbing it with sharpened sticks.

A Blackman picked up a stuffed black iguana and said, "Look! He
is the president of Mexico who arrived by airplane yesterday. Look at
your father! This is your father who came all the way from Mexico
[City] to see all his children [Zinacantecos]." The president of Mexico was represented as an iguana because the iguana happened to be the
largest stuffed animal the junior entertainers had with them.

The visit came to a close with a song by the musicians:

> Tricky jaguar,
> Licentious jaguar.

---

[7] The Zinacanteco's soul "is composed of 13 parts, and a person may lose one or
more parts and require a special curing ceremony to recover them" (Vogt 1965:33).

Hurr-hurr-ves-ves,
   Huh-huh-ves-ves.
What a long beard you have, jaguar;
   What long hair you have, jaguar.
What long hair you have, sitting animal;
   What long hair you have, armadillo.
Tricky jaguar,
   Licentious jaguar . . .
What a long beard you have, jaguar;
   What long hair you have, armadillo.
What a long beard you have, hidden animal;
   What long hair you have, sitting animal.

According to one informant, the Jaguar is called "tricky" because he tried to eat a Chamula boy and "licentious" because of what he does with the stuffed squirrels and sharpened sticks. The "long hair" and "long beard" of the Jaguar mentioned in the song probably refer to pubic hairs and "sitting animal" and "hidden animal" to the vagina.

The senior entertainers arrived en masse about an hour after the junior entertainers had left. After exchanging ritual greetings with the host and other members of the Second Regidor's household, the senior entertainers entered the house to be served rum. Then the two men dressed as Spanish Ladies rose and walked over to one of the women in the *regidor*'s household, saying, "We will comb out your lice."

The woman replied, "Please do."

One Spanish Lady began to comb and exclaimed: "Oh, how many lice you have! It must be because you worry too much. You are worried by your husband and your child. As for me, my husband does not give me cause for concern. Look at our lovely clothes—mine and those of my husband!"

The woman responded, "Yes, I am worried because my child cries all the time and my husband keeps beating me up."

If the woman whose hair was being combed happened to be the *cargo* holder's wife, the Spanish Lady added: "Your lice have multiplied like crazy. You must be worried about your *cargo*."

The *cargo* holder's wife replied, "Well, yes, it is because we don't have enough money."

The Spanish Lady then walked up to a young girl and began to comb her hair, saying: "Oh, you have so many lice. It is because your mother scolds you so much. You are very distraught." While combing the girl's hair the Spanish Lady held her bowl underneath, pretending to catch the lice in it. Then she called over to one of the Spanish Gentlemen, "Kill them, or the lice and fleas will escape!"

The Spanish Gentleman came over to her, took her bowl, and stirred its contents with his index finger. Then he turned the bowl upside down and stamped on the ground beneath it, pretending to kill the lice. When the Spanish Lady finished combing a woman's hair, she held one of her mirrors in front of the woman's face so that she could see for herself if her hair was well combed.

While the Spanish Ladies were combing the spectators' hair, the musicians sang the following humorous song about them:

> Ojalá, María!
>> Ojalá, Chinita!
> Ojalá, Luchita!
>> Ojalá, María!

> María is dancing;
>> Luchita is dancing.
> María is swaying;
>> Luchita is swaying.

> Ojalá, María!
>> Ojalá, Luchita!
> Ojalá, Chinita!
>> Ojalá, María!

> Laughing María,
>> Laughing Luchita;
> Shamefaced María,
>> Shamefaced Luchita.

> I am a woman, I am a woman, I am a woman for sure!
>> I am a girl, I am a girl, I am a girl for sure!
> Pinch away, pinch away, women [the lice]!
>> Pinch away, pinch away, girls [the lice]!
> Comb away, comb away, women!
>> Comb away, comb away, girls!

> I am a woman, I am a woman, I am a woman for sure!
>> I am a girl, I am a girl, I am a girl for sure!
> Spanish, Spanish women;
>> Spanish, Spanish girls.
>
> I am a woman, I am a woman, I am a woman;
>> I am a girl, I am a girl, I am a girl.
> I am a bought woman [i.e., prostitute];
>> I am a bought girl;
> I am a whoring woman;
>> I am a whoring girl.

María, of course, is a Spanish name for women, and Luchita and Chinita are diminutive forms of María. The song mocks the Spanish Ladies' impersonation of Spanish women and suggests that they are prostitutes.

The men costumed as Spanish ladies and gentlemen mock some of the beliefs that Spanish-speaking Mexicans (and probably the Spaniards before them) hold about Indians: that Indians are dirty and infested with fleas and lice. In fact, Zinacantecos pride themselves on their cleanliness, especially in comparison with other Indian groups. They make fun of the vain Ladino women, who are always combing their hair and looking at themselves in mirrors.

To the Zinacanteco, some defining characteristics of Spanish gentlemen are (a) that they are wealthy, (b) that their wealth is displayed in large ranches and numerous cattle, and (c) that they win attractive young women as wives because of their wealth. This stereotype is the theme of joking between the musicians, a Spanish Gentleman, and a Spanish Lady:

Musicians:	Dance well, old Spaniard! Why should you be tired? Your wife knows how to dance better. She doesn't become tired, because she is so young. You, Spanish Gentleman, we don't understand what your wife sees in you, because you are very old.
Spaniard:	Ah, but that's because I have money—I am a rich man. I have a ranch; I have cattle. That's why the girl from Oaxaca [the Spanish Lady]

	wants me. She wouldn't want you, even though you are still young, because you are poor.
Musicians:	Well, we'll ask the Spanish Lady if it is true that you have money—if it wasn't your wife who bought you your clothes.
Spaniard:	Ask her, but she won't tell you that.
Musicians:	Well, Spanish Lady, of what use is your husband to you, since he's so old? Look! He can't dance at all. He has already fallen over because of his age. You are so much younger. You aren't well matched with your husband. Much better that you marry me, for I am much younger than he is.
Spanish Lady:	But I don't want you, because I am accustomed to my husband's ways. He has a lot of money, and he has cattle. That is why I like him, even though he is an old man already. But he is a rich man, and he buys me rings and necklaces. Look—I have a mirror. You would never buy your wives that.
Musicians:	But we don't know who bought you your necklace and rings. It wasn't the stupid old Spanish Gentleman who bought them—perhaps it was your lovers who bought them.

Thus the rings, necklaces, and mirrors worn by the Spanish Lady symbolize her vanity, the wealth of her husband, and her preference for wealth over love in marriage. The musicians' punch line reiterates the theme of their song about the Spanish Lady—that she is promiscuous.

Finale

In the late afternoon of January 22 the junior entertainers leave the San Sebastián churchyard in a group to go to the small chapel (ʔ*ermita*) near the church of San Lorenzo to light candles and pray for forgiveness of any poor *cargo* performance in the past year. They dance for a short time as a last gesture of honor to the saints there and then leave to go to the house where the sacred drum resides for one last night, to honor and guard it. There they build a fire and fling their stuffed animals on it. The "wives" of the *cargo* officials and the "president of Mexico" are thus consumed in flames. As the animals burn, the junior entertainers drink rum, burn candles, and cry, for the end has finally come to their year of *cargo* service.

Encore

The Blackman is one of the most prominent symbols in the ritual humor of Zinacantan (and of other communities in highland Chiapas as well). He plays a major humorous role in two fiestas, Carnaval as well as San Sebastián (see next chapter). In nonritual contexts, people who are especially dark in complexion automatically receive the nickname Blackman, and whoever wears a capelike garment is sure to be drawn into joking interactions which have a Blackman theme.

During each of the principal fiestas (including the fiesta of San Sebastián) two of the *alféreces* complete their year of service and are replaced. The *alféreces* going through a change-of-office ceremony put on long blue or black capes with white collars, green or blue velvet knee breeches, long red stockings, and black hats decorated with peacock feathers. The musicians who are present at this ceremony claim that the *alféreces'* capes resemble the mythical Blackman's wings, on which he carries Zinacantecos off to die in his cave. The musicians begin to joke with the *alféreces*:

Musician: Where do you come from, Blackman?

Alférez: Ah, I come from far away—Guatemala is my homeland.

Musician: Well, what is your homeland like, Blackman?

Alférez: Ah, my homeland is all mountains, grassland, and caves.

Musician: Is your cave light or dark?

Alférez: Well, my cave is very dark.

Musician: Well, how deep is your cave, Blackman?

Alférez:	My cave is very deep. If you venture into my cave you will get lost.
Musician:	Won't you let me see what your cave is like, Blackman?
Alférez:	Ah, but if you venture into my cave you will become blind and lose your way.
Musician:	Ah, no, that wouldn't make me blind. Let me see how you enter it so that I can learn.
Alférez:	If you go into my cave, you will die of fear there, and then you won't be able to return to your country.

The details of the joking are fully consistent with mythical descriptions of the Blackman's habits and habitat. But for the musicians and the *alférez* in question, as well as their audience, their joking has additional humorous sexual connotations. "Cave" is synonymous with "vagina" and "grassland" with "pubic hairs." The musician's request to visit the Blackman's cave is tantamount to asking permission to cohabit with the *alférez*'s wife. In order to show the musician how to enter his cave the *alférez* would have to demonstrate how he performs sexual intercourse.

The musicians tease the incoming *alféreces* of Trinidad and San Antonio because they will perform as Jaguars at the following fiesta of San Sebastián. The musicians joke with them:

Musician:	You, Jaguar! Where is your house? Where do you sleep—in a house or, since you are a jaguar, do you sleep in a cave?
Alférez:	Every house is my house, because I roam through them all at night.
Musician:	But what do you do in the houses when you roam at night? Do you look for food, or do you just wander?
Alférez:	I produce offspring in the houses. All the children are my offspring. People say, "I have a son," but it's not their son—it's the Jaguar's son. They don't

realize that the Jaguar enters [their houses] and produces their offspring.

Musician: You are lying that you wander through the houses. You sleep only in caves.

Alférez: I don't know how to sleep in caves. But you wouldn't know when I come, for I come only at night when you are fast asleep and wouldn't see me. The Jaguar comes to amuse himself there. That's why your houses fall down. He digs under the walls of the house. The Jaguar knocks down the house in the same way that the house of the *síndico* fell down.

Alféreces: Hi, hi, hi, hi, hi.

The "tricky" and "licentious" Jaguar claims to impregnate the wives of Zinacantecos during his nocturnal wanderings. He refers to the house of the *síndico*, which collapsed earlier that week.

Thus the ritual humor of *alféreces* is partly determined by the roles some of them will play or have played during the preceding or forthcoming fiesta of San Sebastián, and stems partly from the capes they wear during their change-of-office ceremonies. In this way the humorous roles of San Sebastián serve as the models for ritual humor in other contexts.

4. ¡Bomba!

The Easter season in Zinacantan, Chamula, and Chenalhó begins with the fiesta of Carnaval and is followed by the Lenten period and Holy Week, which culminate in the Saturday of Glory (*savaro lorya*). However, Carnaval is the only fiesta of the Easter season at which ritual humorists perform. (See Vogt 1969:551–559 for a description of the others.) The sponsors of the fiestas of the Easter season are appropriately called Passions (*pašyon*) because the fiestas commemorate the passion of Christ.

The Passions of Zinacantan, of which there are two in number (senior and junior), wear the following costume: green velvet breeches trimmed with gold braid, red knee-length stockings, high-backed sandals, red turbans, and long-sleeved white shirts. Red woven straps which resemble suspenders cross at the shoulders and are tied around the waist. The Passions carry flags and feather-covered rattles. Each Passion is expected to serve a banquet of beef stew, tamales, coffee, bread, and rum on Shrove Tuesday. The Senior Passion purchases two bulls for this event; his junior buys only one. They must also serve the fermented drink made from brown sugar, a kind of beer called *yakil vo?*, to whoever requests it.

The Passions are accompanied by a Judge (*?alkalte šuves* from Spanish *alcalde juez*), who wears a black robe and a black felt hat and carries a wooden staff as the symbol of his office. Each Passion has an assistant (*yahmayol pašyon*) who watches over the Passions' flags and the Judge's staff when they are not being carried. These assistants wear black robes and red turbans.

The ritual humorists of this fiesta are known by two names: Blackmen (*h?ik'aletik*) or Demons (*pukuhetik*). Their leader, the Father of the Blackmen (*tot h?ik'al*), used to be known as the King of the Jews (Zabala n.d.:14). He wears a thigh-length wool tunic with wide brown and white stripes, somewhat resembling a Moslem kaftan; a black hat; rust-colored knee pants; and a red kerchief tied around his head. He carries a wooden staff and a bull's horn full of brown-sugar beer. The other Blackmen wear Ladino clothes—khaki trousers, shirts, white palm hats—with the exception of one Blackman, who is disguised as a woman and pretends to be the wife of their leader. Although all members of the group are referred to as Blackmen, only their leader blackens his face. These Blackmen bear a superficial resemblance to the Blackmen of the fiesta of San Sebastián, described in the last chapter, but their function and behavior are different. The fact that their leader was formerly called the King of the Jews suggests that they represent the demons, or Jews, whom Zinacantecos believe hounded Christ to his death. Significantly, they are constantly running or giving chase. They are similar to the monkey impersonators of Chamula, who also symbolize the demons, or Jews, who killed Christ (see next chapter).

The passion of Christ is not the only theme that is dramatized during this fiesta. A second major theme is the re-enactment of the Caste War of 1867–1870, when a rebellion led by Chamulas threatened to exterminate the Ladino population of the highlands. The Blackmen represent not only the Jews, who the Indians think were responsible for the crucifixion of Christ, but also the Ladinos, whom Zinacantecos regard as enemies. That is why the Blackmen wear Ladino clothing. On the last day of the fiesta of Carnaval the interethnic struggle which exploded into the Caste War of 1867–1870 is re-enacted in a mock battle. Furthermore, I believe that the Blackmen once played the part of Moors in a Dance of Moors and Christians, but that, after the Caste War, this dance was reinterpreted in terms of the local conflict. The leader of the Blackmen still wears clothes appropriate to the earlier role.

Any Zinacanteco man who wishes to do so may impersonate a Blackman during the fiesta of Carnaval. The leader of the Blackmen, however, is recruited for his role. The elders of the community choose someone known to have a good sense of humor. He retains his position for five or six years; so he is a specialist in ritual humor. The leader of the Blackmen is responsible for teaching the other Blackmen the behavior expected of them during the fiesta. In this sense he truly serves as "father" to all the Blackmen.

K'in tahimoltik, which is the Tzotzil term for the fiesta of Carnaval, means "fiesta of games." It is a period of general license and abandon; those men who dress up as Blackmen or Ladinos enjoy a four-day drunken spree at other people's expense. For four days and four nights they are released from the moral strictures which normally apply to Zinacanteco men. They derive great satisfaction from behaving like evil spirits and impersonating their social superiors, the Ladinos.

The Bomba

The ritual humor of the fiesta of Carnaval emphasizes the Blackmen's impersonation of Ladinos. It is different from anything I have described for other fiestas in Zinacantan and from ritual humor in the other two communities. It is unique in two respects: (*a*) its formal expression is limited to verses called *bombas*, and (*b*) these are recited only in Spanish. *Bombas* correspond to the Spanish verse form *copla* or *verso* (Edmonson 1952:200). The term *copla*

denotes any short poetic composition of a popular character in one single strophe or stanza, as a rule in octosyllabic meter, although shorter meters are also used. In Spanish tradition since the sixteenth century the most common are the *cuartetas*, octosyllabic quatrains with verses 2 and 4 in assonance or rhyme. This octosyllabic quatrain is the modern Spanish *copla* par excellence, the most popular type of the *copla* wherever Spanish is spoken. Next in popularity and importance in Spanish tradition are the sixain, an octosyllabic strophe of six verses, and the *seguidilla*, or quatrain of two heptasyllabic verses that alternate with two pentasyllabic verses. (Espinosa 1935:135)

In Spain and in Ladino communities of Latin America, *coplas* are "recited and sung on festive occasions, at baptisms, wedding festivities, dances, and other merrymaking occasions" (Espinosa 1935:136).

The Zinacanteco equivalent of the *copla* is called the *bomba* because the verses always end with the exclamation "*¡Bomba!*" meaning "Listen!" an interjection used to call attention to a toast (Cuyás 1904: 74). Zinacanteco *bombas* are usually, but not always, quatrains in octosyllabic meter; a few quatrains are in *seguidilla* form with alternating heptasyllabic and pentasyllabic verses.

In Zinacantan, *bombas* are recited only during the fiesta of Carnaval, and they are essential to the performance of the Blackmen, although other celebrators, such as the musicians, the Passions, and the Judge, may recite them also. About thirty different *bombas* are known in Zinacantan, and they are all regarded as humorous. The recitation of *bombas* is congruent with the Blackmen's impersonation of Ladinos. It is appropriate that Ladino impersonators should attempt to be humorous in a characteristically Ladino vein.

Perhaps the most often recited *bomba*, the one first mentioned in all interviews, is as follows:

> En el punto del cerro de Santa Cecilia,
> Oí cantar una golondrina;
> Creí que era mi madrina;
> No, que es mierda de gallina!
> > ¡Bomba!

> On the peak of the mountain of Saint Cecilia,
> I heard a swallow sing;

I thought it was my godmother;
But no, she is chicken shit!

¡Bomba!

This *bomba* is an exception to the rule, for it is in none of the traditional meters. Yet Zinacantecos regard it as a member of the same
genre to which more traditional quatrains belong. The following
bomba is closer to the traditional *copla*; the first two verses are in octosyllabic meter, and the second and fourth verses rhyme:

Qué linda está la luna,
Lucero y la campana.
Qué triste se pone el hombre—
Con chicotones quita la maña.

¡Bomba!

How beautiful the moon is,
The evening star and the bell.
How sad a man becomes—
With blows he erases the deception.

¡Bomba!

It is similar to a sixteenth-century Andalusian *copla*:

¡Qué alta que va la luna
Y el lucero en su compaña!
¡Qué triste se queda un hombre
Cuando una mujer lo engaña!

(Rodríguez Marín 1882:*copla* 6240)

How far above the moon travels
And the evening star in her company!
How sad a man can be
When a woman deceives him!

I suspect that the second line of the Zinacanteco version, which
makes little sense in its present form, was originally identical to the
second verse of the Andalusian version, but became garbled during the
intervening centuries. A number of Zinacanteco *bombas* are so garbled
that they are almost impossible to scan and translate.

I have reinterpreted this *bomba* as follows:

> ¡Qué linda está la luna,
> Y el lucero en su compaña!
> Qué triste se pone el hombre
> Cuan chicotones quitan la maña.
>   ¡Bomba!
>
> How beautiful the moon is
> And the evening star in her company!
> How sad a man becomes
> When blows erase the deception.
>   *¡Bomba!*

A similar, but fragmentary *bomba* begins as follows:

> Qué linda está la luna,
> Jornalero, corniguero . . .
>
> How beautiful the moon is,
> Journeyman, cuckolder . . . [lit., horned]

A key to both *bombas* is found in a New Mexican *copla*, which Espinosa (1935:141, 145) thinks is a variant of the Andalusian version given above:

> Ya la luna tiene cuernos,
> y el lucero la acompaña.
> ¡Ay qué triste queda un hombre
> Cuando una huera lo engaña!
>
> Now the moon has horns,
> And the evening star accompanies her.
> Oh, how sad a man remains
> When a blonde girl deceives him!

The sixteenth-century Spanish poet Góngora used the phrase "half moon" (*media luna*) as a figure of speech to describe a horned object because the half moon resembles the crescent-shaped horns of a bull (Alemany y Selfa 1930:597). Horns also connote cuckoldry, which implies that the moon is a wandering cuckolder. Clearly it is the beautiful moon which is responsible for the woman's deceit.

Other *bombas* refer to courtship, unrequited love, and unfaithful sweethearts or lovers:

> No quieren moler;
> No quieren lavar.
> Y lo pega[n] su[s] marido[s]
> Si no echa[n] huevo[s]!
> > ¡Bomba!

> They don't want to grind [corn for tortillas
> > or tamales];
> They don't want to wash [clothes].
> And they beat their husbands
> If they don't lay eggs!
> > *¡Bomba!*

Here one must realize that the verb "to grind" (*moler*) has several meanings. On one level it refers to the grinding of wheat for bread or corn for tortillas or tamales. But on another level it means "to have sexual intercourse." This interpretation is supported by the fact that "bread" in Spanish (*pan*) and tortilla or tamale in Tzotzil (*vah*) refer euphemistically to the female genitalia. Moreover, a Spanish vulgarism for testicles is "eggs." In this euphemistic context, "to wash" probably refers to the scrubbing action of sexual intercourse.

> Qué oscura está la noche;
> Parece [que] quiere llover.
> Pero mi puta novia no deja entrar.
> ¡Yo creo que está con otro hombre!
> > ¡Bomba!

> How dismal the night is;
> It seems about to rain.
> But my whoring sweetheart won't let me in.
> I think she is with another man!
> > *¡Bomba!*

The first verse is almost identical to a Chilean *copla* (Jijena Sánchez and López Peña 1965:112):

> Ay, qué oscura está la noche,

como que quiere llover;
así está mi corazón
cuando no te puedo ver.

Oh, how dismal the night is,
For it seems about to rain;
That is how my heart is
When I can't see you.

The last verse of this *copla* is similar to another, but fragmentary, Zinacanteco variant:

¡Ay, qué oscura está la noche!
¿Qué dirá mi negrita
Por no ir a ver?
                    ¡Bomba!

Oh, how dismal the night is!
What will my little black girl say
For not going to see her?
                    ¡Bomba!

Another group of *bombas* describe promiscuous behavior on the part of women:

¡Mariquita, no te vayas a un lado!
Te tengo oro;
[Te] tengo plata.
Tu piernita me gusta mucho.
                    ¡Bomba!

Mariquita, don't go away!
For you I have gold;
[For you] I have silver.
I like your little thigh very much.
                    ¡Bomba!

Ay, Mariquita,
Abreme tu[s] piernita[s]
Porque ya me estoy muriendo de frío.
                    ¡Bomba!

Oh, Mariquita,

Open your little thighs to me
Because I am about to die of cold.

> *¡Bomba!*

¡Esta muchacha muy alegría!
¡Aunque me llega día y noche [noche y día],
Sale uno!

> ¡Bomba!

This high-spirited girl!
Whether I arrive day or night,
Someone is always leaving!

> *¡Bomba!*

The Blackmen recite their verses in Spanish, not Tzotzil. This means that their audience (and often the men who recite the *bombas* also) may not understand what is being said, but everyone laughs anyway. However, significant words may be translated into Tzotzil. For example, instead of saying María or Mariquita, the Blackmen may say Maruč or Katal, depending on which promiscuous Zinacanteco girl they want to ridicule.

Several *bombas* specify that the girl in question has a dark complexion, for example:

Ahora un año me fuí en Guatemala;
De allí trajé un mi calzón blanco,
Para enamorar una muchacha morena;
¡Parece que tiene el ojo de gavilán!

> ¡Bomba!

A year ago I went to Guatemala,
Whence I fetched a pair of white trousers,
So that I could win the heart of a dark girl.
She seems to have the eye of a hawk!

> *¡Bomba!*

En esta calle derecha,
Allí encontré una puente elegante,
En donde pasa mi morena.
¡Parece como la orma de una garza!

> ¡Bomba!

> On this straight road
> I discovered a graceful bridge,
> Which my dark girl crosses.
> She seems to have the shape of a heron!
> > *¡Bomba!*

Zinacanteco women are, of course, dark in complexion, and it is appropriate that an Indian so describe his sweetheart. But Zinacanteco men customarily do not recite verses about women and unrequited love. Nor is the structure of the *bomba* similar to that of the metaphorical couplet which is the characteristic Zinacanteco verse form. The *bomba* is a lyric composition with its roots in sixteenth- and seventeenth-century Spain (Espinosa 1935:135); the Blackmen recite *bombas* because they are a Ladino verse form and therefore contribute to the Ladino stereotype that the Blackmen are trying to convey. Many Spanish and Ladino *coplas* refer to dark women; for example:

> Los ojos de mi morena
> Se parecen a mis males:
> Grandes, como mis fatigas;
> Negros, como mis pesares.   (Rodríguez Marín 1927:241)

> The eyes of my dark girl
> Resemble my misfortune:
> Great, like my anguish;
> Black, like my grief.

> ¡Mal haya la ropa negra,
> y el sastre que la cortó!
> Mi negrita tiene luto
> Sin haberme muerto yo.   (Espinosa 1935:140)

> May the black clothes be damned,
> And the tailor who made them!
> My little black girl is in mourning
> Without my even having died.

> ¡Qué malas entrañas tienes,
> al decir que te amo poco,
> Sabiendo, morena ingrata,
> que tu amor me tiene loco!   (Espinosa 1935:140)

> What a bad disposition you have,
> To say that I love you little,
> Knowing, ungrateful dark girl,
> That your love drives me crazy!

Although some of the *bombas* are humorous in themselves, their chief value as ritual humor derives from the support they give to the Blackmen's caricature of Ladinos. The Blackmen take turns reciting *bombas* while dancing, as if in competition with each other, thereby parodying the *copla* contests so popular in Spain and Latin America (Espinosa 1935:138).

The dance and the recitation of *bombas* together form a complex which is similar to the *jarana* of Yucatán: "The couples dance until interrupted by the cry '*bomba*' (bomb). The dancing stops and the person indicated by the caller has to recite a *copla* or *verso*. If the persons attending are particularly talented, some may make up verses on the occasion" (Bork 1949:6–7). A *jarana* which I witnessed in Hocabá, Yucatán, during the 1971 fiesta of Carnaval conforms to Bork's description.

Redfield and Villa Rojas (1934:155) write that the *jarana* is one of the essential features of the fiesta in honor of the patron saint of X-Kalakdzonot, another Mayan community in Yucatán. There, too, the *jarana* includes "the recital by a dancer when challenged to do so, of humorous quatrains (bombas)" (Redfield and Villa Rojas 1934:156).

According to Bork (1949:6), both the dance and the verse forms of the traditional *jarana* are of Spanish origin. Although common in Mayan communities of Yucatán, they are rare among the highland Maya, Zinacantan being the only Mayan community outside Yucatán where, to my knowledge, these forms exist. Although the recitation of *bombas* in Zinacantan may be a vestige of a formerly more widespread distribution of the *jarana*, it is today regarded as something alien—as part of a parody of Ladino customs.

Prelude

Some days before the fiesta begins, the Passions recruit at least ten men each to fetch firewood to be used in preparing the Shrove Tuesday banquet. Each woodman makes three trips back and forth between the Passion's house and the woods. This job takes the better part of a day. At noon the Passion sends them a picnic lunch of dried beef, tortillas, rum, and cigarettes. When the woodmen finish their stint, they return to the homes of the Passions, where they are served another similar meal.

On Friday afternoon the Passions dress in their costumes and go with gifts of coffee, rolls, and rum to the houses of the Judge, the leader of the Blackmen, and their musicians. After the gifts have been presented to the leader of the Blackmen, he too puts on his costume and recites the first *bomba*. The fiesta personnel then return to the house of the Senior Passion, where they eat, drink, and dance until dawn.

On Saturday morning the Passions, the Judge, and the leader of the Blackmen are sworn into office in the chapel of Esquipulas. At this time they receive their symbols of office—the flags, rattles, and wooden staffs. Then they go to the Judge's house to be served gruel.

Ceremonial Visits

Beginning on Saturday afternoon, the Passions, Judge, Blackmen, and musicians go together as a party to visit the homes of the *cargo* holders. First of all, the musicians send two or three Blackmen on ahead to ask the *cargo* holder's ritual adviser for permission to visit his house. Upon arrival, the Blackmen go up to the ritual adviser and greet him as follows:

> Well, grandfather,
>   Lord:
> Are you waiting here for my earth?
>   Are you waiting here for my mud?
> Our father sent us here;
>   Our mother sent us here.
> We've come to ask for a word;
>   We've come to request advice.

"Will you give us permission?" ask our father and the musicians.

The ritual adviser replies:

> They should come!

I am waiting here for their earth;
    I am waiting here for their mud.
Will they be assembled here?
    Will they be united here?
Our father,
    Our mother.

And the Blackmen emissaries say that they will do as instructed:

You will wait there for our earth;
    You will wait there for our mud.
Here in a moment;
    Here in two moments.
Let us fetch our father,
    Let us fetch our mother.

The Blackmen return to their companions and report that they have
been given permission to make the visit. The whole party then troops
off to the *cargo* holder's house. When they arrive, they greet the *cargo*
holder and his ritual adviser. The Passions and the Judge tie their flags
and staff to the cross standing outside the house and then enter to
sing, dance, recite *bombas*, and be served rum. The Passions' assistants
remain outside to guard the sacred objects which have been tied to
the cross.

Midway through the dancing, the *cargo* holder serves strong rum
laced with coffee to the Passions, the Judge, and the leader of the
Blackmen. This drink gives them heat and strength so that they will
not tire from the dancing. It also relaxes their inhibitions so that they
will not be too embarrassed to recite *bombas*. The rest of the Blackmen
are served weak rum because they are only volunteers and do not
sponsor the fiesta.

The Judge is the first to recite a *bomba* and is followed by the Passions, the musicians, and the Blackmen, in that order. Each person recites a different *bomba*. The Blackmen wiggle their hips as they dance.
When a dance ends, the Blackmen shout *"muchacho,"* the Spanish
word for "boy." Ladinos use this term in a patronizing way to refer
to all Indian men, even mature adults.

When the dance is over, the visitors leave, after bidding a formal goodbye to their hosts. The musicians again send several Blackmen on ahead to request permission to visit the next *cargo* holder's house. The visits continue until Tuesday night. The Carnaval celebrants must stay awake throughout this period, for they believe that if they fall asleep before the fiesta has ended, they will die.

Early on Monday morning the Senior Passion serves a meal of meat, coffee, and tortillas to the *mayordomos*, sacristans, and Blackmen, after which pilgrimages are made to the various cross shrines which are located in Zinacantan and on the sacred mountains which surround the valley in which the ceremonial center is situated. Since the ultimate destination of the pilgrims is Mount Calvary (*kalvaryo*), the cross shrines probably represent the Stations of the Cross, and the pilgrimage commemorates Christ's procession from Pilate's house to Calvary Hill (Alston 1912:XV, 569). The Blackmen accompany the *mayordomos*, the Passions, and the Judge on these visits. The Blackmen dance and recite *bombas* while the Passions and the Judge light candles and pray before the cross shrines. The irreverent behavior of the Blackmen contrasts sharply with the solemn rituals performed by the Passions, but it is in keeping with their role as pagan Jews or Moors. The circuit includes a visit to the mountain of Saint Cecilia, the mountain referred to in the Blackmen's favorite *bomba*. Similar visits are made to the three principal churches on Tuesday.

The Banquets

On Monday, after the ceremony on top of the mountain of Saint Cecilia has ended, the *mayordomos* race down the mountainside and up to the top of Mount Calvary, where they have a snack, and then to the house of the Junior Passion where they "hurl themselves at the table, gobble down all the food they can get, then run out and sit down outside innocently awaiting the arrival of the Passions, when they go in formally to eat their meal. They are impersonating robbers of meals" (Laughlin, personal communication, September 12, 1972).

Two ceremonial banquets are served on Tuesday. One takes place at the house of the Junior Passion, where the Carnaval performers eat. The civil and religious officials are served their meal in the chapel of Esquipulas.

The two scribes write notes in Spanish, which they give to the leader of the Blackmen to deliver at the two banquets. The notes ask whether the banquets are still in progress or have terminated. The leader of the Blackmen serves as mailman, running first to the house of the Junior Passion, then to the chapel, and then back to the Passion's house. After delivering his message, the leader of the Blackmen and his "children" return to the chapel to beg for food. The leader of the Blackmen makes what he calls his "chocolate" to offer in exchange for tidbits. He mixes brown sugar and finely ground coffee with rum. The food he receives he passes out to the other Blackmen, who fight over it.

The "Caste War"

The *presidente* decides that the Blackmen should be jailed for their "crimes." A group of Zinacanteco policemen chases them and captures them, but the Blackmen break away and have to be recaptured. The Blackmen run wildly through the crowds in their attempt to escape their pursuers and, when caught, some of them put up a convincing fight. Finally they are captured and taken to the *presidente*, who orders them to be locked up in the jail. The leader of the Blackmen is the last to be jailed.

The Passions and the Judge plead with the *presidente* for the prisoners' release. He grants their request and orders the policemen to release them. Each of the policemen brings out two captives, their wrists tied with rope, and dances with them, holding onto their ropes. Finally the Blackmen are set loose, and they run off to the churchyard to be served rum by the wives of the *cargo* holders.

This incident clearly represents a conflict of some sort. There is a polarization between men wearing Ladino clothes and men wearing Indian clothes. For this reason I think that this conflict represents the Caste War of 1867–1870, when Indians fought Ladinos in an unsuccessful effort to exterminate them.

Postlude

Although called the "fiesta of games," in comparison with the fiestas described in chapters 2 and 3, this fiesta offers relatively little in the way of ritual humor. The *bombas*, of course, are humorous, as are the "caste war" and the impersonation of Blackmen and Ladinos. But it seems as though most of the Zinacanteco's ingenuity with respect to ritual humor is expended in the fiestas of Christmas–New Year's, Epiphany, and San Sebastián. This observation is given added weight when the Zinacanteco fiestas are compared with the fiesta of Carnaval in Chamula and Chenalhó. In those communities the elements of ritual humor which Zinacantecos distribute over three fiestas are concentrated into a single fiesta. In Chamula and Chenalhó the fiesta of Carnaval is truly a "fiesta of games."

I have included Zinacantan's fiesta of Carnaval in this study not only because of its ritual humor, but also because it shares certain themes with the same fiesta in the other two communities. Those themes include the impersonation of Ladinos and Blackmen, the dramatization of ethnic conflict, and elements of the Catholic Passion Play. It is therefore interesting that, although the three communities are neighbors, they have developed those themes in quite different ways.

5. Chamula: Crazy February!

The dominant theme of the fiesta of Carnaval in Chamula is war and conquest. All of the conflicts in which the people of Chamula have participated are telescoped into this one fiesta. For the Chamulas, all conflicts are alike in certain important respects: (*a*) there is the armed conqueror, who arrives bearing weapons, flags, and fireworks; (*b*) there is the battle; (*c*) the conqueror has a mistress. Ostensibly the fiestas of Carnaval, Lent, and Easter commemorate the passion of Christ. There is conflict associated with that event too—the domination of the Jews by the Romans and the crucifixion of Christ. The Chamulas see nothing strange about lumping the passion of Christ with Cortés's conquest of Mexico, the French intervention of 1861–1867 (Dabbs

NOTE: The phrase "Crazy February," which begins the proclamation announcing the fiesta of Carnaval in Chamula, was used by Carter Wilson as the title for one of his novels about Chamula (1966).

1963), the Ladino invasion of Chamula during the Caste War of
1867–1870 (Molina 1934; Pineda 1888), the nineteenth-century
boundary dispute between Chiapas and Guatemala (Orantes 1960),
and the Mexican revolution of 1910–1917. There are certain themes
common to all the conflicts, and it is those themes which are dramatized
during the fiesta.

The several themes of the fiesta are neatly summarized in the proclamation made by the master of ceremonies (ʔ*avito*) a week before the
fiesta begins:

Chamulas!
Crazy February!
Today is the Ninth of February, 1969.
The first soldier came to Mexico [City].
He came to Guatemala;
He came to Tuxtla [Gutiérrez];
He came to Chiapa [de Corzo];
He came to San Cristóbal [Las Casas].
He came with flags;
He came with drums;
He came with trumpets.
Viva! Viva!

Fellow citizens!
The second cavalier came to Mexico [City].
He came to Guatemala;
He came to Tuxtla [Gutiérrez];
He came to Chiapa [de Corzo];
He came to San Cristóbal [Las Casas].
He came with flags;
He came with drums;
He came with trumpets.
Viva! Viva!

. . . .

The last cavalier came to Mexico [City].
He came to Guatemala;
He came to Tuxtla [Gutiérrez];
He came to Chiapa [de Corzo];
He came to San Cristóbal [Las Casas].

He came with fireworks;
He came with cannons;
He came with fifes;
He came with bugles;
He came with flags;
He came with trumpets.
Mariano Ortega and Juan Gutiérrez came with their young lady,
   Nana María Cocorina.
They go together into the woods to make love.
They return eating toffee, eating candied squash, eating
   blood sausage.
Viva Mariano Ortega!

This announcement clearly recapitulates the Spanish conquest of Mexico, beginning with Hernán Cortés's victory in Mexico City, followed by Pedro de Alvarado's journey to Guatemala through Chiapas, and culminating in the conquest of Chiapas by Luis Marín and Diego de Mazariegos. Marín and Mazariegos first conquered the Chiapanecs near what is today Chiapa de Corzo, and then moved into the highlands, where they established a town on the present site of San Cristóbal Las Casas. The Chamulas were one of the last tribes to be subdued by the conquering Spaniards in 1524 (Díaz del Castillo 1904:II, 220–223). Troops were brought in from Tuxtla and Chiapa during the Caste War of 1867–1870 to reinforce the small garrison in San Cristóbal (Pineda 1888:104–105; Corzo 1943:142–143). The Ladinos of Chiapas appealed to the president of Mexico for help, but he refused to send federal troops, perhaps because he was himself an Indian (Flores Ruíz 1939[?]:12). President Juárez did, however, send Mexican troops to help suppress the Imperialist cause during the French intervention, and Mexican soldiers did battle with Guatemalan troops in the border dispute of that period. Finally, in 1917 Chiapas was the scene of armed conflict between the constitutional forces of Mexico led by Carranza and revolutionary forces led by Pineda. Thus the proclamation heralding the beginning of the fiesta of Carnaval in Chamula faithfully accounts for the movement of troops during several periods of crisis.

   Mariano Ortega (historically Juan Ortega) was a political reactionary and an advocate of the privileges of the clergy in the two decades before the Caste War (Cáceres López 1962; López Gutiérrez 1963: 130–228). At that time Mexico (including Chiapas) was embroiled in a struggle for power between Centralist (conservative) and Federalist (liberal) factions (Corzo 1943:109). The people of San Cristóbal sided with the Centralist cause, while those of Tuxtla and Chiapa supported the Federalists. When the French invaded Mexico in 1862, Ortega declared himself in favor of the empire and attempted a military takeover of the state of Chiapas (López Gutiérrez 1963:150–151). On May 7, 1863, he invaded and occupied San Cristóbal, which he held until January 24, 1864 (López Gutiérrez 1963:155; Paniagua 1870:650). As a result, Chamula, which at that time belonged to the department of San Cristóbal, fell under Ortega's domination, as did the neighboring township of San Pedro Chenalhó (*El Baluarte de la libertad*, August 27, 1869:4). It is clear that Ortega's presence was felt in the Indian countryside, for he forced Indians to build fortifications in San Cristóbal, and Chamula Indians are known to have assisted federal troops sent by Juárez to drive out the Imperialists (Paniagua 1870: 626, 635). Furthermore, Ortega's troops are known to have passed through Chenalhó on their way to Tabasco after they had lost a decisive battle against the federal forces (López Gutiérrez 1963:206). The Pedrano myth of the Caste War claims that Juan Ortega was the leader of the Ladino forces which were going to kill all the Indians (Guiteras-Holmes 1961:265). Because of his military activities and his conservative stance, Ortega became identified with the troops that put down the rebellion in Chamula.

Ortega is also identified with the boundary dispute between Mexico and Guatemala, because many of his troops were recruited from Central America and because he used Guatemala as a base for his attacks on the towns of Chiapas. The border dispute concerned the Soconusco area of Chiapas, which Guatemala claimed on the grounds that it had been first pacified by Alvarado in 1524 on his way to conquer Guatemala (Orantes 1960:60). Mexico's claim rested on a decision made by the Spanish Crown in 1790 to incorporate the Soconusco area into the intendancy of Chiapas (Orantes 1960:60).

Gutiérrez was a champion of Federalism and local autonomy for the state of Chiapas during the first half of the nineteenth century. In

1830 Gutiérrez became the governor of Chiapas, and during the next eight years he led Federalist troops in raids throughout Chiapas, including an attack on the conservative stronghold of San Cristóbal.

The symbols of war—flags, drums, trumpets, cannons, and fireworks —are important symbols in the fiesta ritual. Every major event is introduced and terminated by the setting off of cannons and rockets. The flag is the key symbol of this fiesta because it represents the spear which pierced the body of Jesus Christ. The flagstaff is tipped with a socketed metal spear head called "The Head of Our Father" (*shol htotik*), which is tied to the flagstaff with red and green ribbons. The cloth banner and the ribbons represent the clothes of Christ. The banner cloth is of flowered chintz; the flower is the symbol of divinity in Chamula and is in this sense equivalent to the color gold and the halo in Christian symbolism. The adjective "flowery" (*ničim*) is used in contexts in which Christians used the term "divine," for example:

> *ničim yahvalel vinahel,*
> *ničim yahvalel lorya.*
> Flowery [divine] Lord of Heaven,
> Flowery [divine] Lord of Glory.

Jesus Christ is impersonated by religious officials called Passions (*pašyon*). Each of the three barrios is represented by two Passions, an incoming Passion (*hʔočel pašyon*) and an outgoing one (*hlok'el pašyon*), for a total of six Passions in the community. When the Passion carries the flag topped by the lance tip, he is in effect providing the body for Christ, whose head is the lance tip. Chamulas say that "when the Passion walks, Christ walks; when the Passion dances, Christ dances; when the Passion runs, Christ runs." Through the Passion, God returns to earth for the duration of the fiesta. The Passions are required to give three banquets, called *kompiral* (from Spanish *convidar*— "treat, invitation"), during the fiesta. In this way God feeds his children, the people of Chamula, all of whom are welcome to attend the banquets.

The Passion cult is the only cult in Chamula for which the object of devotion is not a saint figure in the church. The emphasis is on impersonation rather than idolatry. The theme of the fiesta is war, and one of the wars being commemorated is the Caste War of 1867–1870, which originated in Chamula. The leaders of this rebellion exhorted the Indians to reject the Catholic saints and, on Good Friday in 1868, crucified a ten- or eleven-year-old boy, Domingo Gómez Checheb, to be worshipped as the Indian Christ (Pineda 1888:76–77). There is abundant evidence that the Christ whom the Passion impersonates is this Indian Christ rather than the Ladino Savior (Bricker n.d.*b*).

Each Passion has a ritual adviser (*yahvaltikil* or *yahvotik*), someone who has served as Passion in a previous year, who advises him on how much food to serve at the banquets and who conducts ritual for the Passion. His role is perhaps the most important one of all, because if the Passion should run out of food, God would be embarrassed and, as punishment, would send rain, which would interfere with the proper celebration of the fiesta.

Assisting the Passions in sponsoring the fiesta are six religious officials called Flowers (*ničim*), also two from each barrio. As mentioned above, *ničim* means "flower," or "divinity," in Tzotzil. God apparently has at least two aspects, a Passion aspect and a Divine aspect. This is in keeping with Mayan tradition, for the ancient gods of Yucatán had multiple manifestations (Morley 1946:224, 231).

Not only do the human impersonators of Christ represent several of his aspects, but so also do the lance tips, which represent his head. The Passions and Flowers of each barrio are entrusted with four metal lance tips and the clothing belonging to them. Each of the four lance tips is a different manifestation of God: two are male and two are female. The male manifestations are the Lord of Heaven (*yahvalel vinahel*) and Little Emmanuel (*bik'it hmanvel*); the female manifestations are the Mother of Heaven (*sme? vinahel*) and Abandoned Woman (*sutemal ?ant*). The latter is so named because she was deserted by her husband (St. Joseph). The Flowers keep the male and female manifestations of God in separate wooden chests because "men and women shouldn't sleep together—who knows what hanky-panky might occur if they slept in the same bed!"

In addition to the flag cloths and ribbons, Christ's clothes consist of miniature shirts, wool tunics, women's head coverings, hats, shawls, and shoes (little brown plastic Oxfords such as might be worn by a child of two). The shoes are cut out at the toes to show that they are worn out. When the lance tips are removed from the flags, they are wrapped in their clothes and put to bed in their chests on mounds of pure white carded sheep's wool.

The Passions of each barrio are accompanied by men called ?ortinaryo (from Spanish ordinario) and komisaryo (from Spanish comisario). "In New Spain [Mexico] from 1522 to 1571 an episcopal Inquisition operated and bishops tried cases as ordinaries, or monastic prelates acted as ordinaries under the omnímoda" (Greenleaf 1965: 139). However, "when the Mexican Tribunal of the Holy Office of the Inquisition was established in 1571, it was refused the right to hear Indian cases. Indians were to remain under the ordinary jurisdiction in the bishopric" (Greenleaf 1965:141). Thus Indian cases of idolatry and bigamy were never handled by Inquisitors, but were dealt with, from the beginning, by bishops "under the portfolio of Ecclesiastical Judge Ordinary" (Greenleaf 1965:138). The Ordinaries were the Inquisitorial judges as far as the Indians were concerned. "The Inquisition archives of Mexico record the final Indian trial of the Mexican colonial period in 1818" (Greenleaf 1965:165), only three years before Mexico achieved independence from Spain.

The Commissary's duties were "to investigate heresy and gather evidence for the central tribunal" (Greenleaf 1969:160). Thus both the Ordinaries and the Commissaries are associated with the Mexican Inquisition, an institution comparable to war in the impact it had on the Indian community. The Inquisition is even more explicitly commemorated in the fiesta of Carnaval in Yucatán (see chapter 9).

The outgoing Passions, Ordinaries, and Commissaries wear similar outfits: red two-piece suits trimmed with gold braid, ribboned necklaces, red knee-length stockings, sandals, and straw hats with red and green ribbons cascading over the brims (plate 11). On the other hand, the incoming Passions and all the Flowers wear black wool robes over white shirts and trousers, ribboned hats, and necklaces. Since in Chamula the color red symbolizes evil, all the fiesta personnel will have to run through fire at the end of the fiesta in order to purge themselves from the evil of having worn red themselves, or from having associated with others who have.

Nana María Cocorina, also called Spanish Lady (*šinolan ʔanť*), is impersonated by a man. She represents Malinche, Cortés's mistress, as well as the presumed mistress of Juan Gutiérrez or Mariano Ortega. The Passions sometimes take the roles of Juan Gutiérrez or Mariano Ortega (because they accompany Nana María Cocorina), and sometimes the Ordinary is called Ortega because his role name begins with the same four phenomes (*ʔortinaryo, ʔorteka*).

Nana María Cocorina wears a man's ribboned ceremonial hat covered with a white plastic cover from which the ends of the ribbons escape, dangling unevenly. Her cream-colored dress, perhaps originally white but now yellowed with age, is worn over a dark-blue skirt. About three inches of blue embroidery at the hem of the dress is the only decoration. She wears men's sandals and white trousers, which can be clearly seen hanging below her skirt. Over her head and shoulders she ties a large white cotton shawl, on top of which she rests her hat. She holds with both hands a lighted censer with which she censes or "feeds" the Passions' flags, for God "eats" only incense (fig. 2).

Each Passion, Ordinary, Flower, Commissary, and Nana María Cocorina is accompanied by courtiers who impersonate monkeys. They are called *mašetik* (Monkeys) or *yahmaštak* (Their Monkeys) [from *maš* "monkey"], because they wear headdresses of monkey fur. The Passions, Flowers, and Ordinaries have four Monkeys apiece; Nana María Cocorina and the Commissaries have only two each.

The costumes worn by the Monkeys are almost identical to the uniforms worn by French grenadiers during the period of the French intervention (Blom 1956:281; Martin 1963:118, 145 right). The Monkeys wear black frock coats trimmed with a long red cross in back and wide horizontal red bands at the waist, wrists, and the bottom of the tails in back. These coats resemble the grenadiers' dark-blue uniforms faced with red (Martin 1963:145 right). Chamulas call these jackets *leva*, which means "draft" in Spanish, with reference to conscripted men or draftees. They recognize the costumes as soldiers' uniforms and sometimes refer to the men wearing the jackets by military titles, such as Captain and General.

2. Nana María Cocorina participating in Dance of the Warriors. (Drawn by Mariano López Calixto)
(1) Acolyte censes the cross here; (2) cross to which flags are tied; (3) "Damn! I don't think my ass is going to fit!" (4) Monkeys circling the Drummer; (5) Passion's flowers are placed here; (6) Censer; (7) Drummer's rum receptacle; (8) Drummer is lying here because he's drunk.

The Monkeys wear brown suede or dark-orange cotton knee breeches over ankle-length white trousers (plate 11). This combination bears some resemblance to trousers worn by some French grenadiers (Martin 1963:145 right). It is possible that the white scarves which the Monkeys tie across one shoulder were once meant to represent the white crossbelts worn by the French grenadiers (Martin 1963:118). The Monkeys carry whips made from bull penises, rather than guns.

The busbylike headdresses of the Monkeys are made of black howler-monkey fur (*baǰ'*) instead of bearskin. They probably also date from the period of the French intervention (see Martin 1963:118, 145 right). They are furthermore decorated with cascades of red and green ribbon streamers, which recall the insignia worn by Ortega's imperial forces (Paniagua 1870:439). Today the material source of the headdress is of greater symbolic importance than its historical association.

The military theme survives, but it is overshadowed by the monkey symbolism. A monkey's tail is attached at the base of the headdress and hangs down to the monkey impersonator's waist.

Some Monkeys blacken their faces with soot and wear sunglasses to further disguise themselves. In this guise they resemble the Blackman impersonators of Zinacantan (chapter 4), Chenalhó (chapter 6), and Huistán (chapter 9). In Chamula mythology the monkey is symbolically equivalent to the *pukuh* (evil spirit) and the *h'ik'al* (Blackman). The *pukuh* is black except for his red eyes and penis; black and red are the colors of the monkey impersonators' jackets. Monkeys, Blackmen, and evil spirits are all symbols of evil and Chamulas make no clear-cut distinction between them in their myths and rituals. I therefore suspect that, before 1861, what Chamulas now call Monkeys were called Blackmen, as they still are today in neighboring Zinacantan, Chenalhó, and Huistán. Apparently Ortega's version of the French intervention had such an impact on Chamula that the Blackman impersonator's costume was changed in response to it. Later the symbolic associations of the fur headdress came to dominate the role, although the military and Blackman themes still remain as two of its components.

This argument is strengthened by the fact that the monkey impersonators of Chamula, like the Blackman impersonators of Zinacantan, also represent the demons, or Jews, whom a Chamula myth describes as the murderers of Christ. The Jews' attack on Christ is symbolized by the Monkeys in the Dance of the Warriors (see below).

Chamulas distinguish between two kinds of monkey impersonators: (*a*) "independent" Monkeys (*šokol maš*), who disguise themselves as monkeys purely for the fun of it, and (*b*) the "dependent" Monkeys who are associated with the fiesta's sponsors and who are called Their Monkeys (*yahmaštak*). Any man or boy in the community may borrow or buy a monkey costume and wear it during the fiesta. The "independent" Monkeys are like the Blackmen in Zinacantan (Carnaval) and the Dancing Ladies of Chenalhó. Carnaval is a time when any man or boy may change his identity for a while, cease to be human, and indulge in animallike behavior—the behavior of monkeys.

The "dependent" Monkeys serve as the courtiers or assistants of the fiesta leaders. They supervise the activities of their servants and lead the men who sweep the plaza and gather firewood for the Passions. Their wives serve as ladies-in-waiting to the wives of the officials— keeping them company, chatting with them, and attending to them when they drink too much.

Both types of monkey impersonators imitate wild monkeys. They dance incessantly, in apparent imitation of the continuous motion characteristic of real monkeys in the forest:

> Throughout the entire fiesta the Monkeys manifest a person-ality which they have adopted in imitation of the nervous and rest-less movements of monkeys.
>
> The Monkeys dance constantly to the sound of the characteristic music of Chamula; they do not cease even when they feel tired and can no longer move their feet; they bend their knees in time with the rhythm of harmonica, accordion, and guitar music; they dance without stopping: when they quarrel, when they drink; their dancing is almost pathological; they keep still only when they fall down overcome by fatigue and alcohol. (Pozas 1959:170; my translation)

The Monkeys make animal noises (*borohó-borohó-borohó*), whistle, and jokingly threaten to seize people, wrap them in their tails, and carry them off into the forest. If someone threatens to chase them, the Monkeys reply that they will escape by climbing trees. They pretend to live on a diet of fruit and leaves. The following is an example of a joking interaction which took place between an "independent" Monkey and some spectators:

Monkey: Look, coward! I have a tail, coward. Look after yourselves, girls. Otherwise I will carry you off to my house. If you like, I'll carry you up to the branch of a tree, coward. You shouldn't approach me too closely, coward, because I'll carry you off to a tree branch, coward, *ha-la-ha, ha-la-ha, ha-la-ha.* I'm tell-ing the truth, child; I'm telling the truth, coward. I'll carry you off to a tree branch, coward. *Ha-la-ho, ha-la-ha, ha-la-ha.*

Girls: [Laughing] Ti, hi, hi, hi; ti, hi, hi.

Monkey: I'll carry you up with my tail, coward. We'll go to
sleep together on the tree branch, coward. But don't
be afraid, coward, *ha-la-ha, ti-ha-la-ha, ti-ha-la-ha.*
I'm telling the truth, coward; I'm telling the truth,
child. I know how to eat seeds; I know how to eat
acorns because I am an animal of the woods, coward.
That's why I have a tail. My mother stayed there in
the tree because she is pregnant. She can't walk.
That's why she stayed in the tree, *ti-ha-la-ha, ti-ha-
la-ha, ti-ha-la-ha.*

Some "independent" Monkeys hang stuffed animals (squirrels,
weasels, iguanas) from their shoulders or wrists or put them in their
pockets. They pretend that the stuffed animals are their children. If a
spectator laughs at him for carrying stuffed animals, the Monkey asks:
"Why are you laughing, bastard? Is it because this [squirrel or iguana]
is your animal-spirit-companion here, bastard? *Horohó-horohó-horohó-
horohó.* Is it because it is your animal-spirit-companion, bastard? Feed
it if you like, bastard! Feed your animal-spirit-companion so it will not
die from hunger. If you feed it, you will die, bastard. *Horohó-
horohó-horohó-horohó.*"

The spectator answers, "I will only feed it if you will feed me too,
bastard."

The Monkey responds to that with: "I'll feed you, bastard. Let's go
to the woods, bastard! *Horohó-horohó-horohó.* I'll feed you, bastard.
First you'll bite the head of your animal-spirit-companion, bastard.
Horohó-horohó-horohó. For it's really the head of your animal-spirit-
companion, bastard. That's why I'm giving it to you to eat, bastard.
Horohó-horohó-horohó."

Chamulas believe that each person has an animal alter ego on which
his life and health depend. If harm befalls the animal, its human alter
ego will become ill. Thus, if the spectator's animal-spirit-companion
dies of hunger, so also will the spectator. On the other hand, if the
spectator eats his alter ego, he will die, for in so doing he will destroy
his animal-spirit-companion.

Some "independent" Monkeys wear jaguar pelts on their backs although they never take part in the ritual of the sacred jaguar pelt (see

below). Perhaps they are parodying the Monkeys who serve the religious officials.

During the fiesta the "independent" Monkeys beg for food and
drink (the Monkeys of the religious officials never do this). They go
up to merchants, singing:

> Cover the eyes;
>   Cover the face,
> Of the Lord of Heaven,
>   Of the Lord of Glory.
>
> Oh, you know of his goodness;
>   Oh, you know of his greatness,
> Of the Lord of Heaven,
>   Of the Lord of Glory.
>
> Your festival has come;
>   Your goodness has come, Lord of Heaven.
> For only three days of your greatness,
>   For only three hours of your goodness,
> For only three days of your festival, Lord of Heaven.
>
> *Horohó-horohó-horohó,*
> Oh, you know of his goodness, son;
> But not every day,
>   Not every hour,
> His goodness,
>   His greatness,
> Of the Lord of Heaven,
>   Of the Lord of Glory.
>
> For only three days,
>   For only three hours,
> His uprightness,
>   His greatness,
> His goodness.
>
> *Horohó-horohó-horohó.*
> Oh, you know of his greatness, son;
>   Oh, you know of his goodness,
> Of the Lord of Heaven,
>   Of the Lord of Glory.

Then the merchant replies: "Go away, Monkey! Go and work first! Go and look for money to pay for your beer!"

The old Monkey replies: "But look son, monkeys don't know how to work. But why are you scolding me? For monkeys don't know how to work. But haven't you seen that monkeys only know how to walk in trees? That's why monkeys don't have any money. They have eaten up all their acorns. That's why they climbed down to look for food in the market. Because they have eaten up all the fruits in the trees. That's why they left to look for fruit to eat, because they know that there is fruit in the market. That's why they came to look for fruit in the market."

The merchant pretends to be convinced by this argument and gives the Monkey alms of beer, locust tree pods, or maguey.

Still another major role in the fiesta is that of *mayol tahimol*. The term *mayol* means "policeman" (from Spanish *mayor*) and *tahimol* means "game." The fiesta of Carnaval is called *k'in tahimoltik* ("fiesta of games"). The duties of the Chamula policeman include serving as errand boy and messenger for the civil officials and summoning people to appear in court. The *mayol tahimol* serves as the Passions' messenger during the fiesta, fetching officials to be sworn into office or to take part in the ritual dance. Each barrio has one *mayol tahimol* (to be referred to from now on as the Messenger). He wears no special costume, but carries a short unvarnished white wooden staff decorated with two red and green ribbon streamers at the top.

The six Passions are expected to play one of three roles: (*a*) Soldier Passion (*soltaro pašyon*), (*b*) Linking Passion (*skaʔbenal pašyon*), and (*c*) Consort Passion (*šinolan pašyon*). The barrios take turns supplying Passions for these roles. During 1968 the Passions of barrio San Sebastián were Soldier Passions, the Passions of barrio San Juan were Linking Passions, and the Passions of barrio San Pedro served as Consort Passions. In 1969 the roles of Soldier Passion were played by the Passions of barrio San Pedro, Linking Passion by the Passions of barrio San Sebastián, and Consort Passion by those of San Juan. The man who plays the role of Nana María Cocorina always belongs to the barrio from which the Consort Passions are recruited.

The highest-ranking Passions are those called Soldier Passions. They march ahead of all the other Passions, accompanied by their Monkeys and the Commissary, Ordinary, and Messenger from their barrio. They are followed by the Linking Passions with their Monkeys, Commissary, Ordinary, and Messenger. Bringing up the rear are the Consort Passions, the female impersonator, and their Monkeys, Commissary, Ordinary, and Messenger.

Chamulas say that the Passions who walk in the middle are called *ska?benal paśyon* because they serve as the link between the Soldier Passions who lead the way and the Consort Passions who lag behind with Nana María Cocorina. Their folk etymology is based on the root *-ka?*, one of whose meanings is "to link" (Laughlin 1973). Obviously this is the same word that I glossed as Lacandon in chapter 3, but because Chamulas do not call these Passions "Lacandon Passions," and do derive *ska?benal* from *-ka?*, I have decided to call them Linking Passions. Their function is to link or join the Consort Passions with the Soldier Passions. The Consort Passions are last because they accompany the "woman," and, as one Chamula informant explained to me, "women, of course, cannot keep up with men."

From time to time the soldier group slows down and waits for the Linking Passions to catch up so that they can salute them by smacking their flags together. Then the soldier group goes up ahead. The middle group waits for the group behind it to catch up in order to greet it and then moves ahead a little faster. In this sense the middle group serves as a link between the very fast group in front and the very slow group bringing up the rear.

Each barrio, then, is represented by two Passions, two Flowers, one Commissary, one Ordinary, one Messenger, and twenty-two Monkeys. The barrio from which Nana María Cocorina is recruited has two additional Monkeys. The cast and setting of the fiesta are diagrammatically represented in figure 3.

Preparations for the Fiesta

The Passions offer three major banquets during the fiesta of Carnaval, the preparation of which consumes large quantities of firewood.

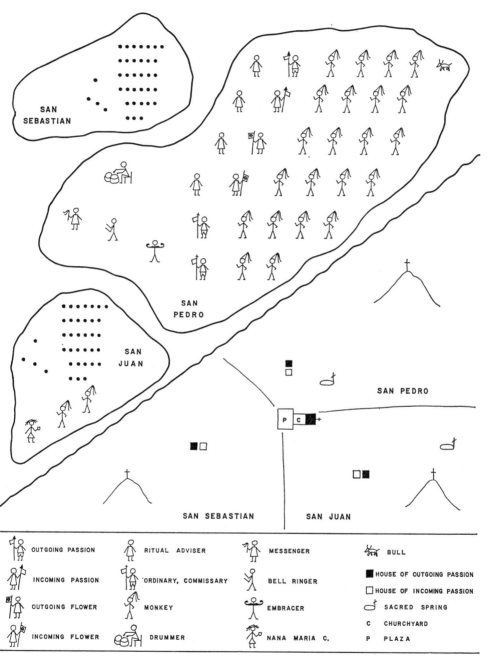

SAN
SEBASTIAN

SAN
PEDRO

SAN
JUAN

SAN PEDRO

SAN SEBASTIAN   SAN JUAN

OUTGOING PASSION	RITUAL ADVISER	MESSENGER	BULL
INCOMING PASSION	ORDINARY, COMMISSARY	BELL RINGER	■ HOUSE OF OUTGOING PASSION
OUTGOING FLOWER	MONKEY	EMBRACER	□ HOUSE OF INCOMING PASSION
INCOMING FLOWER	DRUMMER	NANA MARIA C.	SACRED SPRING
			C CHURCHYARD
			P PLAZA

3. The cast and setting of Carnaval in Chamula.

About three weeks before the fiesta begins, the Passions, together with
their ritual advisers and their Monkeys, recruit men to bring wood for
the fiesta. First, they go to the church to pray, asking God to protect
the woodcarriers from harm, and saying that the wood is for the heat
and light of our Lord:

> Have mercy, my Lord;
>> Have mercy, Jesus.
> Divine Lord of Heaven,
>> Divine Lord of Glory.
>
> Our lowly flesh is bowed down;
>> Our lowly bodies are bent over,
> With [those of] your four Monkeys,
>> With [those of] your four masked ones;
> With [those of] your flower bearers,
>> With [those of] your leaf bearers.
> Divine Lord of Heaven,
>> Divine Lord of Glory.
>
> You are there in the coffin;
>> You are there in the grave,
> Divine Payer [for our sins],
>> Divine Buyer [of our sins] . . .
>
> How much, O Lord;
>> How much, O Jesus,
> Of your firewood should they take out?
>> Of your fire should they take out?
> So they won't be angry;
>> So they won't be disgusted,
> Your born child,
>> Your engendered child.[1]
>
> Let them not be lazy;
>> Let them not be loafers,
> On behalf of your firewood,
>> On behalf of your fire.
>
> That is why they lift it;
>> That is why they raise it,

---

[1] "Your born child" and "Your engendered child" refer to the spectators.

With their axes,
　　With their knives,
With their ropes . . .

May nothing befall them;
　　May nothing harm them,
Your born child,
　　Your engendered child.[2]
So they won't cut their toes;
　　So they won't cut their fingers,
When they lower their feet;
　　When they lower their hands.

Divine Lord of Heaven,
　　Divine Lord of Glory:
This is your firewood;
　　This is your fire;
This is your feast-day;
　　This is your holiday,
My Lord,
　　Jesus . . .

Then they go to the Passions' houses, where they eat a ritual meal. When they finish eating, the same men go to the homes of the wood-cutters to request their assistance on the following Friday or Saturday:

Won't you do me the favor for the sake of his firewood,
　　For the sake of his fire,
Of the Lord of Heaven,
　　Of the Lord of Glory;
For him who bought you [out of difficulty],
　　For him who paid for you [for your guilt]?
For it is his firewood;
　　For it is his fire.

The woodcarriers agree to go, asking when and from where the fire-wood should be fetched. The Passion and his men reply: "You will go early Friday morning, eight days from now. You will know where it will be by the sound of exploding rockets and cannons, the singing of the Monkeys, and the playing of drums."

2 "Your born child" and "Your engendered child" refer to the woodcutters.

The woodcarriers for the outgoing Passions haul wood on the following Friday. Those for the incoming Passions fetch wood on the next day (Saturday). Each Passion recruits approximately thirty men for this task.

At eleven o'clock on the night before the designated Friday or Saturday, the Monkeys and the Passion put on their fiesta costumes and sing while the musicians play:

> We are putting on our tunics,
>   We are putting on our kerchiefs;
>   La, la, li, la, lai, lao;
>   La, la, li, la, lai, lao.

The cannoneer goes outside to set off cannons and skyrockets to herald the robing ceremony. When the Passion and his Monkeys finish dressing, they go outside to dance in front of the cross which stands at the side of the Passion's house. At one o'clock in the morning two Monkeys go off to the woods to meet the woodcutters at the appointed place. The other two Monkeys stay behind with the Passion, his ritual adviser, and the musicians. The Monkeys and their companions run off into the woods toward the place previously selected for obtaining firewood. When they arrive at the designated place, the cannoneer immediately fires off a cannon and skyrockets to signal their arrival to the woodcutters. The Monkeys also blow trumpets to let the woodmen know where they are. The Monkeys dance and sing and shake their rattles. The woodcutters depart from Chamula Center, straggling in to meet the Monkeys at about 2:00 A.M. When the men arrive, they fell a tree, chop it up, split the logs, and carry them off to the Passion's house. Each woodcutter carries six loads of wood. While the men are chopping the wood, the Monkeys dance in the forest. As each woodcutter finishes with his sixth load, he sits down to rest at the Passion's house until the other woodcutters have finished their stint. All the men rest for a while. The Monkeys lead the woodcutters on their trips back and forth between the woods and the Passion's house. They stop from time to time on the road to say: "God the Father, God the Son, God the Holy Ghost, my Lord, Jesus," waving their flags back and forth toward heaven.

After the last trip at 10:00 or 11:00 A.M., the Monkeys walk up to the Passion, saying: "We have returned, Passion. The men have the wood ready."

The Passion and his ritual adviser reply: "Are you back already? Didn't any jaguars bite you in the woods?"

The Monkeys reply: "They didn't bite us because we have tails. We climbed into a tree right away. That's why the jaguars didn't bite us."

The Passion and his ritual adviser laugh: "Ha, ha, ha, ha, ha—so you climbed a tree right away. You are animals of the trees. You know how to climb trees. That's why the jaguars didn't bite you."

The Monkeys add: "Ah, the jaguars couldn't get us because we know how to wrap our tails around the branches of trees. Even if a jaguar were to climb [the tree] he couldn't reach us because we would be on a branch [out of his reach]"—to which the Passion and his ritual adviser respond, "Ha, ha, ha, ha, ha . . . well, sit down for a little while and rest."

Meanwhile, the servants of the Passion are stacking up the firewood to form the walls of an enclosure which will be used as the cooking compound during the fiesta. Then the Monkeys serve rum to the woodcarriers, the Passion, and his ritual adviser. The drinking ceremony is followed by a meal, which the cannoneer signals by setting off fireworks. The woodcarriers are served bowls of beef-belly soup, beans, tortillas, and maize gruel. The Monkeys do not eat with them, because they are expected to dance and sing during the meal. They sing the following song:

> Greasy beans,
> Greasy beans,
> Greasy food,
> Greasy meal.
> La, la, la, lah, la, la, laʔo;
> La, la, la, la, li, la, la, laʔo.
>
> Greasy meal,
> Greasy food,
> Greasy cabbage,
> Greasy turnip greens.
> La, la, ti, la, la, laʔo;
> La, la, ti, la, laʔo.

> Greasy beans,
>   Greasy beans,
> Greasy meal,
>   Greasy food,
> La, la, ti, la, laʔo;
>   La, la, ti, la, laʔo.

They sing "Greasy Beans" three times until the woodcutters have finished eating. Then the Monkeys stop dancing and address the people eating: "There is still a lot of food left, Passion and ritual adviser. So eat up, uncles, older brothers, and younger brothers."

The Passion and his ritual adviser reply: "We are eating well, thank you. It is very good. Our food is greasy. It is delicious—just like Ladino food."

The Monkeys return with: "Ha, ha, ha, ha, ha, wipe off your mouth! It is very greasy. Otherwise flies will come and eat it. There they are eating it now!"

The Passion, his ritual adviser, and the woodmen reply: "I have wiped it off."

The significance of the song "Greasy Beans" is made clear in the exchange between the Monkeys and the banqueters. Beef-belly soup, the traditional dish for this occasion, is regarded as a great delicacy in Chamula. The soup is very greasy because the beef stomach contributes a lot of fat to it. Indians generally do not use grease in cooking. They seldom eat meat, and other food is always prepared by boiling or baking, not frying. On the other hand, Chamulas know that Ladinos fry almost everything they eat. The Monkeys pretend that since the meal is greasy, it is like Ladino food, even though Ladinos do not make beef-belly soup. They joke that the people who are eating the soup are really Ladinos, because their mouths are greasy. They deprecate Indian food, saying that the beef-belly soup is delicious because it is greasy like Ladino food.

When the woodcutters have finished eating, they drink some more rum. Then the Passion and his ritual adviser thank them for carrying the wood:

> Thank you for your trouble on behalf of the firewood,
>   On behalf of the fire,

Of the Lord of Heaven,
  Of the Lord of Glory.

I borrowed your ten toes;
  I borrowed your ten fingers,
For the sake of the firewood,
  For the sake of the fire,
Of the Lord of Heaven,
  Of the Lord of Glory . . .

Then the woodcutters go home. Shortly thereafter the Passion, his wife, and their Monkeys change out of their fiesta clothes and everyone rests.

On the next day, Sunday, at 10:00 A.M., the fiesta personnel inscribe their names in the little book carried by the master of ceremonies, who is known as ʔavito (from Spanish hábito, "habit" [of clergy]) or piškal (from Spanish fiscal, formerly a minor church official). He goes to the house of each Passion, where the Passion and the personnel associated with his household sign their names in order of importance. He then moves on to the houses of the Commissaries and Ordinaries. After all the Carnaval officers for the three barrios have inscribed their names, they go to the plaza and run around it three times. This is not a race, but a trial run or practice for the running the men will be called upon to do during the fiesta the following week. They are testing their endurance and their ability to run without tripping or falling. During the fiesta they will be carrying the sacred flags when they run. If someone carrying one of these flags stumbles or falls down, God will be angry and send rain. The officers try to avert such a calamity by practicing a week before the fiesta begins, to put them in shape for running with the flags. Sometimes one of the older men discovers during this trial run that his heart is not up to so much running. He then has time to appoint a younger substitute to run in his place.

The men run in order, the Soldier Passions leading the way, followed by the Linking Passions and the Consort Passions, who bring up the rear. They are expected to maintain this order whenever they run, for the object of the running is not to "win," but to symbolize Christ running, with the Jews (Monkeys) in hot pursuit.

The only other important event which takes place on this day is the announcement of the coming fiesta, made by the master of ceremonies, in which he summarizes the various conflicts commemorated by the fiesta of Carnaval. The text of this announcement has already been given above.

On Monday the Passions of each barrio send a group of assistants (*hnitvakašetik*) to some cattle-raising area to buy a bull for slaughtering on the following day. This undertaking takes them all day and all night. About twenty-five men go in each group; on the return journey, half of the men walk in front of the bull and half behind it, controlling the animal with ropes. They arrive at the entrance to Chamula Center at about 7:15 A.M. and are met there by the Passions, their Monkeys, and other personnel. They carry on to the center of town, where the bull is forced to run three times around the plaza in front of the church to greet God and inform him that a bull has been obtained for his banquet. One by one, the bull of each barrio is led in front of the church, where the men pray. When all have circled the plaza three times, the bulls are dragged off to the houses of the Passions, where they are tied and thrown to the ground. Their front and back legs are tied together, and with another rope their heads are pulled backward in order to expose the neck arteries which the slaughterers (*hkarnisero*) use as a guide for finding the right place to insert their knives.

Before stabbing the bull in the neck, the butcher asks for mint leaves, which he places in both nostrils to flavor the meat, and for a bucket to receive the blood of the bull. The blood is taken immediately to the cooking compound, a brush-enclosed area not far from the slaughtering post, where all the cooking for the fiesta takes place, to be cooked with mint into a pudding which will be served at midday together with some of the bull's internal organs.

The bull is then skinned, and its internal organs are removed. Next the bull's penis is cut off. The men throw it at small boys asking, "What's this for?" The boys answer, "The bull's penis is used for screwing, for making yourself a child." Everyone (except the women) laughs.

Then someone takes the penis, attaches a stone to it at one end as a weight, and hangs it up on one of the posts which support the porch roof of the Passion's house. There it remains until it has stretched and dried. It will be used as a whip by one of the Monkeys at the next year's fiesta.

The head and feet of the bull are also removed; the head, its nostrils stuffed with mint leaves, is tied to the center post of the porch like a trophy, with ropes encircling its horns. The feet are tied beside the head. Neither the head nor the feet are skinned.

Before the meat is cut up, the Passion's ritual adviser searches out the women among the group who are pregnant. They are requested to bite the brisket of the bull three times to protect the meat from flies and from spoiling. The women are too embarrassed to admit that they are pregnant and dislike it when the men laugh at them for biting raw meat like an animal. The women say, "We are just like dogs biting raw meat." They giggle with embarrassment and blush when the men laugh at them. When the pregnant women finish biting the meat, the ritual advisor offers them liquor as a compensation for their suffering.

The meat is quartered and the quarters are hung by ropes from a crossbeam of the porch roof.

Then the ritual adviser searches for someone to protect the meat from flies with a switch. Some men say jokingly, "Don't kill all the flies, because there are only a few flies, ha, ha, ha, ha." There are, in fact, many flies, and the man chosen for the task is kept busy night and day flicking them off the meat. Three men and boys take turns guarding the meat during the next ten days.

The midday meal on this occasion is substantial: blood soup with large clotted chunks of blood, cabbage soup seasoned with chili pepper, chunks of boiled liver, and tortillas.

During the afternoon six large conical-bottomed pots are brought outside. Each of them is carried in a rope sling by two people. They are placed on their sides in a line directly in front of the cross with their mouths facing the cross. The servants line up water jugs in front of the cooking pots. The two gruel makers (*hʔulavil*) scrub out the cooking pots with water fetched in those jugs. As each cooking pot is scrubbed out, a man and a woman standing behind the pot turn it upside down and coat the outside with lime up to the pot's shoulder. Then it is again turned on its side with its mouth facing the cross. Chamulas believe that the lime coating acts as a conductor and economizes on fuel.

While the bull is being butchered in the morning, the women are hard at work in the cooking compound boiling corn in lime for use in making gruel. In the late afternon the gruel makers and their wives dip the boiled corn kernels out of a large pot, drain them in baskets, and transfer them to four large gunny sacks to be taken to the mill to be ground the next day.

Early on Wednesday the gruel makers go to a mill in San Cristóbal where their corn is ground for the gruel. They load the four gunny sacks of boiled corn on the backs of two horses. When they return from San Cristóbal with the ground corn, they place the sacks of corn dough on the ground in a line facing the cross. The corn dough sits there until evening and begins to ferment in the hot sun.

The gruel-making process takes approximately twenty-four hours. At about 8:00 P.M. on Wednesday the gruel makers begin to separate the cornstarch from the cellulose. They use small baskets as sieves and place them in large cooking pots full of water. The wives of the gruel makers hold the baskets submerged in the pots while their husbands put lumps of corn dough into the baskets. Then the women knead the dough with their hands so that the starch floats free and only the cellulose matter remains in the basket. This they dump into another basket set on a chair in front of them. Then they add more corn dough to the basket sieve and repeat the process until they have used up the four gunny sacks of dough. Throughout the process, which lasts about four hours, the Monkeys dance, the musicians play, and the ritual adviser prays.

They begin to cook the gruel before dawn on Thursday morning. The gruel makers place four large pots in the center of the Passion's house and stack large pieces of firewood around them. Then the gruel makers and their wives begin to pour the liquid cornstarch, which they extracted the night before, into the pot. Each gruel maker, together with his wife, is responsible for two pots. The fire is lighted, and the gruel makers and their wives begin to stir the gruel. The Monkeys, the

Passion, his ritual adviser, and their wives dance at the side of the gruel pots. The gruel makers and their wives sing and dance as they stir the gruel in time to the music. From time to time the ritual adviser prays with the gruel makers and their wives, all holding glasses of rum and facing the door of the house. When they finish praying, they pour the liquor into the gruel pots so that the pots can share in the ritual drinking. "If we didn't serve rum to the pot, it would grumble, it would explode and burn people severely. That's why we have to offer liquor to it, for the pot is accustomed to drinking liquor. But the pot won't explode if it drinks liquor."[3] Similarly, the musicians spray their instruments with rum so that they will not squawk, and the cannoneer sprays his cannon with liquor so that it will explode properly.

The door of the house remains firmly shut while the gruel is cooking, and people go outside only to urinate, for if a cold draft should enter the house, the gruel pots would explode. The people inside dance vigorously as the gruel boils. They perspire so much that the house is like a steam bath. After the gruel is cooked, everyone changes into dry clothing.

The gruel makers cool the gruel by gradually withdrawing wood from the fire until the pots rest only on hot coals. Finally, when the coals have cooled, the gruel is ready. The gruel makers open the door of the house and dip gruel out of the large pots in gourds and put it into smaller pots which are lined up along one wall of the house. Everyone is served a gourdful of hot sweet gruel.

On Friday the sacred kettledrums (*bin*) are washed at the houses of the outgoing Passions. The kettledrum is a clay pot with an everted lip at the top. The mouth of the pot is covered with stretched leather, formerly deerhide, but today more likely to be cowhide. A hole at the side of the pot serves as its mouth (*homol*), into which rum liquor and incense are "fed." The Drummer (*hbah bin*) plays the drum with his finger tips. The drum emits only a faint sound when it is played.

Myths about the kettledrum from Chenalhó (Guiteras-Holmes

---

[3] According to the *Popol Vuh*, some abused plates and pots and grinding stones brought an end to the First Creation by destroying the people who had mistreated them (Edmonson 1971: lines 721–808).

1961:191–193) and Chamula (Gossen n.d.:T-33) suggest that it has an "increase" function, for whenever it is played, food comes out of it. The kettledrum is played at all banquets so that the Passions will not run out of food (plate 12).

Each barrio possesses two such kettledrums. The Drummer is responsible for the drums for life, handing them on to his eldest son when he becomes too old to take care of them himself. The drum is covered with a network of twine which serves as its carrying bag; this bag is removed when the pot is washed.

The kettledrummer is also responsible for another item of ritual paraphernalia, a jaguar skin called *čilon*. A leather band on which a row of cow or sheep bells has been sewn is attached to the pelt at what would have been the living jaguar's neck. A leather strap fastened to the beast's head permits the pelt to be slipped over the head and worn during a dance called *ʔak'ot čilon*, for which the kettledrums provide the only musical accompaniment.

The Messenger fetches all the civil and religious officials, one by one in rank order, to take part in this dance. He has two assistants called the Bell Ringer (*htih čilon*) and the Lifter, or Embracer (*hpetvaneh*). When the Messenger walks up to an official, the Bell Ringer accompanies him, carrying the jaguar pelt, which he slips over the chosen official's head. The Messenger walks in front of the jaguar impersonator carrying his ribboned staff; the Bell Ringer walks behind him, shaking the pelt so that the bells ring. The designated official carries one of the Passion's flags, capped by the "Head of God." He circles the kettledrums in a counterclockwise direction in time to the beat of the drums. Behind the Bell Ringer march several Monkeys also carrying flags (but without the "Head of God"). The Drummer sits on a little chair, his drums resting on a bed of pine needles. The Embracer stands outside the circle waiting for the moment when he will lift the man wearing the jaguar skin. After the jaguar impersonator has circled the drums several times, the Embracer lifts and walks him three steps into the center of the circle, then three steps away from the drums, while he waves his flag in the four cardinal directions, and finally carries him over to the cross, where he sets him on his feet. Immediately the Bell Ringer snatches the jaguar pelt from his head, the Messenger seizes the flag, and both run off to recruit someone else, the next-highest-ranking male present, to take part in the dance. The lifting episode is described as being "raised beside the kettledrum" (*muyel ta bin*) (fig. 4).

The jaguar skin represents God's jaguar, who defended him when the demons (Jews) tried to kill him. Formerly, jaguars wore bells around their necks so that they could signal each other's presence in the forest. That is why there are bells attached to the jaguar skin. Whenever a man puts on the jaguar skin, he is impersonating the jaguar who tried to defend Christ. Therefore, no man can refuse to participate in the dance, for to do so implies refusing to protect God from evil. The jaguar impersonator carries the flag with the "Head of God" on top and protects it from the Monkeys (demons), who follow

4. The Dance of the Warriors. (Drawn by Mariano López Calixto)
(1) Cross to which flags are tied; (2) Senior Monkey; (3) Messenger carrying his staff; (4) the Bell Ringer; (5) Flower's tapster; (6) Messenger's assistant, the Embracer; (7) Drummer; (8) Cannoneer dancing in defense of God.

behind him. When the dance ends, both God and his jaguar are lifted toward heaven, symbolizing the resurrection of Christ.

Gossen offers a somewhat different interpretation of the lance symbol, namely that "the symbolic representations of the sun's head are the metal flagpole tips which are kept in a special chest. Carried on poles with cloth banners by the cargoholders' assistants, the tips form the sun's head" (1970:419). In support of this thesis he points out that the Chamula word for God (*htotik*) is also used to refer to the sun (Gossen 1970:440). Furthermore, Chamulas believe that the demons, monkeys, and Jews killed God (also the sun) "and forced him to ascend into the heavens, thus providing heat, light, life and order" (Gossen 1970:440). This suggests that when the jaguar impersonator, who is carrying the metal-tipped flag, is lifted by the Embracer, the lifting symbolizes the movement of the sun (and Christ) into the heavens.

Some ethnohistorical evidence suggests not only that the dance commemorates the death and resurrection of Christ, but also that it was once a Dance of the Warriors similar to a Yucatecan dance of that name which was also associated with rites occurring during the five unlucky days at the end of the year (Tozzer 1941:114; see chapter 9 for a comparison of the dances). Edward Calnek notes that, in highland Chiapas before the Spanish conquest, "the highest military rank reported seems to be that of *zba chilom*" (1962:76). One of the definitions of *chilom* cited by Calnek (1962:76) is "peón lancero en guerra [lancer in battle]." *Zba* (or *sba* in my transcription) means "head" or "leader"; therefore, the *zba chilom* was probably a lance captain (Calnek 1962:75). In other words, by donning the jaguar skin (*čilon*) the Chamula official casts himself in the role of a soldier defending God. In Yucatán some soldiers wore jaguar pelts when they went into battle (Tozzer 1941:122). This practice may have occurred in Chamula, too, and would explain the military symbolism of the jaguar pelt. In any event, it is appropriate that a Dance of the Warriors would be performed at a fiesta that commemorates military conflicts.

At 4:00 P.M. on Friday, two Monkeys and the servants of the outgoing Passions go to sweep the marketplace, the churchyard, and the road to Calvary Hill free of debris so that when the fiesta celebrators run they will not trip over stones or slip on fruit peels and injure themselves. When the three groups of men arrive at the marketplace, they run around it three times. Then they go to the door of the church, where they pray for a few minutes. When they finish praying, the Monkeys order the servants: "Well, please sweep away the banana peels of our wives. If there are stones which have been used as seats, carry them away so that the father of your sheep will not break his leg—ha, ha, ha, ha." The banana peels which are tossed aside by women on market days have a sexual connotation, for Chamulas recognize an analogy between a banana which is being peeled and the foreskin which is "peeled off" during an erection. The stones are rather large flat rocks which men and women have used as seats on market days. "Sheep" refers to the crowds of people who will gather during the fiesta, because large crowds are thought to resemble herds of sheep. The "father of the sheep" is the ram, the male of the flock, the one who impregnates the ewes, as well as their leader. The "ram" in this context is the Passion, who is the religious leader of the community. It is he who will be running during the fiesta and therefore in danger of breaking his leg. The "leg" he is in danger of breaking is also his penis, for "stones which have been used as seats" may refer to the vaginas of women who have used them as seats.

The sweepers gather up the stones, sugarcane debris, and avocado and banana peels and throw the rubbish out of the marketplace. One of the sweepers jokes as he sweeps: "Gather together your milpa clippings, because the rubbish is very useful. The rubbish is useful because when it is cold at night the child [penis] will die of cold; ha, ha, ha." "Milpa clippings" is a euphemistic term for dog or human excrement which is deposited in the cornfields. The male foreskin (rubbish includes banana peels) keeps the penis warm.

After all the rubbish has been swept out of the marketplace, the sweepers go to Calvary Hill. When they arrive one of them says: "Drink up some water! Do you want hot water [urine] or do you want cold water? Ha, ha, ha, ha."

The Monkeys order: "Come here! Come, let us gather the old potsherds. Have you forgotten that you threw aside potsherds [last year]? Come, let us gather them!"

The servants widen the path to Calvary Hill by cutting away the underbrush and hacking off tree limbs which obstruct the path.

Next they go to the sacred spring called *ni² Ho²*. They clean the spring and decorate the cross there with pine boughs and flowers. The water comes out of a cavern, which the men inspect to determine whether the opening is clogged with sticks or stones. As they clean the entrance to the cave they joke:

First Sweeper: How is your steam bath? Is it in good or bad shape?

Second Sweeper: Well, it's in pretty bad shape because it is full of charcoal.

By "charcoal" they mean the stones which have accumulated in the cave. When the sweepers have finished tidying it up, the Monkeys say to them, "Well, look for three tortillas as the entrance fee for the steam bath, because you have come out very white, because you are real albinos." The men badly need to bathe because they are covered with white dust from having swept out the cave. They jokingly refer to the cave as a steam bath because it is long and narrow like their steam baths. The entrance fee is called "tortilla" (*vah*) or "tribute" (*patan*), but it is actually a stone or potsherd. During the fiesta men and women carry stones or potsherds to throw into the cave as tribute, for if they do not offer three stones to the cave, they will die. The cave is evil and must be placated. The stones which the sweepers sweep out of the cave were offered as tribute the previous year.

The "Lost Days"

Saturday. The fiesta officially begins with the Dance of the Warriors. Shortly after midnight on Saturday the owner of the sacred kettle-drums, the Messenger, and his assistants go to the houses of the Passions of their barrio, where the Dance of the Warriors is performed.

The highlight of the first day of the fiesta is the banquet of dried beef, coffee, sweet rolls, gruel, tamales, and tortillas offered by the incoming Passions. Meanwhile, the households of the outgoing Passions are busy preparing for their banquet the following day.

The main activity at the outgoing Passion's house on Saturday morning is the making of bean tamales (*cenek' ʔul vah*). The Passion's servants lay large boards on the ground in front of the cross, in the same place where the cooking pots were coated with lime on Wednesday. The women of the Passion's household, including the wives of the Passion and his ritual adviser, kneel on either side of the row of boards. The ritual adviser hands out white cloths, one for each board. The women take discs of corn dough, knead and mix them with water, and then spread the dough out on the cloths in a thin layer. When that is smooth and evenly spread out, the women spread black-bean paste on top. Then they turn the cloth up and roll it to form a roll like a jelly or cinnamon roll. This roll is cut into four-finger-width pieces, which are wrapped in banana leaves and tied with twine; later they will be cooked in two large pots in the cooking compound. The wives of the Passion and his ritual adviser work together on five large tamales, called "child tamales" (*ʔololal vah*) because they resemble a child wrapped in a shawl on its mother's back. In the case of the "child tamales," the roll is not cut into pieces. The women wrap it completely in leaves and tie it up with palm strips handed out by the ritual adviser. These "child tamales" will be given to the other Passions as gifts during the banquet on the following day.

Not all of the corn dough is made into bean tamales. Perhaps half of it is made into simple corn tamales (*pať'*), the corn dough being formed into small lumps and wrapped in leaves.

When the tamales are ready the wives of the Monkeys go to the banquets of the incoming Passions to receive their gifts on behalf of the Passion's wife. The wife of one Monkey carries a basket covered with an embroidered cloth. In this basket she will carry back her Passion's share of the incoming Passion's banquet. Shortly after arriving at the incoming Passion's house, she is approached by a woman carrying a similar cloth-covered basket. In it are a bull's heart smeared with red anatto pigment, six hard-boiled eggs coated with the same substance, a "child tamale," a pitcher of sugar water, a gourd of gruel, a bird-shaped piece of bread, tortillas, and a bottle of rum. This food is all transferred to the basket brought by the wives of the Monkeys, and the empty basket is returned to its bearer.

While the gifts are being presented to the women, the men of all three barrios are participating in the Dance of the Warriors. The banquet lasts for several hours, but the wives of the Monkeys stay only long enough to receive a drink of gruel before returning to their Passion's house. Later in the day they will make trips to the houses of the other two incoming Passions to receive the same gifts.

Sunday. The outgoing Passions' banquets are considerably more elaborate than those of the incoming Passions the day before. Late on Saturday the cook (*hʔayovil*) cuts meat off one of the quarters of beef hanging from the porch roof. He cuts the meat up into tiny pieces and cooks it in a broth flavored with chili pepper, tomatoes, and onions. This beef stew forms the main course of Sunday's banquet and is served with tortillas and bean tamales. Each guest receives three tiny pieces of meat in his bowl of soup. The first course is gruel, and the third course is sugar water and sweet rolls.

The outgoing Passion of barrio San Pedro had invited me to be his guest during the fiesta and at his banquet. The banquet began at about 10:00 A.M. on Sunday, February 16, 1969. Earlier the Passion and his Monkeys had gone off to the church to pray. They returned with the Passions from the other two barrios and their Monkeys, running up the hillside in front of the Passion's house. At the head of the procession marched the Commissary of San Pedro with his Monkeys, followed by the outgoing and incoming Soldier Passions and their Monkeys. The next group in line was from barrio San Sebastián, the middle, or linking, group. The Consort Passions with Nana María Cocorina brought up the rear. When they arrived at the house, Nana María Cocorina stood with her Monkeys at the very rear, somewhat apart from the Passion groups. After all the Passions had begun circling the kettledrums, she advanced with her Monkeys, carrying her smoking censer.

The Passions, Monkeys, and Commissaries circled only the kettledrums of their own barrio. Thus, there were three circling groups—

the Soldier Passions' group nearest the cross; the Linking Passions' group to the left of and behind the Soldier group if one is facing the cross; and, finally, the Consort Passions' group in back. The three groups formed the vertices of a triangle. Nana María Cocorina joined the Consort Passions' group which was circling the kettledrums of barrio San Juan.

Nana María Cocorina takes part in the Dance of the Warriors, but the Embracer does not lift her at the end of the dance. Nor does she carry one of the flags with the "Head of God" on top; instead she continues to carry her censer. After she has circled the kettledrums three times, she approaches the drums, stops in front of them, and waves her censer over them three times with a circular motion. Then she turns around and dips her buttocks over the drums three times, suggesting the thrusting movements of sexual intercourse. The expression *?ak'be ve?el* means both "to feed" and "to have sexual relations with." Chamula men refer to the genital organs of a woman euphemistically as the "meal" (*sve?el*) of her sexual partner. Thus Nana María Cocorina "feeds" the drums both spiritually and sexually.

Chamulas, like Zinacantecos, believe that women can tame or "cool" male or "hot" objects like bulls and guns by exposing their genitals to them (see chapter 2). All Chamula accounts of the Caste War of 1867–1870 (and some Zinacanteco, Pedrano, and Ladino accounts also) mention that women as well as men fought against Ladino soldiers during that conflict. According to one account: "Even the women fought in the war. They were not afraid. The women were prepared there. As for the women, they lifted up their skirts so that the guns would not fire. Wherever they came, they lifted up their skirts in order to cool the guns, in order to cool the guns. They lifted up their skirts. They stuck out their rears at the guns so that the guns would not fire." A Pedrano account of the Caste War claims that, when the Ladinos fired their guns, the bullets entered the anuses of the Chamula women and thus the men were saved. In any case, Chamulas believe that the men fought with spears, machetes, and pikes, and that the women fought only with their sex organs.

Nana María Cocorina's role in the Dance of the Warriors is exactly the one attributed to Chamula women during the Caste War of 1867–1870. She does not carry a spear (flag), but exposes her genitals to the drum, which is one of the objects Chamulas associate with war.

The spectators laugh and comment on the actions of Nana María Cocorina: "Oh, but the lady is doing an obscene thing—she is putting her skirt into the head of the drum!" They call out to the Messenger: "Don't pull the tit of our younger sister [Nana María Cocorina]. Her breast is full of milk because she is pregnant. And don't poke her stomach, because she is already several months pregnant!"

The Messenger replies: "Never mind if her breast bursts. Someone can drink her milk. But her child is already very big. Who knows if it won't soon be born."

Nana María Cocorina laughs: "Well, never mind if my child is born. We'll look for another [head of] cabbage which can be stuck in; ha, ha, ha."

Nana María Cocorina is pregnant because she made love with Mariano Ortega and Juan Gutiérrez in the woods, as announced by the master of ceremonies the week before:

> Mariano Ortega and Juan Gutiérrez came with their young lady, Nana María Cocorina.
> They go together into the woods to make love.
> They return eating toffee, eating candied squash, eating blood sausage.

When she finishes participating in the Dance of the Warriors, Nana María Cocorina goes over to the bench in front of the cross to join the Passions, Commissaries, and Ordinaries seated there. As she approaches the bench, the Passions laugh and one of them calls out to her, "Come here, lady, for I feel very cold. Come sit here!" He wants her to sit beside him and warm him with the wool clothing customarily worn by women.

While they are sitting on the bench, a Monkey walks by and tells Nana María Cocorina: "If you like, I will marry you. I will make you my wife."

Nana María Cocorina answers: "I don't want to. I already have a husband here—the Passion."

But the Monkey insists: "Niece, if you like, I will marry you."

But Nana María Cocorina is equally firm: "I don't want to. I already have a husband here—the Passion. Look, Passion, you are my husband, you are the Passion. He wants to embrace me."

Now the Passion indignantly enters the conversation: "Why are you embracing my wife?"

The Monkey replies, "Because that's what you and I agreed to."

The Passion responds, incensed: "How could I have agreed to it? Why are you behaving like a monkey? Why are you treating my wife in this fashion? I am here. Now I am going to hit you! Why are you embracing my wife?"

The spectators laugh.

Sometimes the Monkey addresses the Passion first:

Monkey:	Passion!
Passion:	What?
Monkey:	Well, *alférez* Passion, what is on your mind? Take this! Drink some soda pop!
Passion:	Well, what's this soda pop for?
Monkey:	Oh, nothing. Just give me your younger sister as you promised.
Passion:	No, she's not my sister. She's my wife. Well, look, Monkey, if she were really my sister and not my wife [then it would be all right]. Isn't it true, lady, that you are my wife?
Nana María C.:	Oh, no! Look, Passion! The crazy Monkey wants to embrace me.
Monkey:	Lady, I'll embrace you with all my heart, because I'll marry you. Take this *lima* [citrus fruit]! ⁴ What do you want? Do you want money? Or, if not, would you like some oranges?

⁴ Customarily a suitor offers citrus fruits, such as oranges and sweet limes, as gifts to his fiancée during courtship.

Nana María C.: Well, Monkey, tricky Monkey, you should be beaten. Here is my husband, the Passion. Well, look, Passion. Look, the Monkey wants to embrace me. Look, Passion, at the crazy Monkey. He wants to wrap me up in his tail and carry me off to the woods. Look at that licentious Monkey. He wants to embrace me. Look, Monkey; then come here next to me.

Passion: Look, girl! Well, how many husbands do you have? I am your husband. I am the Passion. Monkey, why are you taking my wife away? Why are you giving her a present?

Monkey: Well, lady, it's true that I'll marry you.

Nana María C.: Well, I don't want to. You should be whipped. Well, now I'll really hit him. I don't like what he's saying. What I say is true—that you are the Passion, that you are my only husband.

Monkey: But what is all this fuss about? After all, you agreed to it.

Passion: I agreed to what? What are you saying that I agreed to?

Monkey: Only that you said that I could marry her.

Passion: Well, how can you marry her? I bought her.

Monkey: Well, then, but didn't you agree to it?

Passion: Then you must have seduced my wife. Then go and put him in jail!

Sometimes the participants in the joking include the Messenger, the Commissaries, and the Ordinaries:

Messenger: Look, *alférez* Passion! Now the jaguar is going to eat you up! [waves jaguar pelt at Passion]

Passion: Why is the jaguar going to eat me up? Now I am going to shoot you!

Messenger:	Don't shoot me, because we are just cele-brating a fiesta.
Commissary:	Well, Passion, will you give me the lady?
Passion:	Well, Commissary, why are you asking me for the lady?
Commissary:	Look, Passion, you can't keep the lady all for yourself.
Passion:	But look, why are you asking me for her? Look, Commissary, I bought the lady.
Commissary:	Well, that doesn't matter. Let's see if she wouldn't like to speak to me. Lady!
Nana María C.:	What's on your mind, Commissary?
Commissary:	Nothing. Wouldn't you like to marry me?
Nana María C.:	Well, why have you come to marry me? As if I didn't already have a husband!
Commissary:	So what if you already have a husband! I thought you had many husbands!
Nana María C.:	Well, what do you think I am? That I have many husbands like a dog? I have only one husband here—the Passion.
Ordinary [Ortega]:	Passion, when will you give me the lady?
Passion:	What do you mean by "you will give me the lady"?
Ordinary:	Well, look, Passion, I am thinking of marrying the lady.
Passion:	How can you take her from me? I bought her. Well, look, Ortega, if it means that you are planning to take her from me by force, then I will have you put in jail!

Here the Conqueror (Ortega) tries to steal the wife of the conquered Passion for his mistress.

Monday. On Monday the Passions recuperate from their banquets of Saturday and Sunday. Their servants are busy cooking food for another banquet to be served at the sacred springs the next day. The Passions visit each other, but serve only rum. This day is called Monday of Drinking Water (*luneš ʔuč' Hoʔ*).

Tuesday. At 4:00 A.M. on Tuesday, the wives of the outgoing Passion, his ritual adviser, and the Monkeys go outside behind the cross to bathe. They wash at this early hour so that they will not be observed. They drink two liters of rum and joke with each other as they wash their feet, faces, and hair:

Ritual Adviser's Wife:	Wash your legs well, wives of the Monkeys. Otherwise the Monkeys won't desire you.
Monkey's Wife:	Ha, ha, ha, ha. Who cares if he doesn't want me. It's much better that way.
Ritual Adviser's Wife:	Would you like your reciprocal [wife of incoming Monkey] to take your place? Would you like a younger girl to take your place? You would have to go home. No, it's better that you wash your legs well so that the Monkey won't abandon you. Otherwise he will cry.
Monkey's Wife:	Ha, ha, ha, ha. Well . . . it would be better if he found someone else. I wouldn't cry if my husband looked for another wife. I'd just look for another husband too. He isn't the only man [in the world].
	[The man guarding the meat overhears them.]

Man:
What are you doing? You are laughing too much. Is someone tickling you? Are your husbands there tickling you?

Women:
Come here, too! Come here and wash a little! You are just sitting there with your meat. Isn't your flesh giving off a bad odor? If you like, come here and wash. Otherwise worms may enter your meat [flesh]—hi, hi, hi, hi . . .

Man:
I think you should wash your legs well. If you don't wash your legs well, they will stink. Otherwise, animals [in semen] will enter if you don't wash your legs well.

Women:
Never mind that. Hold your nose, or the stench of your meat will overpower you—hi, hi, hi, hi, hi.

Man:
I like the odor of meat. That's why I don't want to hold my nose, for the flesh is my meal.

Women:
Well, then, take care that worms don't enter your meat—hi, hi, hi, hi, hi, hi.

Man:
Worms won't enter me, because I am sitting next to the fire. You have no fire [i.e., you are dead]. Perhaps worms will invade you. You won't be able to stop them. And if not, flies will enter right away—ha, ha, ha.

Women:
The worms won't enter us either. We have some medicine of our own against them. We have poison [rum]. We will kill the flies right away— hi, hi, hi, hi, hi.

This interaction is humorous because of the multiple meanings of *veʔel* ("meal," "food," "sexual intercourse") and *bek'et* ("meat," "flesh"). By this time the meat hanging from the porch rafters has begun to rot, and the stench is overpowering. The women are purposely ambiguous in their teasing about whether it is the rotting beef that smells or whether it is the man's body. The man counters that it is the women's dirty flesh that stinks. The "animals" referred to are either maggots which infect the meat or the small creatures which are believed to inhabit the sexual fluids.

When they have finished bathing, the women change their clothes and go with their husbands to the plaza to join the fiesta celebrators from the other barrios. When the men have run around the plaza three times, they light pine torches and form processions to their respective Mount Calvarys. There they dance the Dance of the Warriors until sunrise.

Mount Calvary is the most important of the many cross shrines visited by the Passions during the fiesta of Carnaval. The cross shrines probably represent the Stations of the Cross, and the pilgrimage to Mount Calvary commemorates Christ's procession from Pilate's house to Calvary Hill (Alston 1912:XV, 569).

Meanwhile, the Passions' servants are completing the final preparations for the last banquets. They carry food and serving dishes to the sacred spring of their barrio. There are two sacred springs in Chamula, one a shrine maintained by the residents of barrio San Juan, and another associated with the other two barrios. The servants set up benches for the Passions to sit on and serve a meal of beef stew, gruel, bean tamales, sweetened water, and bread rounds to all the spectators.

While the spectators are eating near the sacred spring of barrio San Juan, the Passions' Monkeys round up some "independent" Monkeys and children to take part in the "war" between Mexico and Guatemala, or between the Carrancistas and Pinedistas. The participants form two lines—one on the hillside above the sacred spring and one in the valley below. The men on the hillside represent Mexico (or the Carrancistas), and those in the valley represent Guatemala (or the Pinedistas). Mexico has fifty men and Guatemala has forty men. They

1. The Bull "gores" Grandfather. (Photo by Frank Cancian)

2. Grandmother helps Grandfather mount his horse. (Photo by Frank Cancian)

4. Grandfather, writhing in pain, is assisted by Grandmother. (Photo by Frank Cancian)

3. Grandfather gets to his feet after having been "gored" by the Bull. (Photo by Frank Cancian)

5. Some Junior Entertainers: *left to right*, Spanish-Moss Wearers, Plumed Serpents, Lacandons. (Photo by Frank Cancian)

6. Jaguars and Blackmen. (Photo copyright by Gertrude Duby de Blom)

8. Jaguars and Blackmen climb the Jaguar Tree. (Photo by Frank Cancian)

7. Plumed Serpent with ear of corn in his beak. (Photo copyright by Gertrude Duby de Blom)

10. Blackman dancing with stuffed iguana and squirrels. (Photo by Frank Cancian)

9. Blackman carrying stuffed squirrel. (Photo by Frank Cancian)

11. Outgoing Passion with his Monkeys. (Photo copyright by Gertrude Duby de Blom)

12. The sacred kettledrum of Chenalhó. (Photo by Marcey Jacobson)

13. A group of Monkeys. (Photo copyright by Gertrude Duby de Blom)

14. Monkeys set fire to thatch. (Photo copyright by Gertrude Duby de Blom)

15. Running over burning thatch, Messenger leading the way. (Photo copyright by Gertrude Duby de Blom)

17. Crossbacks and Lacandon Woman. (Photo by Marcey Jacobson)

16. Blackman in monkey-fur headdress. (Photo copyright by Gertrude Duby de Blom)

20. Masked woman. (Photo copyright by Gertrude Duby de Blom)

19. Masked woman and masked *fiscal*. (Photo copyright by Gertrude Duby de Blom)

18. Masked performer. (Photo copyright by Gertrude Duby de Blom)

21. Flags of *regidores* and *regidor* impersonators. (Photo copyright by Gertrude Duby de Blom)

22. Cowboys leading Bull. (Photo copyright by Gertrude Duby de Blom)

23. Dancing Ladies and Red Buttocks. (Photo copyright by Gertrude Duby de Blom)

24. Procession of Pedrano women. (Photo copyright by Gertrude Duby de Blom)

25. Passions of Chenalhó (*left*, incoming; *right*, outgoing). (Photo copyright by Gertrude Duby de Blom)

26. Blackman (*right*) and Limey Asses. (Photo copyright by Gertrude Duby de Blom)

28. Monkey kidnaps boy in Larráinzar. (Photo copyright by Gertrude Duby de Blom)

27. Group of Limey Asses. (Photo copyright by Gertrude Duby de Blom)

30. Above: Volador Dance in Chichicastenango. (Courtesy of the Middle American Research Institute, Tulane University)

29. Left: Dance of Moors costume in Chinautla. (Courtesy of the Middle American Research Institute, Tulane University)

31. Dance of Moors in Chichicastenango. (Courtesy of the Middle American Research Institute, Tulane University)

32. Dance of Conquest in Tactic. (Courtesy of the Middle American Research Institute, Tulane University)

33. Dance of the Moors in Ixtapalapa. (Courtesy of the Middle American Research Institute, Tulane University)

34. Dance of Old Men in Pátzcuaro.
(Courtesy of the Middle American
Research Institute, Tulane Univer-
sity)

35. Pig's Head in Telchaquillo. (Photo
by author)

decide who will be called General, Colonel, Captain, and Sergeant.

The men pelt each other with lumps of horse dung collected earlier in a nearby pasture. After blowing trumpets, the two armies charge at each other three times. The first time, Mexico loses; the second time, Guatemala loses; the third engagement ends in a draw. When the "war" ends, the thirsty soldiers rush over to the spring for a drink of water.

Formerly, this battle took place at the second sacred spring also. The men of barrio San Pedro lined up on one side and the men of barrio San Sebastián on the other. But in 1969, the battle took place in barrio San Juan only.

After the battle between the Mexicans and the Guatemalans is over, the Monkeys round up a group of men and boys to look for roof thatch. They seek out an abandoned house, remove the old thatch from its roof, and carry it to the plaza in front of the town hall. They carefully arrange the thatch in a five-meter-wide track running from the atrium of the churchyard to the opposite end of the plaza. This track is called the "path of God." At about 2:30 P.M. the Monkeys begin to light the thatch with matches (plate 14). The thatch blazes up and then dies down, leaving a thin bed of glowing coals. At this point, the Passions and all their assistants run back and forth across the coals three times (plate 15). No one else is permitted to step on the thatch; the Monkeys apply their whips to the backs of whatever animals and unauthorized people stray onto the "path of God" so that they will not block the way of the men carrying the flags.

According to Gossen, Chamulas believe that, after having tried, unsuccessfully, to burn God, "all the Jews jumped into the fire and died" (1970:417). The monkey impersonators symbolize the Jews, or demons, who harrassed Christ. That is why they must run over the fire. Their associates must also run over the coals because they have become tainted with the Monkeys' evil during the fiesta of Carnaval. If they do not run through fire at this time, their ghosts will go to hell after they die. But if they run through the fire while they are still alive, they will not receive further punishment after death. It is clear that the fire-walking rite symbolizes going through hell.

After the fire-purification rite is over, some men entertain the spectators by trying to ride live bulls which the Passions have provided for this purpose. The spectators laugh as one man after another is thrown to the ground. Finally, someone succeeds in riding a bull, much to the delight of the audience. The crowds begin to disperse after this event.

Wednesday. This is the last day of the fiesta and the first day of Lent. Formerly, the Passions served a banquet of fish and potatoes in honor of "Fish-Eating Wednesday" (*melkuliš htiʔ čoy*), but now they economize by serving leftover beef, tamales, and tortillas. The Passions of barrio San Juan make an attempt to keep the tradition alive by placing three fish on a table as a symbol of the occasion, but they serve their guests beef, as do the Passions of the other two barrios.

Conclusion

The fiesta of Carnaval is, for Chamulas, a period of license and evil which marks the end of the old year. It is a time for men to release their inhibitions by impersonating monkeys. The "independent" Monkeys engage in an orgy of drunkenness and violence, blindly quarrelling with friend and enemy alike and beating them with their whips. I observed several quarrels in the Passion's household, even among women, brought on by lack of sleep and excessive ritual drinking. By the time the fiesta ended, the Passion's wife had quarrelled with me and with the wife of her husband's ritual adviser, with the result that the ritual adviser's wife returned to her home in a huff. Thus the fiesta is marked by real, and not just symbolic, social disruption, which must be repaired during the following year. In a very real sense much of social value is "lost" during the fiesta of Carnaval.

6. Pandora's Box

The fiesta of Carnaval in San Pedro Chenalhó begins exactly four weeks after the fiesta of San Sebastián. The Carnaval celebrators assemble during the earlier fiesta to make an announcement in which they warn the people of Chenalhó of what they should expect in a month's time:

> Fellow citizens!
> Look now! Look here!
> Here in a month's time everything will happen!
> The Monkeys are coming;
> The Turks are coming;
> *The* fiesta is coming.
> Everything will come:
> Animals, jaguars.

Don't sin too much!
Danger will come;
Evil will come;
Turks will come;
The French are coming;
Blackmen will appear;
The Crossbacks will appear;
The Abductors will appear;
Evil will appear.
Every possible horror will come in thirty days' time!

This announcement foretells the arrival of the Blackmen (*h²ik'aletik*), the Crossbacks (*hkurus patetik*), and the Abductors (*htakeletik*). The Blackmen, known also as Turks, Monkeys, and Frenchmen, wear blackface and ribboned monkey-fur headdresses which resemble those worn by the monkey impersonators in Chamula (plate 16). There are six Blackmen in all: two are called "Ladinos" (*hkašlan*); the other four pretend to be the dogs of the Ladino Blackmen (Guiteras-Holmes 1946:168).

Turks, monkeys, Frenchmen, Blackmen, and Ladinos are all symbols of evil in Chenalhó. The Turks, who controlled the Christian Holy Land for centuries, symbolize the evilness of all that is non-Christian. The French, on the other hand, are evil in a political rather than a religious sense, having intervened in Mexican affairs between 1861 and 1867. Blackmen and monkeys are cast in evil roles in the mythology of highland Chiapas. When a Pedrano woman has a miscarriage, she says that a monkey is to blame—that it has stolen her foetus (Guiteras-Holmes 1961:105). The Pedrano fears that if he goes outside at night he will be seized by a Blackman and carried off to his cave. In the Pedrano myths, Blackmen are sometimes referred to as Ladinos (Guiteras-Holmes 1961:189). Ladinos, of course, are the Pedrano's traditional enemies, notorious for their cruelty and exploitation. The Pedrano's hatred of Ladinos was expressed in Chenalhó's active participation in the Indian rebellion of 1867–1870 (Molina 1934:382). Not surprisingly, the Blackmen's performance dramatizes some of the uglier aspects of ethnic relations in highland Chiapas.

The Crossbacks, of which there are two, walk about almost nude. Their only garment is a pair of white shorts. What they lack in clothing, however, they make up for in body paint: their torsos, front and back, are decorated with crosses and the rest of their bodies with circles. The circles faintly resemble the markings of jaguars (plate 17), hence the reference to "animals" and "jaguars" in the announcement of their impending arrival made during the fiesta of San Sebastián. This jaguarlike effect is achieved with red anatto, yellow ochre, and white lime pigments.

The Crossbacks are the consorts of a female impersonator known as *me? hka?benal*. I have already explained, in chapter 3, that the word *ka?benal* is probably derived from the name of a Lacandon chief. The Tzotzil word *me?* means "wife" or "female." In this context I believe that *me? hka?benal* should be glossed as Lacandon Woman.

The people of Chenalhó tell a myth about a man called *hka?benal* who ate people and whose daughter married the Pedrano culture hero, Ohoroxtotil (*Ahau rioš totil*, "Lord, God, Father"), the mythical figure credited with ridding the world of jaguars (Guiteras-Holmes 1961: 182). Pedranos believe that this culture hero is God himself (Guiteras-Holmes 1961:182).

The Lacandon Woman pretends to be the wife of the Crossbacks. This suggests that the Crossbacks symbolize Christ on his journey to Calvary Hill with the cross on his back. The white crosses painted on the backs of the Crossbacks represent the actual wooden cross carried by Christ, and the circles on their bodies represent his wounds. Even their seminude state is consistent with this theme.

Pedranos no longer identify the Crossbacks with their culture hero or with Christ, but they sometimes do view their painted blotches as wounds or sores. For example, Guiteras-Holmes (1946:166) mentions that at the fiesta of Carnaval in 1944, a Crossback approached her and, pointing to the circles painted on his body, told her that he had ringworm and asked her for some medication.

What remains unexplained is the puzzling fact that the Crossbacks also represent jaguars. In the course of time the slayer of the jaguars has become identified with his victims! The painted wounds have been reinterpreted as the markings of a jaguar.[1]

The Lacandon Woman wears the typical Pedrano woman's costume—dark-blue cotton skirt and embroidered blouse. Like the Crossbacks, she paints her arms and legs with anatto pigment and ochre. In imitation of a woman's long hair she winds a red-and-blue striped band several times around her head, leaving a long end dangling like a woman's braid. Formerly, Pedrano women bound their hair with such woven strips of cloth. The Lacandon of Zinacantan's fiesta of San Sebastián also wears such a false braid.

Both the Lacandon Woman and the Crossbacks carry in their hands bunches of weeds (plate 17), with which they pretend to cure other fiesta celebrators and spectators of hypothetical illnesses.

The two Abductors wear red knee-length breeches, red jackets, and white shawls. Their woman companion, another female impersonator, decks herself out in the woman's costume typical of Chenalhó: dark-blue skirt, white cotton blouse embroidered with wool, shawl, and strings of gold beads. This trio poses as the enemies of the Blackmen; on Monday and Tuesday nights of the fiesta they pretend to flee from the Blackmen, who chase them from house to house.

A third group of entertainers is referred to as the k'oh ("masked") group. There are five masked figures: two piškal k'oh, two kapitan k'oh, and one rehirol k'oh. Their masks are made of leather, in which holes for their eyes and slits to represent their mouths have been cut; horsehair whiskers are glued to their chins (plates 18 and 19). They are accompanied by the me? k'oh, a female impersonator who pretends to be the wife of the rehirol k'oh. She does not wear a mask, but sports a dark-blue skirt, shawl, wool-embroidered white blouse, red-and-blue striped braid, and strings of gold beads (plate 20).

Piškal, kapitan, and rehirol are Tzotzil corruptions of the Spanish terms fiscal ("lay church official"), capitán ("captain"), and regidor ("town councilman"). Regidores are, at present, members of the town

---

[1] Munro S. Edmonson (personal communication) informs me that the jaguar has exactly this role in the Popol Vuh, the sacred book of the Quiché Indians of highland Guatemala, and in the Jaguar Deer Dance of the Quiché town of Rabinal (see chapter 9).

government of Chenalhó, but the position of *fiscal* has become obsolete. The position of captain is a *cargo* in the civil-religious hierarchy. Two captains take office during the fiesta of San Sebastián and end their terms of office at the end of the fiesta of Carnaval. The two captain impersonators carry stick horses with which they mock the horse races of the real captains, which take place on Sunday during the fiesta of Carnaval. *Regidores* are the officials who swear new *cargo* holders into office. The two *regidor* impersonators mimic the gestures of the *regidores* when they anoint the *cargo* holders and their wives on the first day of the fiesta. The *regidores* carry large silk flags, one white and the other red, which they wave over the *cargo* holders who are being sworn into office. The *regidor* impersonators carry small coarse cotton flags in the same colors, parodies of the flags carried by the true *regidores* (plate 21). The *fiscal* impersonator and his consort take the roles of the *cargo* holder and his wife in the anointing ceremony. In other words, the members of the masked group are humorous counterparts of some of the members of the civil-religious hierarchy of Chenalhó.

Still another group of entertainers consists of the Cowboys (*hvakero*) and the Bull (*toro*), who wears a framework constructed of saplings and reed mats over his head. The face of the Bull is made of paper and topped with horns (plate 22). The bull impersonator holds onto a bar at the front of the frame with which he directs the movements of the Bull. The Cowboys wear either Ladino clothes or soldiers' costumes and carry ropes and guns (plate 22).

Pedranos, like Zinacantecos and Chamulas, distinguish between Carnaval roles to which men are appointed and roles that are voluntary. In Chenalhó, too, the five "lost days" commemorated by the fiesta of Carnaval provide the men of the community with their only opportunity to assume a new identity. Pedrano men, however, have two choices open to them: they may put on women's clothing and pose as Dancing Ladies (*ʔanṭil ʔak'ot*), or they may assume the role of Red Buttocks (*ṭahal čak*), so named because they wear red knee-length breeches. The Dancing Ladies and Red Buttocks of Chenalhó are functionally equivalent to the "independent" Monkeys of Chamula and the Blackmen or Demons of Zinacantan. Although the performances of

the "independent" Monkeys of Chamula and of the Blackman impersonators at the fiesta of Carnaval in Zinacantan are similar to those of
the Blackmen of Chenalhó, the latter are appointed to their positions
and therefore are functionally (and thematically) equivalent to the
"dependent" Monkeys of Chamula and the Blackmen who perform at
the fiesta of San Sebastián in Zinacantan.

The role of Dancing Lady is by far the most popular choice in Chenalhó. The men who choose this role wear the typical Pedrano woman's
outfit plus sunglasses, turbans, and ribboned hats (compare plate 23
with plate 24). The costumes of the Red Buttocks are like those of the
Abductors: white shawls and red breeches and jackets (plate 23). The
Red Buttocks carry harps, rattles, violins, and guitars. They pretend to
be the husbands of the Dancing Ladies and serve as their partners when
they dance.

Here, as in Chamula and Zinacantan, the *cargo* holders who sponsor
the fiesta of Carnaval are called Passions (*pašyon*). There are eight
Passions who preside over the festivities in Chenalhó: four enter office
at the beginning of the fiesta, and four finish their terms of office at the
fiesta's end. The four pairs of incoming and outgoing Passions do not
at present represent any barrio divisions as do their counterparts in
Chamula, although it is likely that they did at some time in the past.

The outgoing Passions wear gold-trimmed red knee-length trousers,
white shirts, high-backed sandals, and black capes. Fringed white
shawls with wide red borders are folded diagonally in two and draped
over their shoulders, the point of the triangle falling in back. They
wrap similar pieces of cloth around their heads as turbans, on top of
which they set broad-brimmed black felt hats decorated with ribbons.
The incoming Passions wear white shorts and shirts and black wool
robes left unsewn at the sides. They, too, wear shawls, but they fasten
them at the back so that the point falls in front. Their headgear is like
that of the outgoing Passions, but they wear sandals without backs. The
outgoing Passions carry long white staffs tied with red and green ribbons; the incoming Passions carry unornamented staffs (plate 25).

The captains are dressed like the outgoing Passions in red jackets,
knee-length breeches, and black capes (plate 25). They are called

"captains" because they lead younger men on horseback in cavalry charges on the first two days of the fiesta of Carnaval.

Properly speaking, the fiesta of Carnaval begins with the fiesta of San Sebastián a month before. At 10:00 A.M. on the main day of the fiesta of San Sebastián, the four incumbent Passions announce the fiesta of Carnaval, which is to take place in four weeks' time. This is the first occasion for the Carnaval personnel to get together and perform their acts (although they are not yet in costume), and it is at this fiesta that the Passions serve their first ritual meals, to which they invite the civil authorities.

The Passions serve pork at their banquets. The civil officials are the first to be served; only much later will the Blackmen be given their portions. The hungry Blackmen walk up to the civil officials, calling out "*kuč, kuč*," the call used to summon pigs to eat. Of course the pig in question is already dead and does not respond, but the amused officials offer the Blackmen tidbits of meat as a reward for their humorous behavior. If beef instead of pork were being served, the Blackmen would pretend to call a bull, shouting "*toro, toro.*"

It is the duty of the Blackmen and the *fiscal* impersonator to go to the town hall during the fiesta of San Sebastián to inform the civil and religious officials of the date on which the fiesta of Carnaval will begin. It is then that they give their preview of coming attractions, announcing the impending arrival of Turks, Frenchmen, Blackmen, Abductors, Crossbacks, and wild animals. They end their proclamation with:

> They will offer a little entertainment;
> They will offer a little joking;
> They will evoke laughter
> On the roadway,
> In the square.
> They will celebrate the festival;
> They will celebrate the holiday,
> Of our father Jesus,
> Of our father the Nazarene.

With these words the prophets of doom calm the fears of their fellow townsmen, suggesting that the forthcoming fiesta has its mirthful side as well. Their announcement signals to the men of the community that it is time to ready their Dancing Lady or Red Buttocks disguises so that they will be prepared to take part in the Fiesta of Games when the time comes.

Preparations for the Fiesta

The Passions come to the ceremonial center "to fast and pray every twenty days during the sixty that precede Carnaval" (Guiteras-Holmes 1961:97). Starting eight days before the fiesta begins, the Passions must be sexually abstinent. If it should rain during the fiesta it means that a Passion has sinned: he has quarrelled with someone or has engaged in sexual relations with a woman. "If he is jealous, or ill tempered, or has not provided sufficiently, his wife will weep and her tears will bring on the rain; if harsh words are spoken, the earthenware vessels will crack and break to pieces" (Guiteras-Holmes 1961:98). When this happens the guilty Passion goes to dance and pray at the foot of the saint in the church so that the rain will cease. In the past, the guilty Passion received a dozen lashes as punishment if it rained during the fiesta. But now the *presidente* no longer whips him. Instead, by praying and dancing, the Passion tries to make amends for his wrongdoing.

Two or three months before the fiesta the Passion recruits men to cut and stack firewood to dry. Then during January the Passion recruits between fifty and seventy men to haul the wood to his house in the ceremonial center. A week before he needs the wood he goes to the homes of the woodmen to request their assistance. The men may work for as long as a week, carrying four loads of wood a day. They are fed beans, corn gruel, and chili peppers in return for their labor. The wood is used in cooking food for the large banquets offered by the Passion.

Cooking begins a week before the fiesta. The Passion has recruited helpers, who live at his house for seven days. During the time they work for him the Passion provides his helpers and their children with room and board in exchange for their labor. The helpers make corn dough, corn tamales, bean tamales, and "dry," or baked, tortillas. On the Wednesday before the fiesta begins, a gruel specialist (*me? ?ulavil*) makes the sweet, slightly fermented cornstarch drink (*?ul*) which is traditionally served at this fiesta. On the same day, the woman who supervises the making of tortillas (*vahobil*) directs her helpers in boiling corn kernels in lime. When they are soft, the women carry them to the riverside to rinse them. On Thursday before the fiesta the women grind the softened kernels into a dough, which they will make into tamales on Friday. Also on Friday the outgoing Passions slaughter their bulls. The blood is used for making blood sausage.

The fiesta begins on Saturday and lasts for five days. Once Pandora's box has been opened, the evil represented by the fiesta entertainers spreads over the town. First come the masked figures, who are the chief entertainers on Saturday. On Sunday the Blackmen dominate the scene with their gory slaughter of two turkeys. By Monday evening three new groups of entertainers have appeared: (*a*) the Crossbacks and the Lacandon Woman, (*b*) the Cowboys and their Bull, and (*c*) the Abductors, who the Blackmen claim have kidnapped their sister or wife. No new groups appear on Tuesday, but several of Monday's events are repeated. On Wednesday, the last day of the fiesta, the entertainers remove their costumes and the fiesta celebrators prepare to return to their hamlets.

The Fiesta

Saturday. Two important events occur on Saturday, the first day of the fiesta. In the morning, the civil authorities go to the house of each Passion, where they swear the *cargo* holders and their wives into office. In the late afternoon the captains and the horsemen recruited by the Passions make a test run with their horses to determine whether they can keep their seats. The masked figures play major roles in both events, mocking the inauguration of the Passions and the horsemanship of the riders.

The two top-ranking *regidores* swear the Passion and his wife into office. The *regidores* carry silk banners, the poles of which are topped with Lorraine crosses. The Passion and his wife kneel side by side on reed mats while the *regidores* wave their flags three times over them. To their right are the *fiscal* impersonator and his "wife," also side by side, with the two *regidor* impersonators standing in front of them holding crude banners without crosses on their poles. When the Pas-

sion and his wife kneel to receive the benediction, the female impersonator lies down on her back while the *fiscal* impersonator spreads his
legs and squats over her in the position for intercourse (Guiteras-
Holmes 1946:149–150).

During the display of horsemanship in the afternoon the captain
impersonators stand to one side, mounted on their stick horses, and
mimic the performance of the real captains. As the captains gallop by
on their horses, their impersonators run alongside, dragging their stick
horses under them. At the end of the performance, the captain impersonators insist on receiving gifts of liquor along with the captains and
their horsemen.

Sunday. In the morning the Blackmen amuse themselves in the marketplace by begging food from the vendors there. One Blackman walks
up to a vendor saying, "Offer alms on behalf of our father the Nazarene!" He requests some coriander to feed to his turkey. If the vendor
does not answer, the Blackman helps himself to coriander, bananas,
peanuts, or *chicha*. The vendor does not become angry, because she
expects the Blackmen to steal from her that day. If the vendor resists,
the Blackman threatens to carry her off (Guiteras-Holmes 1946:154).
The Blackmen return to the town hall, carrying their stolen goods,
which they present as a gift to the *presidente*.

At noon the four outgoing Passions offer a banquet, to which they
invite the civil officials. The *pièce de résistance* at this meal is beef stew.
As usual, the civil authorities receive their portions before the other
guests. In a replay of their performance at the Passions' banquets during the fiesta of San Sebastián, the hungry Blackmen hover around the
table calling the animal being served, this time a bull, so that they will
receive their portions ahead of schedule. They call *"toro, toro"* to the
amusement of the other guests, who indulge them with tasty morsels
from their own bowls.

The high point of the day comes at 4:00 P.M., when the captains
display their riding skill by torturing two turkeys. The Blackmen tie a
rope between two posts which they had earlier set up in front of the
town hall. Then they hang two live turkeys by their feet from the rope,
halfway between the two posts. The captains approach the dangling

turkeys on horseback at a gallop, reaching for their feathers and gradually depluming them alive as they race beneath them. The Blackmen stand beside the posts, raising and lowering the rope so as to place the birds within and beyond the reach of the horsemen. The riders pass beneath the turkeys twelve times, each time pulling out some of their feathers and scattering them on the roadway.

After the twelfth gallop, the Blackmen seize the turkeys and decapitate them, meanwhile exclaiming to the onlookers:

> Look, people!
> Look at Andrés Luis Turkey Belly!
> He is utterly depraved!
> Look!

A Blackman picks up the neck of one of the turkeys and moves it rapidly back and forth through a circle formed with his thumb and index finger, shouting:

> If you have behaved in this shameless fashion—
> Just you wait and see!
> Your fate will be the same as Andrés Luis Turkey Belly's.
> He came to a quick end because of his depravity.

The turkey's neck represents the penis of Andrés Luis Turkey Belly; the hole formed by the Blackman's thumb and forefinger symbolizes a vagina. The turkey represents a real person who has sinned, for the name Turkey Belly (č'ut tuluk') is a Pedrano surname. The obscene gesture with the turkey's neck suggests the immoral behavior which led to Andrés Luis Turkey Belly's downfall. As the Blackmen manipulate the turkey's neck in this fashion, they announce to the crowd:

> The Turks are coming;
> The Monkeys are coming;
> The fiesta is coming.
> We will dance!
> The Blackmen are coming!
> Produce a child [like this]!
> Produce a son [like this]!
> Look! Look! Look!

Then the Blackmen carry the turkeys' necks back and forth along the
road three times, shouting:

> Don't be embarrassed!
>   Look!
> One of our people died—
>   Andrés Luis Turkey Belly!
> Because he was so tricky;
>   Because he was so unruly—
> He is dead.
>
> Look, you-all!
> Don't learn how to be tricky!
>   Don't learn how to steal!
> He has sinned.
>   His head is broken off here.
> It doesn't pay to sin!
>   It doesn't pay to steal!
> Because Andrés Luis Turkey Belly is very tricky.

This performance is repeated in the houses of the Passions and captains as well as in front of the town hall and at the riverside. When the
Blackmen arrive at a Passion's house, they hang the turkey's body on
a wooden hook suspended from the rafters, saying:

> Look at poor Andrés Luis Turkey Belly!
> He died;
>   He met his end,
> Because he sinned so much.
>   The poor thing!

Then they take the turkey's decapitated body and put it on the ground.
They repeat their performance with the neck of the turkey. They cry
and pray over the turkey's carcass just as people pray over their dead
during the fiesta of All Saints. They throw themselves on their knees
and line up five candles beside the turkey's body. As they offer their
candles they sob and wail:

> Why didn't you grow up?
>   Why didn't you mature?
> Why did you look for trouble?

Why did you seek out evil?
Why did you do all that,
Andrés Luis Turkey Belly?

They look at its head; they look at its body.

You were finished;
You died forever,

they say, crying profusely. They go through this routine at the house
of each Passion and captain. When they finish their rounds, they leave
their turkey's body at the house of the second Passion until the next
morning, when they will cook it and serve it in a banquet.

Monday. At 11:00 A.M. on Monday, the Blackmen carry firewood
and a large clay pot to the porch in front of the town hall, where they
will cook the turkeys they killed on the afternoon before (Guiteras-
Holmes 1946:160). The masked figures are in charge of cooking the
meal, which is served as a banquet at 2:00 P.M. The female impersonator of the masked group cuts up the turkey meat into short narrow
strips to be cooked in the pot brought by the Blackmen. When it is
ready, she places three miniscule pieces of the meat in each eating
bowl and pours soup over them; the Blackmen serve the meat-flavored
broth to the civil authorities and to whoever else wants to participate
in the banquet. This meager meal is a parody of the Passions' banquet
of the day before, where each guest had received three generous chunks
of beef—not microscopic bits of turkey. Although advertised as a
"banquet," the entertainers' meal consists of little more than liquid
refreshment.

Monday is also the day when the Lacandon Woman and her two
male companions, the Crossbacks, first appear at the fiesta. All three
figures carry in each hand bundles of weeds, with which they "cure"
the spectators and the civil and religious officials of magical fright
(plate 17). In curing the illnesses called *komel* and *ši^ʔel*, the Pedrano
shaman customarily brushes his patient's body with branches to "seize"
or "absorb" the illness from his body. The fright or shock occasioned
by falling on the ground or into the water or by the sight of something

fearful causes part of the victim's soul to leave his body and become
"lost." *Komel* is the term applied if the patient is a child, and *ši?el* is
applied to an adult patient (Guiteras-Holmes 1961:135–138).

The Lacandon Woman and her Crossback companions go up to Passions, alcaldes, and other people and ask them:

> Are you suffering from magical fright?
> Have you experienced soul loss?
> If so, we will cure you of your illness.

They wave their bunches of weeds over their "patient," pretending to
restore the missing part(s) of his soul. After passing their weeds over
his body several times, they address their weeds: "What have you received?" meaning, "Have you absorbed his illness?"

In the late afternoon the Bull and the Cowboys arrive on the scene.
The fiesta personnel split up into two groups: each group includes two
incoming and two outgoing Passions. The Bull, the Blackmen, the
Crossbacks, and the Lacandon Woman go with one group of Passions.
The Red Buttocks and the Dancing Ladies join the other group
(Guiteras-Holmes 1946:166–167). One group takes the high road
and the other group takes the low road, and they run around the town
three times. They meet at the riverside, where the Cowboys and the
Blackmen ensnare the Bull with their ropes. The Cowboys aim their
rifles and shoot the Bull, which lies there sprawling face-up while the
dancers, the Lacandon Woman, and the Crossbacks jump over it
three times. This event is called "lost at the riverside" (*č'ayel ta
?uk'um*) because the Bull was chased out of town, shot, and left to die
at the riverside.

That evening the Blackmen go looking for their "enemies," the
Abductors, who hide in the houses of the Passions and captains. For
this event the Crossbacks are also treated as Abductors. Thus there are
two groups of fugitives from the Blackmen's "justice": (*a*) the Lacandon Woman–Crossback trio and (*b*) the two Abductors and their
prisoner. Each group visits the home of each Passion and captain
separately. The two figures dressed as men pretend to have abducted
the woman, who the Blackmen claim is their sister or wife. When they

arrive at a *cargo* holder's house, the fugitives hide themselves by lying on the floor, with the "woman" in the middle, and covering themselves with a reed mat. The people in the *cargo* holder's house pretend not to notice them.

The six Blackmen split up into two groups of three men each. One by one the groups go to the houses of all the *cargo* holders, where the fugitives have hidden themselves. Each of the Ladino Blackmen goes with a different group. The other two Blackmen in each group pretend to be dogs, one called Sargento and the other Gachipín.[2] They bark and walk about on all fours. Thus each group represents a Ladino with his two dogs who hunt down fugitives from justice.

When the Blackmen arrive at a Passion's (or captain's) house, the Ladino Blackman knocks at the door, calling out:

> Well, Passion, did you see a woman and two men running away?
> My wife (sister) ran away.
> I am looking for my wife (sister).
> They have sinned;
>   They are evil people.
> They abducted the woman;
>   They kidnapped the woman.
> Open the door, Passion!
> We will search for them;
>   We will look for them,
> Because she is my wife (our sister).
> They shouldn't have kidnapped the woman.
> We are looking for them.
> Open the door!

But the Passion refuses to open the door of his house. He says, "You can't enter here, Ladino."

The house is tightly locked up. One of the "dogs" climbs up onto the roof of the house and enters under the eaves. He then unlocks the door and lets his companions in. The three Blackmen, with the two "dogs" on all fours, pretend to search for the fugitives all over the

---

[2] "Sargento" means sergeant, a Ladino military title, and "Gachipín" is probably a corruption of *gachupín*, a term of reference for peninsular Spaniards during the colonial period.

house. "Bastards, are you here, Abductors?" they say upon arrival. They pretend not to notice the fugitives right away. The dogs look in every corner, within the large pots, under the bed, in the garbage, and behind the door. They sniff at various girls to embarrass them. Finally one of the dogs begins to scratch the mat. The Ladino takes a stick and lifts off the mat, revealing the criminals lying below in an embrace. "Here are the bastards!" say the Blackmen. Sometimes the fugitives pretend to sleep; sometimes they are lying in the position for sexual intercourse (Guiteras-Holmes 1946:168). When they finish their search, the Blackmen seize the Abductors and beat them with their ropes and whips. They fall upon them and maul them, pretending sexual intercourse with the one who is disguised as a woman. Meanwhile the Ladino announces to everyone present:

> Watch carefully how this is done!
> Look, children, so you will know how to do this when you grow up!

When they tire of punishing the Abductors, the Blackmen pretend to make chili pepper sauce (*vokol ?ič*), which they will offer as a gift to the people in the *cargo* holder's house. Into an old broken pot goes whatever garbage they can find: a dry banana leaf, some peppers, floor sweepings, or lime water (Guiteras-Holmes 1946:169). The Blackmen stir up the fire and pretend to cook the sauce. Then they offer it to the Passion's helpers, addressing them as in-laws, uncles, and older brothers, as though the Passion's relatives were their own.

In the meantime the fugitives have left to hide in the house of another Passion. The Blackmen stay behind awhile to make their chili pepper sauce and to joke with the members of the first Passion's household. They take a tumpline belonging to the wife of the Passion and put it on her head. "Do you approve of what the Abductors did?" ask the Blackmen, reprovingly. They throw a mat on the Passion's wife, insinuating that she was the woman who was lying on the mat between the two Abductors when they arrived. The Blackmen pretend to attack the Passion's wife because she protected the criminals and refused to open the door for the representatives of "justice." Then the Blackmen leave to go look for the fugitives at another house.

Tuesday and Wednesday. On Tuesday, two of the events from the previous day are repeated. In the afternoon, the Bull is again chased through the town and to the riverside. Then the Cowboys go from house to house trying to sell their Bull. Finally the outgoing Passions pretend to buy the Bull (Guiteras-Holmes 1946:171).

In the early evening the Blackmen resume their pursuit of the fugitives. By midnight all the fiesta personnel have gathered in front of the town hall. One by one, each of the Passions goes to the porch of the town hall, where the Ladino Blackmen beat them with their monkey-fur headdresses, scolding:

> What did you do?
>> What was your work?
> You made passes at your older sister;
>> You made passes at your aunt;
> Perhaps you made passes at everyone!
>> Why did you sin so much?

In this way the Passions pay for their sins. Then come the Dancing Ladies and the Abductors, followed by the Crossbacks. Each one is flogged with a monkey-fur headdress. Carnaval was a period of excesses and obscene behavior. People must be punished for dancing too much, for lewdness, and for impersonating women. With these beatings the period of license ends. Now purged of their sins, the fiesta celebrators remove their costumes, say their goodbyes, and return to their homes in the hamlets.

The Prophecy Fulfilled

Thus the dire predictions announced during the fiesta of San Sebastián have all come to pass during the five "lost days" of Carnaval. The terrifying performances of the Monkeys, Blackmen, Turks, Frenchmen, and Ladinos are enough to dislodge the soul of even the most stouthearted Pedrano who witnesses their cruel torture of turkeys and their merciless tracking down of fugitives. These shocking incidents provide an apt context for the mock curing ceremonies of the Crossbacks and the Lacandon Woman.

In this period of chaos the Pedrano moral order is disrupted, what is sacred is made profane, and the boundaries of permissible behavior are relaxed. The Blackmen corrupt the youth with their grisly pantomime of Andrés Luis Turkey Belly's sins and with their realistic demonstrations of sexual intercourse in the homes of the Passions and captains. The masked figures, too, do their best to upset the moral order of Chenalhó with their sometimes obscene parodies of religious ritual. And even the ordinary man in the street flouts the traditional mores when he disguises himself as a woman and temporarily frees himself from the strict Pedrano canons of masculinity.

The Mayan calendar is cyclical, and even bad things must come to an end. After five days and five nights the fiesta celebrators reluctantly remove their disguises and assume the burden of morality again. The Monkeys, Turks, Blackmen, Frenchmen, Ladinos, Jaguars, Crossbacks, and Lacandon Woman return to the earth to await the moment when the prophecy will release them again to "offer a little entertainment," to "offer a little joking," and to "evoke laughter" at the Fiesta of Games.

7. The Moral Dimension of Ritual Humor

An essential ingredient of ritual humor in Zinacantan, Chamula, and Chenalhó is the impersonation of women, animals, mythical creatures, Ladinos, and deviant members of the community. Each character chosen as the referent of impersonation is the symbolic locus of a set of qualities or character traits which the members of these communities regard as evil.

In all three communities, humorous roles are those which involve behavior which deviates from norms. Elsewhere (Bricker 1968) I have shown that the basic principle underlying all Zinacanteco humor is that Zinacantecos will always laugh at deviant behavior. Thus, to understand Zinacanteco humor, it is necessary to know the Zinacanteco behavioral norms. Gossen (1970:204) believes that the same principle is implicit in Chamula humor. I did not have the opportunity to col-

lect data concerning the relation between norms and humor in Chenalhó. However, the data presented in chapter 6 suggests that some
Pedrano humor, at least, is based on deviations from norms as well.

In Zinacantan there are two dominant thematic foci of humor. One
theme concerns the "self" which the Zinacanteco presents to others.
Goffman has pointed out the relation which exists between self, demeanor, and deference: "It is therefore important to see that the self
is in part a ceremonial thing, a sacred object which must be treated
with proper ritual care and in turn must be presented in a proper light
to others. As a means through which this self is established, the individual acts with proper demeanor while in contact with others and is
treated by others with deference" (1956:497). Conversely, when the
self is *not* presented in a proper light to others (i.e., when the individual does not "act with proper demeanor while in contact with
others"), other people may treat him without deference. Nondeferen-
tial treatment in Zinacantan means ridicule, defamation, or legal punishment.

The "self" which the Zinacanteco presents to his community should
conform to the norms which govern language, wearing apparel, and
posture. Zinacantecos are not the only Indians in highland Chiapas
who speak Tzotzil, but their intonation pattern and certain dialectical
differences in pronunciation and vocabulary distinguish them from
neighboring Chamulas and the more distant inhabitants of Chenalhó.
The Zinacanteco who speaks differently from other Zinacantecos will
be mocked by his fellow townsmen, as will the Chamula who speaks
idiosyncratically (and presumably also the Pedrano).

The Indians of highland Chiapas all wear clothing which distin-
guishes them from other Indian groups and from such non-Indians as
Ladinos and foreigners. The inhabitants of Zinacantan, Chamula, and
Chenalhó speak disparagingly of members of their communities who
change into Ladino clothes and try to enter the mainstream of Mexican
national culture. This ethnocentricity is reflected in their ritual humor
(see chapter 8).

Among the Indians of highland Chiapas, as in our own society,
"clothes make the man." Clothing is recognized as an integral part of

the individual's body image. For example, when a Zinacanteco is ill, both his body and his clothing must be ritually cleansed (Laughlin 1962:130). Thus, in order to present himself in a "proper" light to others, the Zinacanteco must observe certain rules relating to his appearance—rules which apply to both his clothing and his body.

One such rule is that his body and his clothing should be clean. Clothing need not be new and may be torn and patched, but it must be clean. Washing clothes is the woman's task, but men are held responsible for keeping the clothing they are wearing from becoming soiled. The humorous nickname Old Ashy-Knees (*tan ?akan mol*) was applied to an old man who was always warming himself beside the fire but never washed the ashes off his legs. A woman was given the nickname Bushy (*č'et*) because her hair was messy—"she never washed or combed her hair, just like a woman from Chamula." Chamulas have a reputation in Zinacantan for being dirty.

However, Chamulas, too, have standards of cleanliness, noncompliance with which invariably invites ridicule. The humorous nickname Dirty-Eared Man (*?ik'al čikin vinik*) requires no explanation. The Chamula woman with dirty hair is not likened to a Zinacanteco woman, but is equated with the wife of the Blackman, for a "good" woman in Chamula is one who has clean hair, face, legs, and arms, and does not have many fleas. Similarly, if a Chamula man wears dirty clothes, people will laugh at him, claiming that his clothes resemble the rags women use to wipe out frying pans.

Chamula women, unlike Zinacanteco women, make a point of going about in rags, because when they wear new clothing, people ridicule them for being in pursuit of men. New clothing does not have that connotation in Zinacantan.

Another set of rules refers to body carriage and posture. There are "proper" ways of sitting and walking which differ for each sex. In both Zinacantan and Chamula people are ridiculed if they are bowlegged or pigeon-toed, if their legs are crooked, and if they are lame or hunchbacked. They make jokes about any kind of physical abnormality:

> *Question*: Do you know why that man sways from side to side, just like a horse?

Answer: He sways from side to side when he walks, because
he fucks too much. He sways from side to side because he broke his leg [penis].

Little variation is permitted in the wearing of the tribal costume. All
the items of the costume must be worn whenever the Zinacanteco or
Chamula appears in public, and they must be properly draped. There
are at least ten joking terms in the Zinacanteco dialect which describe
pants which hang improperly (Laughlin, personal communication).
One man was given the nickname Pointed Pants (*pah veš*) because his
pants were too long. Another man was called Old Flapping Clothes
(*lič k'uʔ mol*) because he did not fasten down the sides of his tunic,
which flapped like a woman's skirt in the wind. Similarly, in Chamula
the man who does not belt his tunic can count on being the butt of
ridicule.

There are, of course, some aspects of "self" over which the individual has no control, but if they depart from the community's norms,
they too may stimulate laughter. There are a host of derogatory nicknames in Zinacantan and Chamula which refer to unusual or deformed
body traits: Bearded (*ton sat*), Bony (*bak*), Black Face (*hʔik'al sat*),
Hairy Nose (*tot niʔ*), Bulging Head (*tom hol*), White Hair (*sak
hol*), Crooked Arm (*šot k'ob*), Droopy Eyelid (*maʔ sat*), Fat Neck
(*kut'unuk'u*), Spoon Mouth (*leč ʔe*), Big Ass (*muk'ta čak*), Barrel
Belly (*len č'ut*), Crane Legged (*luš ʔok*). The Chamulas call men
with beards or with long hair demons, because demons are thought to
be hairy.

The person who conducts himself with proper demeanor is also one
who performs competently the various roles he is called upon to play.
This means that men should not behave like women, nor women like
men. It also means that, in public life, men should perform their duties
of office properly, whether they be shamans or civil or religious officials. In Zinacantan, those who fail to perform their roles satisfactorily
may expect to be ridiculed, not only in humorous gossip and nicknames, but also in ritual humor (see chapter 3).

The second focus of Zinacanteco humor pertains to deviant sexual
behavior. Homosexuality, promiscuity, sodomy, adultery, impotence,

transvestism, celibacy, incest, and wife-beating all provide fuel for humorous gossip and nicknames. Some of these are apparently topics of humor in Chamula (Gossen 1970:119) and Chenalhó (see chapter 6) also. It is possible to infer some of these themes from the humor of female impersonators.

The image of womanhood which female impersonators try to con· vey is not that of the typical Indian woman. It is of the Indian woman who deviates from the role behavior appropriate for women or of the Ladino woman who symbolizes qualities which Indians disdain. The grandmother impersonator of Zinacantan exaggerates the deviant behavior of women by playing exceptionally well the role he is most familiar with—that of a man. The incongruity of men dressed as women pretending to do women's work serves to ridicule women who do not perform the woman's role adequately and who thus seem as awkward as men doing women's tasks. The Grandmother's humor, then, serves to define role boundaries for women.

Uncontrolled sexuality is another theme of ritual humor. People guilty of this character defect are equated with such animals as dogs and squirrels. An interpretation of this animal symbolism is provided in the next chapter.

The Spanish Lady, Nana María Cocorina, and the Lacandon Woman all symbolize qualities which Indians disapprove of, but attribute to Ladinos. The Spanish Lady publicizes her vanity and preoccupation with personal finery and trinkets. Nana María Cocorina and the Lacandon Woman are notorious for their promiscuity. Nana María Cocorina is unfaithful to her husband (the Passion), having gone off into the woods with Mariano Ortega and Juan Gutiérrez. The Lacandon Woman is abducted by the Crossbacks.

Blackmen (*hʔik'aletik*), monkeys (*maꭍetik*), demons (*pukuhetik*), Jews (*huraꭍetik*), and jaguars (*bolometik*) are malevolent creatures in the mythologies of all three communities. Although myths concerning monkeys are thematically different from those concerning Blackmen, Jews, and demons, the people of Chamula view these creatures as functionally equivalent in the sense that they are all evil. The Monkeys of Carnaval symbolize both the demons or the Jews who are reputed to have killed Christ and the Blackmen. They paint their faces black in imitation of the Blackmen, and the red banding on their jackets is said to symbolize the red eyes and penises of the Blackmen. Zinacantecos likewise equate Blackmen with demons and Jews, while Pedranos equate monkeys with Blackmen (their Blackmen wear monkey-fur headdresses like those worn by the Monkeys of Chamula). In other words, the three communities share a common fund of mythical symbols with shared meanings. The symbols are functionally the same in their representation of evil, but each one represents a different aspect of evil. Each community has drawn from this common pool of symbols a different aspect of evil to elaborate upon during the fiesta of Carnaval (and San Sebastián, in Zinacantan).

The myths which feature these symbols provide the contextual details of behavior and dress which the human impersonators imitate. The monkey impersonator of Chamula jokes about his diet of leaves and fruit and about his ability to climb trees and walk on limbs. He copies the nervous movements of monkeys and is noted for his incessant motion. He imitates the cries of monkeys.

Blackmen in Zinacanteco myths are noted for their hypersexuality, their ability to fly, and their habit of living in caves. Significantly, Blackmen at the fiesta of San Sebastián are preoccupied with the sexual activities of religious officials, and their humor is based on this theme. The *alférez* who is entering or leaving office is called Blackman because his black cape resembles the wings of Blackmen. Thus his putative ability to fly is the thread which runs through his joking. His exchange with the musicians is humorous because the mythical idiom permits a sexual interpretation of which both the performers and their audience are well aware. The Blackman's cave is equated in their minds with the vagina of the *alférez*'s wife. Metaphorically his statement that there is a lot of grass at the mouth of his cave means that his wife has thick pubic hair. When the musician asks to visit the Blackman's cave, he is really slyly asking to have intercourse with the *alférez*'s wife. When he asks to be shown how to enter the cave, he is asking the *alférez* to demonstrate how he performs sexual intercourse. Thus, the *alférez*-Blackmen also emphasize the sexual theme by making puns with Tzotzil words for "cave" (vagina) and "grass" (pubic hair). Because these figures are drawn from a mythology with which all members of the community are familiar, much can remain unsaid in the joking of the performers, thereby facilitating punning.

The Blackman of the fiesta of Carnaval (in Zinacantan) is better regarded as a demon, a Jew, or a Ladino.

The Blackmen of Chenalhó are noted for their preoccupation with sexual matters. It is they who seek out the Abductors and pretend to copulate with them.

Chamula differs from Zinacantan and Chenalhó in its characterization of the jaguar. All three communities have myths which describe jaguars devouring men. The jaguar impersonators of Zinacantan and Chenalhó (Crossbacks) play deviant roles. In Zinacantan they pretend to want to eat a Chamula boy; in Chenalhó they play the role of Abductors. But Chamula has another myth in which the jaguar defended Christ. It is this myth which is dramatized at the fiesta of Carnaval in Chamula.

It has already been pointed out that in these three communities humorous behavior is behavior which deviates from norms. The mythical creatures mentioned above are all known for their deviant behavior. Therefore, the more successful people are in impersonating these creatures, the more deviant behavior they perform, and the more humorous they seem to their compatriots. Impersonation is role-playing of a special kind. The better the role is played, the more humorous it is, because it is a deviant role.

The masked figures of Chenalhó, the Grandfathers and Grandmothers of Zinacantan, and Nana María Cocorina in Chamula are a special class of impersonators. All of them make fun of the ritual behavior of religious officials. In Chenalhó and Zinacantan these buffoons mock the change-of-office ceremonies of *alféreces*. In Chamula, Nana María Cocorina profanes the symbolic defense of Christ in the Dance of the Warriors. They are humorous because they represent the antithesis of appropriate behavior. The contrast between what is deviant (and therefore humorous) and what is normative (and therefore not humorous) is clear because the performances take place side by side or one after the other. There is no tradition of mythology to provide an implicit reference point for evaluating the behavior; the ongoing rituals of the officials furnish that standard.

The impersonator must appear and behave in a way which enables his audience to recognize the referent of impersonation immediately and unequivocally. There is, however, no effort to make costumes which accurately duplicate the appearance of the person or figure in question. The costumes consist of diagnostic elements, such as fur and tail in the case of an animal, blackface in the case of a Blackman or a demon, and skirt, blouse, and shawl in the case of a woman. Other costume items may conflict with the image being conveyed, but that is apparently of no consequence. The fact that a female impersonator wears men's sandals, trousers, and hat is unimportant; what counts is that he wear the three basic components of the woman's costume: skirt, blouse, and shawl. Similarly, the monkey impersonator of Chamula does not wear a monkey costume. His fur hat (or mask), at the base of which a tail is attached, is sufficient for his identification as a monkey.

The impersonator in these communities is often the locus of more than one role, for in ritual humor time is ignored, and functionally equivalent roles from different periods are treated as variations on a theme. Thus the monkey impersonators of Chamula represent not only monkeys, but also French soldiers, demons, and Jews. And the Blackman impersonator is Blackman, Turk, monkey, Frenchman, and Ladino in Chenalhó, but Blackman, Moor, demon, and Ladino in Zinacantan. This collage effect is made possible by the economy in costuming. In Chamula, a diagnostic headdress suffices in defining the monkey role; other costuming details define the Frenchman, soldier, and demon roles. Blackface is a defining characteristic of the Blackman role in Chenalhó and Zinacantan. Another diagnostic criterion in Zinacantan is a black cape.

Although details of costume are essential in defining a role, they do not necessarily make that role humorous. The monkey impersonator is not humorous by virtue of his costume alone, but because he also *behaves* like a monkey. He hoots and whistles; he flicks his tail back and forth; he imitates the quick nervous gestures of monkeys. Thus a humorous role is defined by certain diagnostic behavioral traits as well as by costume elements.

This selection in favor of only the most diagnostic (and therefore the most deviant) traits (most deviant from the Indian's point of view) is, of course, what makes the performances humorous. If the monkey did not deviate from human norms of behavior and appearance, it would not be a monkey (see next chapter). Similarly a woman who did not value trinkets would not be a Ladino, but an Indian. Zinacantecos, Chamulas, and Pedranos seem to equate difference with deviance. Therefore, a representation of difference (species difference or otherwise) is necessarily deviant or immoral and therefore humorous, for the essence of ritual humor is disguise—the impersonation of difference.

This type of symbolic representation corresponds to the literary device called *kenning*, through which an object or an idea may be implied by mentioning several of its qualities or attributes. Many examples of kenning occur in the prayers of Zinacantan, Chamula, and Chenalhó. In Zinacantan, for example, the synonyms "earth" and "mud" connote "arrival," while the parallel expressions "the cause for fear" and "the cause for shame" together refer to "rum." The Passions of Chamula do not thank their woodmen for their "help," but for having borrowed their "ten toes" and their "ten fingers." And the entertainers in Chenalhó are said to perform "on the road" and "in the square," rather than "in public."

Since in kenning an innocent-sounding phrase can connote something obscene, it has great potential as a humorous device. The mock curing prayer recited during the Christmas-Epiphany season in Zinacantan derives its humorous effect from kenning. "Bone" and "muscle" together connote "penis," and "place" and "hole" together connote "vagina." Similarly, "stick" refers to "penis" and "devilish flesh" to "vagina." A song sung at the fiesta of San Sebastián in Zinacantan is rich in sexual (and humorous) innuendoes. "Long hair" and "long beard" connote "pubic hair," and "sitting animal" and "hidden animal" are euphemisms for "vagina."

Miguel León Portilla, who has studied kenning in a number of Mexican Indian languages, including Maya, cites as an example of this device "skirt-and-blouse which implies woman in her sexual aspect" (1969:77). Female impersonators in highland Chiapas use the same symbols in defining their roles. Thus, what can be called kenning in verbal ritual humor is represented as impersonation in its nonverbal form.

When the traits which are imitated are distorted or exaggerated, the result is caricature, parody, or burlesque. The change-of-office ritual is parodied both in Zinacantan and Chenalhó, but by means of quite different symbols. A case in point is the flag, which is an object of parody in both communities: the Zinacanteco Grandfathers symbolize the flags of the *alféreces* with rattles, while the *regidor* impersonators of Chenalhó carry crude imitations of the real *regidores'* flags. There is, of course, less similarity between a rattle and a flag than between a flag and an imitation of it, however crude, but the rattle and the flag do share one feature in common—the fact that they are both mounted on sticks—which is sufficient for the analogy to be recognized. Clearly, parody is only meaningful if the object or action which is being imitated can be recognized in the distortion. For this reason, to cite another example, the mock prayer recited in "curing" the Grandfathers and Grandmothers of Zinacantan retains the couplet structure and some of the verbal formulae characteristic of the real curing prayer at the same time that some phrases undergo modifications with obscene connotations. Thus the symbols used in parody combine normative features with deviant ones.

In parody, what is normally regarded as moral or sacred is distorted so as to appear immoral or profane. For example, the crab-apple necklaces of the Grandfathers resemble the rosaries of the *alféreces* in their shape and the manner in which they are worn, but they differ in qualities such as hardness, edibility, and size. Similarly, when the jaguar impersonator of Zinacantan puts on a curing robe at the fiesta of San Sebastián, he chooses a bottle of intoxicating rum to symbolize the gourd water whistle which the Zinacanteco shaman uses in recalling the missing parts of his patient's soul. These distortions have the effect of profaning otherwise solemn ceremonies.

Norms, like other items of culture, change over time, and ritual humor must change also if it is to remain meaningful as humor. Either new symbols must be introduced or old symbols must be reinterpreted.

A striking example of reinterpretation may be inferred from the ritual humor of the fiesta of Carnaval in Zinacantan. What was obviously once the Zinacanteco version of the battle between Moors and Christians has been reinterpreted to symbolize hostile local ethnic relations and the hoped-for victory of Indians over Ladinos (rather than Christians over Moors). With the exception of the leader of the Blackmen, all the Blackmen are costumed to look like Ladinos. Only the name Blackman is retained as a vestige of the earlier significance of the battle. While the defeat of the Moors no longer has any significance in Zinacantan (if it ever did), Zinacantecos would relish a victory over Ladinos. Similarly, the mock battle which commemorates the Caste War in Chamula has been reinterpreted in terms of the Mexican Revolution of 1910, when the opposing sides in the local expression of the conflict were called Carrancistas and Pinedistas. Through such reinterpretation ritual humor adjusts to changes in norms and historical events.

But these dramatic changes are exceptional, resulting from occasional major national and local crises. Ritual humor is essentially conservative, even though the communities of highland Chiapas do not use written texts which might help to standardize performances of ritual humor. A very different situation exists in the Guatemala highlands, where fiesta performers must memorize their lines from written texts. Written texts help to maintain uniformity from year to year, although new copies of the manuscripts are frequently made when the old ones are about to disintegrate from constant use, and errors can and do creep in (Gillmor 1942:3; Bode 1961:227). Moreover, when errors render the script unintelligible, the performers or copiers often improvise (Bode 1961:227). Nevertheless, the opportunities for change are much greater in highland Chiapas, where there are no such written texts to refer to.

In the absence of manuscripts, uniformity is maintained by role specialization and the institution of ritual advisers. In Chenalhó, the same men are chosen to perform as Blackmen, Lacandon Woman, Crossbacks, and masked impersonators year after year. In Zinacantan, those ritual humorists who are not specialists are coached by ritual advisers (*totil me⁊il*), men who have passed at least two *cargos* and who are therefore familiar with the duties entailed by their positions. "The Ritual Adviser is a master of ceremonies for the cargoholder. He knows what, when and how tasks must be done, and tells the cargoholder or his helpers to do them. He knows what things are needed and tells the others to get them" (Cancian 1965:42). The efforts of the ritual adviser help to ensure that, even though the role of a ritual humorist is enacted by a different person each year, the behavior is always essentially the same.

The man who assumes the role of leader of the Blackmen in Zinacantan retains his position for five or six years. He serves as the ritual adviser for the other Blackmen during the fiesta of Carnaval. The Blackmen do not have individual ritual advisers to teach them ritual humor, because they are not *cargo* holders but have volunteered to take part in that one fiesta only. Therefore, the leader of the Blackmen, who is a specialist in ritual humor, functions as ritual adviser for all the Blackmen.

The men who are recruited for the "dependent" Monkey roles in Chamula are also specialists, but the role of "independent" Monkey is purely voluntary. As a result, the humor of the "independent" Monkeys is the more variable. The Passions have ritual advisers (*yahvaltikil* or *yahvotik*), men who have previously passed Passion *cargos*, who teach them their roles.

Ritual humor which takes mythical creatures, animals, and institutionalized cultural roles as models is relatively immune to change, but when actual members of the community are the object of caricature, the themes which are dramatized depend on the nature of their transgressions. For example, in 1969, I retaped the humor of the entertainers at the fiesta of San Sebastián in Zinacantan, which I had taped for the first time in 1966. The 1969 performance of the senior entertainers, who represent roles rather than individuals, was virtually identical to the 1966 version. But the Blackmen's performance with stuffed squirrels was somewhat different. A new routine was added in 1969 to ridicule a man who had run away to the lowlands to avoid assuming the duties of a policeman. Since men who work on plantations in the lowlands heat their food in discarded oil tins, one Blackman carried a pint-sized oil can from which he pretended to feed his stuffed squirrel.

Quantitative as well as qualitative fluctuations in ritual humor reflect the yearly variations in *cargo*-holder performance. Zinacanteco informants say that in years when few *cargo* holders default, there is simply less humor. In "good" years there are more stuffed squirrels available than delinquent *cargo* holders to be symbolized. The extra squirrels are used to represent the children of errant *cargo* holders. Thus the general nature of the ritual humor remains the same, although the details change to accommodate yearly variations in religious performance.

In summary, the two major ingredients of ritual humor are impersonation and a preoccupation with behavior which departs from cultural norms. Outsiders, evil mythical creatures, animals, and deviant members of the community provide the models for humorous impersonation. Because of their preoccupation with morality, the inhabitants of Zinacantan, Chamula, and Chenalhó lump everyone whom they define as evil or deviant in a single category. That is why the impersonator is often the locus of multiple roles and models.

The techniques used in impersonation include realistic imitation, exaggeration, and distortion. In the first case, what is humorous is the fact that a Zinacanteco, Chamula, or Pedrano disguises himself as a symbol of evil. Likewise the referent of distortion or exaggeration is always some norm or standard. Morality is therefore always implicit in humorous impersonations.

8. Metaphors of Social Criticism

In Zinacantan, Chamula, and Chenalhó, public disapproval of deviant behavior is expressed in ritual humor and humorous gossip. Often in ritual humor the offending party is symbolized as an animal of some kind, whether in the form of animal impersonation or ritual paraphernalia. Implicit in this use of animal symbols are beliefs which the inhabitants of the three communities hold regarding some innate differences which they think exist between human beings and other animate creatures in their universe.

They believe that people differ from animals in their possession of the faculty of reason and in their capacity for feeling shame. Human beings are capable of doing what is right and proper, because they are born with reasoning ability and because they are responsive to ridicule. Animals, on the other hand, act only on impulse, because they lack these reflective capabilities. "Reason" for these Indians seems to mean knowledge of the rules of etiquette—that is, knowledge of the proper way to speak to, act toward, and behave in the presence of other people.

Human beings know that there are some classes of people with whom sexual intercourse is forbidden. The exogamic restriction applies to parents, lineage relatives, and ritual kinsmen. Animals do not possess this knowledge. That is why male dogs mount any bitch who presents herself to them, including their mothers and litter mates. Human beings should know that most kinds of behavior, and sex in particular, have their proper time and place. Animals mate on impulse.

Therefore, animals are inferior to people, because they are incapable of knowing the difference between right and wrong behavior. Animals, like the malevolent mythical creatures described in the last chapter, are symbols of deviant behavior. It follows, then, that statements comparing humans with animals are insulting, and that impersonations of animals are humorous.

Leach (1964:28) has dubbed the class of verbal ridicule "in which a human being is equated with an animal of another species" *animal abuse*. In highland Chiapas, two factors govern the choice of species which are referred to in animal abuse: familiarity with the particular animal in question and recognizable similarities between that species and the object of ridicule.

The species which are most often referred to in animal abuse are the domesticated mammals. The most familiar animals are those which Zinacantecos, Chamulas, and Pedranos keep around their home sites: dogs, cats, pigs, cows, chickens, sheep, and horses. Mammals are, of course, physically more like humans than birds are and therefore have characteristics which "more readily lend themselves to anthropomorphic symbolism" (Lévi-Strauss 1966:54). Some wild mammals, such as squirrels, frequent human habitation areas, and, as a result, their habits too are familiar to people.

Some types of deviant behavior or physical abnormalities are more relevant stimuli for animal abuse than others. Dogs are the symbol of sexual licentiousness because they are highly visible and are free to roam in search of bitches in heat. In Zinacantan, people with insatiable, indiscriminate, and uncontrolled sexual appetites are invariably compared with dogs. When the details of illicit, adulterous, or incestuous relationships become known to the community at large, those who gossip about them refer to the malefactors as dogs. In Chenalhó, "men and women who fall in love too frequently are said to have been born on the 'day of the dog' " (Guiteras-Holmes 1961:130). Zinacantecos who are accused of being witches receive the nickname Goat (*čivo*) because witches are believed to have the power to turn themselves into goats at night. Chamulas call people who have not been baptized Monkey (*maš*) because they believe that the unborn (and unbaptized) child is a monkey and that baptism is the rite which makes him a human being. Zinacantecos and Pedranos share this belief. Some physical traits are thought to resemble those of animals. Thus a man with a bulging head is called Agouti (*volov*), and another man is called Pig (*čitom*) because his nose is thick and flattened. Still another man, who has a thin sharp face, is called Chicken Face (*sat kašlan*). The inhabitants of Chamula have nicknamed an obese woman Pig (*čitom*), and several people with long spindly necks or legs are referred to as White Heron (*sak ʔičil*) for obvious reasons.

Animal abuse is the chief metaphorical device for expressing social criticism at fiestas in the three communities. In Zinacantan (fiesta of San Sebastián), the wives of delinquent religious officials are represented by stuffed squirrels. The monkey impersonators of Chamula symbolize the Jews who killed Christ. In Chenalhó, the Blackmen, who pretend to be dogs, realistically simulate intercourse with the Abductors.

Zinacanteco informants explain that the wife of the delinquent religious official is symbolized by a stuffed squirrel because she is a shameless woman. Like an animal, she has no understanding of when intercourse is appropriate. The choice of a stuffed squirrel is particularly apt in this context, for Zinacantecos observe that squirrels seem to "cross themselves like people do" and they "look upward at heaven when they cross themselves." What better animal to have represent the wife of an errant *religious* official than one which seems to make pious gestures![1]

---

[1] According to Munro S. Edmonson (personal communication) "squirrel" means vagina in Quiché.

The monkey symbol of Chamula is polyvalent in meaning. To interpret it requires knowing not only that Chamulas recognize a fundamental dichotomy between animals and human beings, but also that the domain of human beings is differentiated into better and worse categories. There are two major ethnic groups in highland Chiapas: Indians and Ladinos. Indians are further differentiated into tribal groups, each with its own distinctive customs, dress, and dialect. Ladinos form a single ethnic group, which is stratified in terms of classes. In Indian society, the individual is the reference point of social classification, not the group. Moving outward from Ego, there are Ego's domestic group, his lineage, his hamlet, his township, his ethnic group (Indian), and his nationality. Each of these groups contrasts with other taxonomically equivalent groups of which Ego is *not* a member.

Both Chamulas and Zinacantecos are conscious of differences among people from different hamlets in dialect and clothing style. They note also the major dialect or language differences and bizarre clothing of people from other tribes. They are furthermore acutely aware of themselves as Indians in contrast with the usually lighter-skinned mixed-blood Mexicans. On this level major differences of occupation, customs, clothing styles, and language (not just dialect) may be added. Ego regards members of other domestic groups in his lineage as "better" than those of other lineages, members of his own hamlet as "better" than inhabitants of other hamlets, and so on. Ego ridicules all people who are different from him. He ridicules Chamulas (or Zinacantecos) from other hamlets when they pronounce words differently or use a slightly different vocabulary. The different costumes of Indians from other townships furnish topics for humor as well. For example, Zinacantecos ridicule the men of Ixtapa, another Indian community, because they wear long trousers. They claim that virility is expressed by the wearing of shorts; therefore, the Ixtapanecos, who wear long trousers, must be impotent. Similarly they mock the Ixtapaneco women, who do not wear belts but merely fold and tuck the tops of their skirts in at the waist. They claim that Ixtapaneco women are more easily seduced than Zinacanteco women because they do not secure their skirts tightly with belts. Non-Indians, such as Ladinos, are mocked because of their abundant body hair, their distinctive body odor, and their different values (see below). Zinacantecos and Chamulas apply ridicule toward all people who do not follow their behavior codes—members of their community, Ladinos, and American anthropologists. Always implicit in their ridicule is the assumption that people who are, in their terms, immoral, are like animals.

In terms of this social classification, the farther one is removed from Ego's domestic group, the closer he is to the animal world. Gossen (1970) has pointed out that one of the parameters of this ethnocentrism is spatial remove from Ego, and that this classification is extended to mythical creatures—Indians believe that Jews occupy the outer reaches of the earth and are practically animals. Morality, ethnocentrism, geography, and social classification are therefore alternative ways of expressing the same message. Viewed in these terms, it is appropriate that Chamulas impersonate monkeys as symbols both of evil and of Jews.

The dog impersonations of the Blackmen of Chenalhó serve two purposes. On the one hand they symbolize uncontrolled sexuality; on the other hand, they dramatize the cruelty of Ladinos, who hunt down their enemies with bloodhounds. Here again one symbol has multiple meanings, calling to mind both morality and the context of dealing with unscrupulous Ladinos, both of which are realities of the Indian's life.

Ladinos are economically and politically dominant in the region and have been so since the Spaniards first established a permanent settlement at San Cristóbal Las Casas. Ladinos and Indians are "interdependent partners in an economic system where the Indians generally act as producers of agricultural products and consumers of industrial goods, while the Ladinos appear as traders and producers of industrial and handicraft wares and consumers of Indian cultivated food" (Siverts 1969:106). The Indian communities specialize to some extent in the manufacture of such handicraft goods as ceramic wares, woolen robes and sashes, furniture, musical instruments, cordage, charcoal, firewood, and salt. Most Indians grow corn and beans for their own needs, but some communities located at lower elevations specialize in the production of bananas and other fruits adapted to that ecological niche.

Ladinos use economic transactions as occasions for "expressing symbolically their superiority over the Indians by engaging in aggressive bargaining behavior, even when both parties realize that the economic outcome will not be affected. The messages being communicated are loaded with expressions of Ladino superiority and Indian inferiority in a social situation. In general, the marketing behavior tends to express the basic patterns of social stratification in highland Chiapas" (Vogt 1969:119). This is in sharp contrast to the procedure used in economic transactions which occur directly between members of two Indian communities, which is similar to that used in asking favors: "Bargaining, to be sure, often takes place, but for many types of transactions there is also a pattern of requests accompanied by the presentation of rum, chicha, or beer and by ritual drinking that appears to be necessary to seal the bargain" (Vogt 1969:120).

The nature of the symbiotic relationship between Indians and Ladinos reflects the different value they place on manual labor. Ladinos have always viewed farm labor with disdain and regard those who engage in it as their social inferiors. To the Indian, maize agriculture is the only respectable occupation for a man to pursue.

Ladinos maintain political control over Indian affairs in two ways: (a) the secretary of the Indian township is usually a Ladino (Chamula is a very recent exception), and (b) the men elected to the town's political offices must be approved by Ladino authorities in San Cristóbal (Gossen 1970:66–69). The latter policy has tended to undermine the authority of the monolingual elders of Indian communities, in whom leadership was traditionally vested, because the younger men who also speak Spanish are therefore more capable of dealing with the Ladino world and are supported for political office by Ladino authorities.

In their ritual humor Indians ridicule Ladino values and Ladino claims to superiority. The Spanish Lady and Spanish Gentleman in Zinacantan's fiesta of San Sebastián represent Indian stereotypes of Ladinos. Ladinos are people who regard Indians as uncivilized and dirty. The Spanish Lady lives up to this stereotype when she offers to comb lice out of an Indian spectator's hair. True to form, the Spanish Gentleman stamps on the putative "lice" in disgust. Yet Ladinos are not alone in feeling revulsion against filth. The Zinacanteco and Chamula term for Ladino (and formerly for Spanish) woman is šinulan (or šinolan), a word Indians say is derived from the root šin-, which means "bad odor," and can refer to the odor of skunks.[2] Each group has its own (but different) standards of personal hygiene—Ladinos are repelled by vermin, while Indians are more sensitive to odor.

The Spanish Lady and Gentleman of Zinacantan also epitomize the Ladino values of wealth and conspicuous consumption, which are the antithesis of Zinacanteco values. The Spanish Lady says that she prefers to marry an ugly old man because he is wealthy enough to buy her jewels and trinkets. To the Indian, wealth should be spent on public ceremonies which are of benefit to the entire community, not on personal adornment. Lol ʔUč, the delinquent *cargo* holder, is ridiculed because he behaved like a Ladino—he spent his money on necklaces and ribbons for his wife, instead of on his *cargo*. The Ladino, represented by the Spanish Gentleman, is by implication placed in the same category with the errant religious official.

The characterization of Ladinos is realistic in additional respects. When the Spanish Gentleman brags of his wealth, he mentions ranches and cattle rather than the cornfields valued by Indians. In Chamula, the Monkeys make fun of the Ladino diet, which they describe as greasy. It is true that Ladino cuisine depends heavily on frying, while that of the Indians relies on boiling and baking.

Ladino women are portrayed as promiscuous. This may be due to the fact that Indian marriages tend to be more stable than Ladino unions, and that in comparison with lower-class Ladino women, Indian women lead more secluded lives. Lower-class Ladino families tend to be matrifocal, in contrast to Indian households, where there is a strong patrilineal bias.

The political and economic inequalities which characterize relations between the two ethnic groups were satirized in the performance of the junior entertainers of Zinacantan (fiesta of San Sebastián, 1966), when the Blackmen announced that the president of Mexico, who was represented by a stuffed black iguana, had come to the fiesta. The implications of this comparison were not simply animal abuse. The iguana, like the president of Mexico, was unique in several respects. It was the

[2] It might also simply be a Mayanization of the Spanish word *señora*, as is the Quiché word, *šnul* (Edmonson, personal communication).

largest stuffed animal in use that year. It was therefore appropriate that the iguana represent the nation's leader and that the smaller animals represent his political inferiors, the Zinacantecos. Furthermore, as one informant explained, the black iguana is a comparatively rare species, and therefore comparable to the president, who seldom appears in public (at least as far as Indians are concerned). Finally, the iguana was the only lowland animal used in the performance; the squirrels used to represent Zinacantecos are highland species. Clearly the stuffed animals in question symbolize two sets of antithetical qualities:

Squirrel	Iguana
small	large
common	rare
Zinacanteco	Ladino
citizen	president
child	father
highlands	lowlands
inferior	superior

Many of the Zinacanteco's social actions are governed by these distinctions. He acts as an equal with members of his own community, but he behaves in a subservient manner in the presence of Ladinos. Within the Zinacanteco community people are ranked by age. A father treats his child as a Ladino treats Indians—paternalistically. Political inequality is expressed both in the contrast between citizen and president and in that between Indian and Ladino. And, finally, the highland/lowland dichotomy is represented in the differential exploitation of the two environments by Zinacantecos. They build their homes in the highlands but raise most of their crops on land rented from Ladinos in the lowlands. In general, Indians inhabit the highlands, and Ladinos the lowlands, a pattern which has its roots in the colonial period (Metzger n.d.:13).

Although the superiority of Ladinos over Indians, of the president of Mexico over his electorate, and of the father over his child is indisputably expressed by the two sets of animal symbols, the Blackmen at the same time depict even the Ladino, the president of Mexico, and the father as no better than animals. In terms of the larger context of Zinacanteco symbols, the important polarities are:

good	*bad*
human	animal
reason	impulse
Indian	Ladino
highland	lowland
boiled	fried

Thus, whoever is symbolized by an animal is marked as deviant or evil. To the Zinacanteco, moral superiority is of far greater importance than political or economic advantage. In this way the Blackmen isolate and ridicule the status quo relations with which Zinacantecos must cope in their daily lives.

The six Blackmen of Chenalhó are known also as Ladinos. In keeping with the low opinion with which Indians regard Ladinos, four of the Blackmen also pretend to be dogs. The metaphor is an apt one, because on numerous occasions Pedranos who have challenged Ladino authority have been hunted down and murdered. One of my informants, Manuel Arias Sohóm, was forced to flee Chenalhó several times to escape murder at the hands of Ladinos.

Animal symbols are frequent in ritual humor because ritual humor is concerned with lapses in morality, and animals symbolize deviant behavior. Ladinos are often represented metaphorically as some species of animal because, as members of a different ethnic group, they do not observe the moral codes of Zinacantan, Chamula, and Chenalhó. Thus social classification, ethnocentrism, ethnozoology, and morality comprise the common understandings from which these metaphors spring.

9. Ritual Humor in Space and Time

Ritual humor seems to be pervasive in Middle America and is common in many parts of North America as well (Steward 1931:188). Three themes of ritual humor which are characteristic of highland Chiapas are apparently distributed very widely in North and Middle America. They are (*a*) ridicule of public officials, (*b*) parodies of important ceremonies, and (*c*) "caricature and burlesque of foreigners" (Steward 1931:189).

The American Southwest and Middle America share the symbols of ritual humor discussed in chapters 7 and 8. Documentary evidence from central Mexico, from the Yucatán Peninsula, and from highland Guatemala suggests that these symbols were pre-Columbian in origin (Durán 1967; Anderson and Dibble 1951; Tozzer 1941; Means 1917; Lizana 1893; Edmonson 1971). My analysis of the ritual humor of three com-

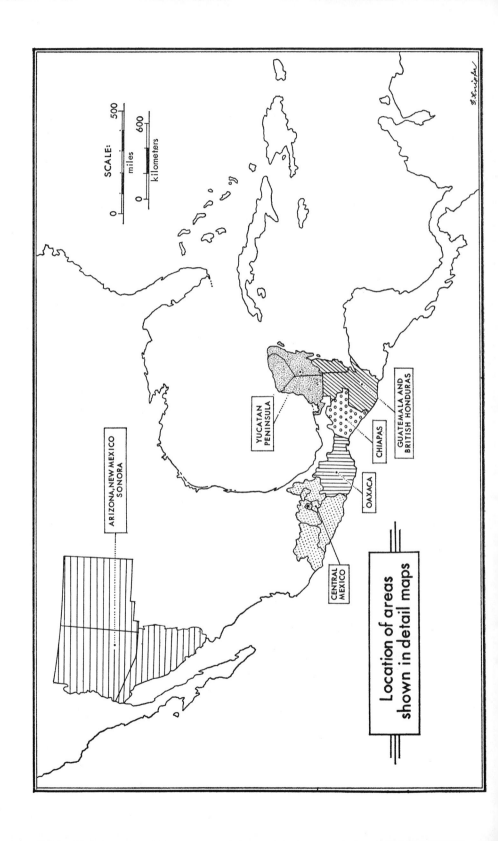

SCALE:

0   miles   500

0   kilometers   600

ARIZONA, NEW MEXICO
SONORA

YUCATAN
PENINSULA

GUATEMALA AND
BRITISH HONDURAS

CHIAPAS

OAXACA

CENTRAL
MEXICO

Location of areas
shown in detail maps

munities of highland Chiapas may therefore be useful in interpreting ritual humor in other parts of Middle America in both its present and pre-Columbian manifestations.

Highland Chiapas

No descriptions survive of the ceremonial dances and dramas which took place in highland Chiapas before the arrival of the Spaniards (Calnek 1962:57). I have provided detailed descriptions of the ritual humor of three modern Mayan communities: Zinacantan, Chamula, and Chenalhó. Data from other communities in highland Chiapas are less complete but suggest that the basic patterns are similar.

The young men of the village of El Bosque, in the district of Simo-jovel, go around to Ladino houses before Carnaval asking for clothing, which they use to impersonate Ladinos during the fiesta. They whiten their faces with starch, carry rattles, dance, and shout. On Carnaval Sunday, Monday, and Tuesday they visit the houses of the *mayordomos* and *alféreces*, who serve them *chicha* and bean tamales (Cáceres López 1946:36).[1]

Late on Tuesday afternoon they gather near the church and dance around a circle of lighted bundles of straw. The dance continues until the straw is completely consumed by the flames (Cáceres López 1946:36). The Indians of this town originally came from Chamula (Gossen 1970:68).

Frank Miller, who witnessed the 1958 fiesta of Carnaval in Huistán, a Tzotzil-speaking township to the east of San Cristóbal, reported two types of "clowns": Limey Asses (*tan čak*) and Blackmen (*hʔikʼaletik*). Apparently, any male inhabitant of Huistán, even one ten years old, was free to dress up as one of these characters. Some Limey Asses were naked from the waist up and painted their torsos with lime, while others wore white T-shirts as a substitute for white paint. They wore a variety of hats, including those of army officers and of the type commonly worn by Ladinos (plates 26 and 27). Some Limey Asses tied bright print scarves over their faces or shoulders, letting them hang free in back (plate 26). Many wore sunglasses in imi-

---

[1] I am grateful to Gary H. Gossen for bringing this reference to my attention.

tation of Ladino men. Almost all carried harmonicas, which they played incessantly. A few carried guitars or whistles. One man carried a toy plastic pistol, which he pointed at people. Another man, who spoke in a high falsetto voice, wore a woman's skirt and shawl, but a man's shirt and hat. Although Miller does not say so, it seems likely that the Limey Asses were impersonating Ladinos (and white men), for they painted their bodies white and wore some Ladino-type clothing.

The Blackmen were distinctive with their dark-brown or red leather masks, moustaches, and beards (plate 26). They, too, wore bright scarves and carried musical instruments. One Blackman wore a skirt and shawl. "Two or three of the clowns had stuffed squirrels which they shoved in people's faces" (Miller n.d.). Miller reports that the clowns joked, but he made no record of their utterances.

There was one monkey impersonator in Huistán who wore the characteristic red-and-black frock coat and monkey-fur headdress and played an accordion. Unlike his Chamula counterpart, he wore a pink mask.

The costumed performers of Huistán, then, are strikingly similar to those of Zinacantan, Chamula, and Chenalhó. The fiesta of Carnaval in Huistán, too, is an occasion for men to assume a new identity temporarily. Huistán shares with Chamula and Chenalhó the monkey impersonator and with Zinacantan and Chenalhó the Blackman impersonators. The costumes of the Limey Asses of Huistán resemble the outfits of the Ladino impersonators of the fiesta of Carnaval in Zinacantan and El Bosque. These figures are comedians, but we do not know if their humor follows the same pattern as the ritual humor of other communities.

The road which connects the ceremonial centers of Chamula and Chenalhó passes through the ceremonial center of the township of Mitontic (map 1). According to one informant from that township, the fiesta of Carnaval in Mitontic has affinities with the same fiesta in the other two communities: monkey impersonators with conical headdresses of monkey fur; a female impersonator called Dancing Lady (ʔanṭil ʔak'ot) with whom men joke; and the performance of a Dance of the Warriors (ʔak'ot čilon), complete with jaguar skin.

To the west of Chenalhó lies another Tzotzil-speaking township, San Andrés Larráinzar. Holland (1963:71) reports that some men in Lar-

ráinzar dress up as monkeys during the fiesta of Carnaval to commemorate the First Creation, when the priests were transformed into monkeys
and escaped death in the Flood by climbing into trees. Plate 28 shows
such a monkey impersonator kidnapping a boy. Also in Larráinzar, a
man dressed in an *alférez* costume "rides" an imitation horse. His role
is probably similar to that of the masked captains of Chenalhó, who
carry less elaborate stick horses.

About twenty miles due south of Huistán, in the Tzeltal-speaking
sector, lies the township of Amatenango, where, until recently, Ladino
impersonators performed at the fiesta of Carnaval:

> Until five years ago, a group of masked jokers visited the houses
> of the captains of the fiestas. They wore Ladino clothing, includ-
> ing vest, pants, and shoes, and they hid their faces behind masks
> or painted them black. They danced a "Ladino dance" (paired
> couples), first in the church and then in the houses of the al-
> fereces. While dancing, they made sexual allusions about unmar-
> ried women. Their joking emphasized their strangeness to the
> villagers; for example one of the jokers might say, "You do not
> know what type of person I am. An airplane made me." They car-
> ried small stuffed animals which they made "cry." Pretending they
> were the husband of a woman, they would go to her and tell her
> to take care of her "baby." The woman speaker would sometimes
> respond to their jokes, saying, "Who are you? You are not good
> looking, you little black boy. You must be from Germany or from
> the other side of the water." (Nash 1970:224)

There are striking similarities between the joking of the Ladino impersonators of Amatenango and that of Blackman impersonators in
Zinacantan. Some common themes are animal abuse, the association
of Ladinos with evil Blackmen, and sexual allusions about unmarried
women.

Female impersonators are the ritual humorists of Carnaval in Oxchuc
and Tenejapa, two other Tzeltal-speaking townships to the northeast
of San Cristóbal. They dress as Indian women in skirts, blouses, and
belts and are accompanied by men masked as Ladinos, in blue denim
overalls, who pretend to be their husbands (Castro 1962:44; Cámara
Barbachano 1966:126, 169–170). In Tenejapa the female imperson-

ators are called Dancing Ladies (ʔanṭil ʔakʼot) and the Ladino impersonators are called Ladinos (kašlanetik) (Cámara Barbachano 1966:126). The female impersonators engage in sexual joking with the officials and spectators (Cámara Barbachano 1966:126, 170). The Ladino impersonators carry wooden knives and rifles with which they pretend to attack the spectators who try to touch their "wives" (Castro 1962:44).

Tenejapa and Oxchuc share with Zinacantan and Chenalhó bull impersonators whose costumes are pole frameworks covered with reed mats (Cámara Barbachano 1966:125–126, 170). In Tenejapa the Bulls are ritually killed on the last day of the fiesta of Carnaval (Cámara Barbachano 1966:126).

Finally, Redfield and Villa Rojas, who visited Tenejapa during the fiesta of Carnaval about thirty years ago, report that there were "three personages carrying the dried bodies of, respectively, a wild cat, a rodent called saben [weasel], and an iguana. Villa was informed that these animals are used in a later festal pantomime in which the alfereces enact a sowing, and in which these animals are represented as performing their characteristic mischief" (1939:115). Judging from the function of such animals in fiestas in other communities of this region, their "characteristic mischief" was probably obscene.

Highland Guatemala

According to Fray Bartolomé de Las Casas (1967:II, 219–220), ritual humor was an integral part of fiestas among the Maya of highland Guatemala at the time of the conquest. This tradition survives today in modern Mayan communities of highland Guatemala, where, as in highland Chiapas, ceremonial buffoons entertain public officials in their homes (La Farge and Byers 1931:109). In Jacaltenango a group of dances performed during the fiesta of Carnaval are parodies of the nonhumorous Cortés and Deer dances. The comic versions of those dances have the same names, but preceded by the term cil- meaning "rags or old clothes or anything old" (La Farge and Byers 1931: 109). According to the Popol Vuh, rags are a symbol of poverty and dejection. At one point during their visit to hell, the heroes, Hunter

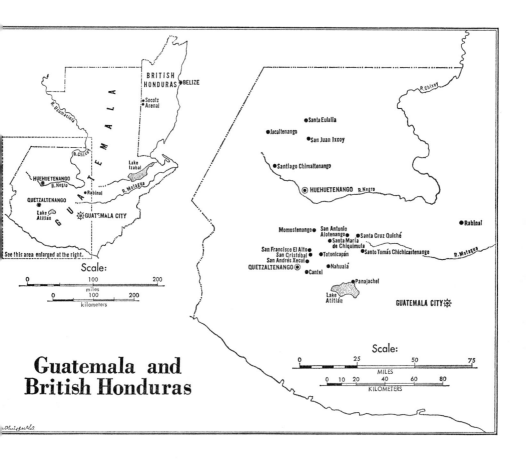

BRITISH
HONDURAS ●BELIZE

●Socotz
●Arenal

●Santa Eulalia

●Jacaltenango
●San Juan Ixcoy

●Santiago Chimaltenango

Lake
Izabal

HUEHUETENANGO
R.Negro

⊙ HUEHUETENANGO   R.Negro

QUETZALTENANGO
Lake
Atitlán

●Rabinal

⊙GUATEMALA CITY

●Rabinal

See this area enlarged at the right.

Momostenango●   San Antonio
                   Alotenango●   ●Santa Cruz Quiché
                   ●Santa María
                     de Chiquimula
San Francisco El Alto●   Santo Tomás Chichicastenango
San Cristóbal●   ●Totonicapán   R.Motagua
San Andrés Xecul●
QUETZALTENANGO⊙   ●Cantel
                 ●Nahualá

●Panajachel
Lake
Atitlán

GUATEMALA CITY⊙

Scale:

0   100   200
       miles
0   100   200
     kilometers

Scale:

0   25   50   75
            MILES
0 10 20   40   60   80
         KILOMETERS

Guatemala and
British Honduras

and Jaguar Deer, appear as beggars dressed in rags. The Lords of Hell summon them to appear before them and entertain them. At first Hunter and Jaguar Deer refuse to do so, saying that they would be ashamed to appear in such company because of their ugliness and mean appearance. Finally persuaded, they entertain the Lords of Hell with the Screech Owl, Armadillo, and Weasel dances (Edmonson 1971:lines 4252–4393, chaps. 37–40).

Similar parodies of serious dances take place in Santa Eulalia (La Farge 1947:85). They are called, in Spanish, *baile gracejo* ("graceful dance"), but La Farge points out that in the Kanhobal language they are called *kanal koq*, which means "masked dance" (1947:85). "There were ten dancers, all having comic masks of native make, two of which represented women and one, worn by the chief comedian, covered with heavy whiskers. All wore Ladino clothes, and some wore shoes. . . . There was a good deal of business with an old monkey-skin, more or less coarse play with the 'women,' various orations, and roughhousing with members of the crowd" (La Farge 1947:85). This would also be a fairly accurate description of the Blackmen of Zinacantan and perhaps of the masked figures of Chenalhó as well. A dance of the same name is performed in the Quiché towns of Momostenango, Santa María Chiquimula, Santa Cruz Quiché, Totonicapán, San Francisco el Alto, San Cristóbal, San Andrés Xecul, Cantel, Nahualá, Santo Tomás Chichicastenango, and San Antonio Alotenango (Lothrop 1929:5–6). "In Momostenango there takes place the simulated rape of a man dressed as a woman. In Chiquimula they shout aloud much spicy gossip, and describe in intimate detail the family life of various individuals, which the spectators receive with roars of laughter" (Lothrop 1929:8–9).

In Santa Cruz Quiché, one of the dancers is dressed in a fur-trimmed suit and carries a fox slung across his shoulders (Reynolds 1956:34). On Corpus Christi in Panajachel, on Lake Atitlán, Blackman impersonators carry stuffed squirrels, which they hold in their arms "as if they were babies. The tail of the squirrel is placed as a moustache or beard on the masks of the dancers" (Sol Tax, quoted in Redfield 1936:239).

Another animal associated with festal clowns in highland Guatemala is the monkey (Redfield 1936:239). The *Popol Vuh* is explicit as to what the Quiché find humorous about monkeys:

> Really the monkeys' appearance was funny, all potbellied
>   at the bottom
>   With the edges of their stomachs bulging.
>   (Edmonson 1971:lines 2837–2838)

. . . .

> All red was the mouth
>   And stupid their faces.
> Bushy were their mouths;
>   Bristling were their mouths.
> Their eyes blanched,
>   As they blinked at them.
> And when the grandmother saw them,
>   The grandmother burst into laughter.
>   (Edmonson 1971:lines 2851–2858)

According to Edmonson (1971:notes to line 2837), the Quiché find obesity highly amusing and have a rich vocabulary to describe it.

The monkeys in this description were once the older brothers of the heroes Jaguar Deer and Hunter. In return for mistreating their younger brothers, they were transformed into monkeys. Because their grandmother laughed at their humorous appearance and behavior, they were doomed to live forever as monkeys in the forest. Jaguar Deer and Hunter comforted their grandmother for her loss, saying that their older brothers would not be forgotten but would be impersonated in masked dances by the Quiché people (Edmonson 1971:lines 2740–2900).

In his travels through highland Guatemala between 1888 and 1895, Carl Sapper observed a performance of the Dance of Howler and Spider Monkeys, which by then had been syncretized with the story of the temptation of Eve: "A number of Howler and Spider monkeys in the forest hear the clamor of a great festival among men; they set out to inquire about the reason for it and on the way meet a Serpent, which invites them to enjoy some apples, with which he had previously deceived Eve in Paradise. But the Howler and Spider monkeys resist the temptation and banish the Serpent by appealing to Mary; they dance in honor of St. Paul and bring him various kinds of fruits as offerings" (Sapper 1897:331; my translation). This dance drama was still being performed in San Juan Ixcoy, Momostenango, and Rabinal in 1960 (Edmonson 1971:notes to line 2877). Thus the prophecy continues to be fulfilled.

The monkey is also associated with the Volador Dance, for which a pole the height of a tree is erected and "in which costumed men, suspended by ropes from a frame surmounting the pole, revolve slowly till they reach the ground" (Redfield 1936:236). In Chichicastenango, two monkey impersonators, called *machines*, accompany the men who go off to the woods to chop down a tree to be used in the Volador Dance (plate 30). Like the monkey impersonators of Chamula, the *machines* imitate the behavior of monkeys: "When they reach the tree, the *machin* climbs up and sits in the very top of the tree and they begin to cut the tree below him. When the tree is just about to fall he springs into another tree, turning somersaults. They are never quiet one moment" (Bunzel 1952:425). The Monkeys of Chichicastenango behave like evil spirits: "The *machines* carry combs in their pockets, and when they see women, they run after them, combing themselves. This is bad, for then the hair of the woman will not grow" (Bunzel 1952:425).

Termer (1930:451) documents the performance of this dance in Santa María Chiquimula and Nahualá until 1919 and notes that it was also once performed in Totonicapán but had been discontinued by the time he arrived in the region.

The Volador Dance was performed in highland Guatemala and central Mexico at the time of the conquest (Fuentes y Guzmán 1882:151–154; Clavigero 1787:401–402; Durán 1967:194). Fuentes y Guzmán, who wrote his history of Guatemala during the seventeenth century, reports that the first person to climb the pole was the monkey impersonator (*mico*), who made ludicrous grimaces (Fuentes y Guzmán 1882:153).

Clowning that resembles the ritual humor of the Blackmen and Jaguars of Zinacantan occurs in Santiago Chimaltenango on New Year's Day when the public officials change office. Two buffoons, one dressed as a Mexican and the other as a woman, whip the new officers and "jeer at them about their duties" (Wagley 1949:90). The "woman" carries a stuffed wildcat in her arms (Wagley 1949:135). For the fiesta of Santiago, the patron saint, two men dress up in Ladino clothes and mimic Ladinos. Still another group of ceremonial buffoons in Chimaltenango are the Ugly Ones (*feos*), who blacken their bodies and wear only a loincloth; ". . . the *feos* are said to dance wildly and with abandon. They become vulgar and imitate intercourse with each other, or with any passing woman; they pretend to defecate and . . . some actually urinate as they dance. They made sexual remarks about the members of the audience" (Wagley 1949:117). The behavior of the Ugly Ones contrasts sharply with that of the Pretty Ones (*bonitos*), who wear dresses decorated with ribbons and frills. They are dainty and feminine in their dancing. These dances take place on Easter morning.

The themes of war and conquest, which are so important in Chamula's fiesta of Carnaval, appear in the Dance of the Conquest which is popular in this region of Guatemala (plates 29, 31, 32; Wagley 1949: 56; Wisdom 1940:451–452; La Farge and Byers 1931:99; Bode 1961: 290; Bunzel 1952:424). There are several variants of the basic themes. In Chichicastenango the war between Alvarado and the Quiché is enacted (plate 31). Among the Chortí it is called the Dance of the Huaxtecs and represents the battle between Cortés and the Huaxtecs, who are called Blackmen. A man impersonates Cortés's interpreter, Malinche. Humorous sex play (which may be similar to that which occurs with the Spanish Ladies of Chamula and Zinacantan) goes on continuously between Malinche and the male characters (Wisdom 1940: 452). Two variants of this dance are performed in Jacaltenango, "the Cortés relating to the Conquest of Mexico . . . [and] . . . the Moors telling of the wars between the Spaniards and the Moors" (La Farge and Byers 1931:99).

The ritual humorist of the Dance of the Conquest is called Don Quirijol or Crijol (Bode 1961:213). He adds a touch of humor to an otherwise solemn presentation by falling in love with both of the Quiché king's daughters and insisting that one woman would not be enough to feed and clothe him (Bode 1961:221).

Conflict was apparently a dance theme even before the conquest, for the Rabinal Achí, which is without obvious European elements, represents a war between the Quiché and the Rabinal (Brasseur de Bourbourg 1862). This dance could have been easily adapted into a Dance of the Conquest, with the Spaniards substituting for the Rabinal warriors.

The bullfight theme is well represented in highland Guatemala (Bunzel 1952:200; La Farge 1947:84; La Farge and Byers 1931:110; Wagley 1949:105). In Santa Eulalia the man who pretends to fight the bull is also a clown (La Farge 1947:84).

The ritual humor of highland Guatemala thus has close affinities with the ritual humor of highland Chiapas. Particularly striking is the similarity in the use and interpretation of animal symbolism, especially that of the monkey. Other parallels, such as the dances of the Conquest and mock bullfights, are to be expected because of the common exposure to Spanish culture in both regions.

Yucatán Peninsula

Several ethnohistorical documents describe the ritual humor of the Mayas of the Yucatán Peninsula at the time of the conquest or shortly thereafter. Landa mentions that at Chichen Itzá there were two stages where "farces were represented and comedies for the pleasure of the public" (Tozzer 1941:158). Antonio de Ciudad Real in the Ponce *Relación* speaks of "some masked men who, dancing and making very sightly gestures and mummeries also imitated, very naturally, the song of certain nocturnal birds of that country: there was music of flutes and trumpets. They were accustomed to have players for the feasts, and they had their trappings for it" (Tozzer 1941:179 n.).

In the twelfth song of Dzitbalché, lines 11 to 14 refer to the arrival of musicians and singers (*h'pax-kayoob*), dancers (*h'okotoob, ziitboob*), comedians (*hpaal-Ɔaamoob*), contortionists (*h²ualak-zut*), hunchbacks (*h²ppuu z*), and spectators (*nac-yoob*) to celebrate with great joy the end of the five melancholy unlucky days at the end of the old year and to welcome the coming of the new year (Barrera Vázquez 1965:71).

Fray Diego López de Cogolludo, writing in 1668, describes "babblers" who impersonate priests and "repeat fables and ancient Histories . . . The babblers are apt to be graceful at mottoes and in the witty say-

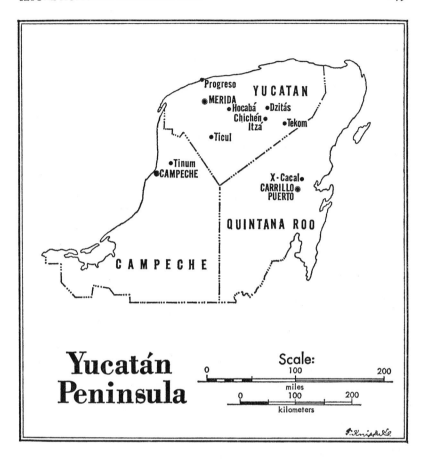

Yucatán Peninsula

Scale:
0   100   200
miles
0   100   200
kilometers

ings which they tell to their elders and Judges if they are over-rigorous, ambitious, avaricious, laying before them the events that have taken place and even that which concerns the officer's own duties. They thus speak to the officer's own faces, and sometimes they rebuke them with a single word. . . . They call these Farfantes [buffoons] *Balzam*, and they apply the word metaphorically to him who is talkative and scurrilous; and in their representations they mimic birds" (Means 1917: 14). The Motul dictionary translates *ah bal Ɔam* (*ah bal t'am*) as "representante de comedias," that is, "comic performer" or "buffoon." These buffoons, like the Blackmen of Zinacantan and Chenalhó, functioned as social critics. It is not clear whether priests are included among those whom they chastise, but if so, it would be appropriate that they impersonate them. As priest impersonators the *balzam* resemble the Lacandon Woman and Crossbacks of Chenalhó, who pretend to cure public officials of magical fright.

Although there are no references in these accounts to the imagery in terms of which these insults were couched, there is evidence that animal symbolism was a device for phrasing insults in other contexts. Roys notes that many of the references to animals in Maya prophetic literature "stand as the symbols for something else and that the reference is not to the actual animals" (1933:196). He cites examples that indicate that the animal terms refer to human beings: " 'There is no kinkajou, there is no fox, there is no weasel to suck men's blood; there are no pernicious rulers.' 'The rulers shall be cut off, when the claws of the eagle are cut, when the backs of the kinkajou and the fox are clawed and torn.' 'Then the burrowing opposums who are greedy for domin- ion shall bite one another' " (Roys 1933:196–197). Roys identifies "these unwelcome individuals" as the Toltec rulers of Yucatán, who invaded the Maya area at about A.D. 950 (1933:196–199). The jaguar, the coyote, the puma, the kinkajou, and the eagle are all symbols of warriors in Central Mexico (Roys 1933:199). Roys points out that the association of the weasel "with ideas pertaining to military affairs is shown by certain expressions found in the Motul dictionary. '*zabim-be*, *ah-zabim-be*: a look-out, sentinel and spy, when no battle-line has been formed; also to keep a look-out.' '*zabin-katun*: look-out or sentinel, when the battle-line has been formed, and to keep a look-out in this manner.' Literally *zabim-be* means the weasel of the road and *zabin- katun*, the weasel of the army" (Roys 1933:199–200). The animal terms in this context are used in an insulting manner which stresses the rapacious nature of the hated rulers; a more pleasant future is prophe- sied when there will be no "pernicious rulers," who at the time of the prophecy were characterized as weasels who "suck men's blood."

Social criticism continues to be an important aspect of ritual humor at fiestas in Mayan communities of the Yucatán Peninsula. At one fiesta, in X-Cacal (Quintana Roo), some men who are chosen to play roles in a mock bullfight are ridiculed: "For example, one who was known to be heavy and awkward at dancing was entitled the 'true master of the dance'; his wife, who had a very serious, grave countenance was designated as 'she who laughs much'; another, somewhat inclined to avarice, was called 'he who hands out cigarettes'; a man known to be henpecked was called 'the seller of eggs' and his wife 'she who keeps the money of the eggs,' and so on with the rest of the characters" (Villa Rojas 1945:127).

In Hocabá (Yucatán) during the fiesta of Carnaval, a buffoon ridicules rich, but stingy, members of the community and dishonest businessmen who make a practice of selling goods at high prices to poor people. The clown complains that the rich men do not give their wives any money for buying food, but spend all their money on clothes. He berates rich men for hiring workmen but refusing to pay them. He also mocks men who seize women at the mill, beat their wives, or fight in the street.

Landa describes a rite in honor of Kukulcan called *chic kaban* (Tozzer 1941:158). Roys has pointed out that one meaning of *chic* is "coati-mundi." He believes that it is reasonably possible to "consider the Kukulcan ceremony as an early type of one of the annual patron saint festivals, in which the *chic*-clown takes a prominent part" (quoted in Tozzer 1941:157). Coati impersonators perform at fiestas in many modern Mayan communities of the Yucatán Peninsula:

> On the day of the annual fiesta in Dzitas, it is customary for two men, known as *chic*, to act as buffoons. One wears short trousers, an old torn shirt, a tattered woven bag, and a feather headdress. The other is dressed, also in tatters, as a woman. These men go about the village blowing on conch shells "to announce the fiesta." As they go about, small boys run and hide, and are careful to keep out of their way. If the *chics* catch a small boy, they remove his clothes and rub a little gunpowder and fat in his anus. At Tizimin there are similarly-dressed festal clowns. When the festal food is distributed, these "*chics*" amuse the crowd by pretending to stuff the mouths of onlookers with the food, and then wiping the faces of these. . . . In the *barrio* of Santiago [Mérida], at least as late as the eighties of the last century, the *chic* amused the crowd with his ridiculous costume and his clownish antics. As a

part of his performance he lassoed men, and "fined" them before letting them go. These "fines" were used to help defray the expenses of the fiesta. (Redfield 1936:241)

A woman performed as the coati impersonator (čiik) during the 1971 fiesta of Carnaval in Hocabá. She, like the coati impersonator of Dzitás, wore short trousers, an old torn shirt, an apron, and an old torn straw hat trimmed with turkey feathers. She appeared at the dance on Monday evening, carrying a rope with which she lassoed dancers in order to extort money from them. When she succeeded in capturing a man, the coati impersonator dragged him off to a "priest," who asked the man which girl he wanted to marry. Usually the prisoner was too embarrassed to answer, but the coati impersonator forced him to name a girl by tightening the rope around his waist. The girl was fetched and the Priest married them in a mock wedding ceremony, after announcing, "Tonight I will marry you, and tomorrow night I will divorce you!" Afterward the man had to pay the Priest from one to five pesos for his services. The priest impersonator makes fun of unscrupulous priests who charge exorbitant fees for performing the sacraments.

According to Pacheco Cruz (1947), the coati impersonator plays an important role in the Dance of the Pig's Head (kub-pol) in rural Yucatán. In addition to singing lugubriously, playing tricks, and grimacing, he begs for alms, holding out a gourd, and shakes a rattle with which "he calls the pig" (Pacheco Cruz 1947:130). This is reminiscent of the antics of the Blackmen of Chenalhó when they want to be served pork or beef.

Coati impersonators appear also at fiestas in X-Cacal (Villa Rojas 1945:127) and Socotz (northwestern British Honduras [Thompson 1930:111–112]). Villa Rojas describes them as clowns, requiring "a person of wit and humor who can make his audience laugh, doing amusing stunts and imitations of the pisote [coati]" (1945:127) to assume that role. It is possible that what Stephens called fiscales during his visit to Ticul (Yucatán) in February, 1841, were coati impersonators (Stephens 1843:65–69). They carried whips with which they lashed the girls dressed as mestizas (Stephens 1843:65–66). At one time they mockingly attacked a high official in the village, and, "in the capricious and wanton exercise of their arbitrary power, [they] rushed across, seized him, dragged him to the center of the floor, hoisted him upon the shoulders of a vaquero [cowboy], and pulling apart the skirts of his coat, belaboured him with a mock vigour and earnestness that convulsed the whole company with laughter. The sides of the elevated dignitary shook, the vaquero shook under him, and they were near coming down together" (Stephens 1843:66).

Redfield has pointed out that "to the Maya of Yucatan 'chic' is apparently both 'buffoon' and 'coati' " (1936:239). He notes that several Maya terms for animals connote human beings with undesirable traits: ". . . as 'pig' also means 'glutton,' and as *mono* [monkey] also means 'mimic' " (1936:240). In other words, the coati impersonator is therefore analogous to the monkey impersonators of Chamula and Chenalhó and to the Blackmen of Zinacantan, who use stuffed coatis and squirrels to symbolize the deviant behavior of certain public officials.[2]

Animal symbolism is especially in evidence during the pig ceremony of Socotz: "A man, who is supposed to represent a hog, then lifts it [the cooked hog] on his shoulders and proceeds to make a tour of the village. In the course of his tour he visits nine houses, at each one of which he grunts like a hog. Occasionally he lies down and rolls about like the animal he represents. . . . In short the whole business is an elaborate buffoonery" (Thompson 1930:113). Plate 35 shows the decorated pig's head that was used in the Dance of the Pig's Head which was performed in Telchaquillo (Yucatán) during the fiesta of Concepción in December, 1971.

The Motul dictionary lists the names of nine comedies: "The Sponger or Parasite" (*ah con cutz*),[3] "The Pot Vendor" (*ah con*

---

[2] Redfield (1936) has demonstrated the frequent association, in Middle America, of small animals, especially furred animals, with ceremonial buffoonery and with the erection of ceiba trees or poles. This association may be observed today in Zinacantan during the fiesta of San Sebastián, when Jaguars and Blackmen climb the Jaguar Tree to throw stuffed squirrels, monkeys, and coatis back and forth to each other, meanwhile shouting obscenities (see chapter 3).

[3] Barrera Vázquez (1965:11) translates *ah con cutz* as "El Vendedor de pavos silvestres" (The Vendor of Turkeys). While it is true that the Motul dictionary

cum), "The Cacao Grower" (*ah pakal cacau*), "The Footstool of Heaven" (*ah can che caan*), "The Chili Pepper Vendor" (*ah con ic*), "The Vendor of Snares" (*ah con tzatzam*), "The King of the Mountain" (*ah cuch uitz*), "The White-Beaked Macaw" (*ah cakal chil mo*), and "The Small White-Haired Boy" (*ah cakal hol paal*) (Barrera Vázquez 1965:11). In Zinacantan a ritual humorist called White Head (*sak hol*) performs during the fiesta of San Sebastián. The vending theme survives today in X-Cacal (Villa Rojas 1945). On the occasion of the principal annual fiesta, a dance with the head of a pig takes place:

> A man representing the owner leading his pig, stepped forward shaking a gourd rattle; he held a cord which was attached to the head of the pig. Next followed the man carrying the pig. . . . The man leading the dance began offering the pig for sale, saying "who wants to buy this pig from me?" Two men, acting as purchasers, responded by offering a very low price. The mock sale continued with comic haggling and exaggerated remarks about the excellence and defects of the animal. The merriment reached a climax when the bearer of the head, pretending to be the pig, cut the cord with his teeth and escaped from the spot leaving the "transaction" in midair. Pursued by his "owner" and by the musicians who run out to look for him, the pig was brought back and the dance resumed until the eighteen ritual turns were completed. Then the organizer of the fiesta "bought" the "pig," saying, "I am placing one hundred cigarettes on this table as payment for this pig which I have bought today." With this the dance ended. (Villa Rojas 1945:124)

Similarly, on the last day of the fiesta of Carnaval in Chenalhó, the Cowboys go from house to house trying to sell their Bull. Eventually

---

translates *cutz* as "pava desta tierra (*Melleagris oscellata*)," i.e., "turkey," it translates *ah con cutz* as "el que come de mogollón, yendo de casa en casa diciendo que tiene hambre para que lo conbiden," or "someone who sponges on others, going from house to house saying that he is hungry so that he will be fed." Roys (1943:30) concurs with my interpretation, saying that the name of one of the comedies is "the parasite." Perhaps more significant is the fact that begging continues to be a humorous theme in some communities (see below).

the outgoing Passions pretend to buy the Bull, offering them liquor as payment (Guiteras-Holmes 1946:17).

Still another theme suggested by the list of preconquest Mayan comedies is that of the parasite or sponger. The Monkeys of Chamula and the Blackmen of Zinacantan and Chenalhó put on such a farce during the fiesta of Carnaval, going up to vendors in the market and begging for food and drink.

Female impersonators abound at fiestas in Yucatán today, but only one Spaniard saw fit to mention them at the time of the conquest (Lizana 1893:41). About seventy years ago Starr noticed that at the carnival in Progreso (Yucatán), "young men dressed in women's clothes, with faces masked or painted, wandered about singly, addressing persons on the street in a high falsetto voice with all sorts of woeful stories or absurd questions" (1908:324–325). The female impersonators of Hocabá put on false breasts and a variety of costumes, including dresses, bikinis, and ballerina outfits. They speak in high falsetto voices. Mariquita, the star female impersonator of Hocabá's fiesta of Carnaval, pretends to be a homosexual, and much of the joking at this fiesta concerns the activities of homosexuals in Mérida. At one point Juan Carnaval, the villain of the fiesta, an effigy of whom will be burned at the end of the fiesta, escapes from jail. The following conversation then takes place between the Judge and an unspecified member of the crowd:

Man:	Ay, ay, sir, Judge, I've just come to tell you that Juan Carnaval has escaped!
Judge:	How did he escape, sir?
Man:	I couldn't see very well. They let María Victoria out [from jail].
Judge:	Is she the artist who sings so well in the movies?
Man:	No, sir, the person of whom I am speaking is an artist of the sixty-sixth south zone [of Mérida]. They say that they [artists] pay men to go with them—that they speak like women.

Judge:	Did the divers board the bus and go off to Progreso?
Man:	No, sir, he entered the hotel with a drunkard.
	[A woman comes running up.]
Woman:	Ay, ay, sir, I just came to tell you that Juan has been captured.
Judge:	Who captured him, then?
Woman:	My husband, sir.
Husband:	Here he is.
Judge:	But Juan, aren't you ashamed to go about with people of this kind?
Juan Carnaval:	No, sir, because if it were not for them, I would be dead now from hunger, because my wives don't work to support me. The little crabs, on the other hand, even buy me chewing gum.
Judge:	But Juan, do you mean to say that you found them in the sea?
Juan Carnaval:	No, sir, they frequent Hidalgo Park [in Mérida]. They approach men and kiss them.
Judge:	But Juan, if you say that they are divers, does it mean that they just go down in the water?
Juan Carnaval:	No, sir, I am telling you that he is above on the wharf, tangled up with a drunk.

There are many puns in this exchange. *Artista* means "actress," but the man takes it in the sense of homosexual or transvestite. The sixty-sixth south district is the red-light district of Mérida, where homosexuals hang out. The noun *b'usóob'* means both "diver" and "homosexual." That is why the Judge asks whether the homosexuals took the bus to Progreso, the nearest seaport. Homosexuals are called "crabs" (*haib'aóob'*) because their effeminate gestures resemble those of crabs moving along the beach. The Judge takes "crab" in the sense of "shellfish" when he asks Juan Carnaval whether he found them in the sea.

Juan Carnaval, on the other hand, takes "crab" in the sense of "homo-sexual" and replies that he found them in Hidalgo Park, a park in Mérida frequented by homosexuals.

The Judge continues to interrogate Juan Carnaval until the end of the fiesta, forcing him to confess sins of homosexuality, polygamy, and wife desertion, all of which Juan Carnaval tries to rationalize with humorously weak arguments. The main theme of the fiesta is the Inquisition and death by burning at the stake. A subordinate humorous theme is deviant sexual behavior, performed by female impersonators.

In Socotz, the coati impersonator wears woman's clothing (Thompson 1930:111–112), as do some of the dancers in the Deer Dance (Thompson 1930:103). In nearby Arenal, "half the men dress up as women and half as old men with faces blackened" during the pig ceremony (Thompson 1930:113).

The *uayeb* days in Yucatán correspond to the five "lost days" of the Chamula calendar, when the fiesta of Carnaval occurs. Some of the *uayeb* rites are very similar to those which take place in Chamula at that time of the year. A dance called the Dance of the Warriors (*holcan okot*) or the War Dance (*batel okot*) took place in Yucatán in some years during the *uayeb* days (Tozzer 1941:144). As many as eight hundred men performed in this dance with long warlike steps, carrying little banners (Tozzer 1941:94). This dance resembles the Dance of the Warriors of Chamula in its temporal setting, its theme, and its paraphernalia.

The first day of each year in the Maya "vague year" calendar could have one of four names: Kan, Muluc, Ix, and Cauac (Coe 1965:99–100). The *uayeb* days of the Ix years were marked by two events which have analogues in Chamula's Carnaval. The color of the Ix years was black, and the idol associated with those days was called Black Uayeyab (*ek uayeyab*). There occurred during this period the Dance of the Devil or Dance of the Demons or Dance of the Underworld (*xibalba okot*) (Tozzer 1941:147). Black Demons are central figures in the fiesta of Carnaval of Chamula.

The *uayeb* days of the Ix years ended with a Fire-Walking Rite which is, in its details and function, strikingly similar to the thatch-burning ceremony of Chamula:

After this, for the celebration of this festival, they made a great
arch of wood in the court, filling it on the top and on the sides
with firewood, leaving in it doors for going in and out. After this
most of the men then each took bundles of sticks, long and very
dry, tied together, and a singer, mounted on the top of the wood,
sang and made a noise with one of their drums. All danced below
him with great order and devotion, going in and out through the
doors of that arch of wood and thus they continued to dance until
evening, when each one leaving his bundle, there, they went home
to rest and eat. When the night fell, they returned and many people
with them, for this ceremony was held in great esteem among
them, and each man taking his torch they lighted it and each one
for himself set fire with them to the wood, which at once blazed
up and was quickly consumed. When there was no longer anything but coals, they levelled them and spread them out wide, and
those who had danced having come together there were some who
set about passing over those coals barefoot and naked, as they
were, from one side to the other, and some passed over without
harm, but others got burned and still others were half burned up.
And they believed that in this was the remedy for their calamities
and bad omens and they thought that this service of theirs was
very pleasing to their gods. (Tozzer 1941:148–149)

The *Relación de la Ciudad de Valladolid* gives a better description of
the men who ran through the fire:

They were also accustomed at certain times of the year to make
from extremely large pieces of wood a heap of it the height of the
stature of a man, and higher, and more than twenty-five feet in
length and breadth; and forming a procession of many Indians
with their kind of torches made of certain rods which burn well
when tied on a stick, they come to where that pile of wood is and
all break their torches on the place where the wood is, some (of
the) pieces of stick remaining in the hand. They carried off the
latter as relics. This wood having been kindled, it made a great
bed of red hot wood half an *estado* high of hot coals of the size
that the wood had been, and they beat it and broke it down so that
the fire should be level. And at the quarter (*cuarto*) of dawn the
same procession came bringing the priest before it clad in their

kind of alb with many small snail shells sewn on the lower part, and their kind of chasuble, a miter on his head; there were depicted on it many faces of demons. With his acolyte he came to the place where the bed of hot wood was, which could not be approached nearer than a stone's throw, and when he arrived he carried a hyssop with many tails of vipers and poisonous snakes tied on it, and, the acolyte bringing to him a vessel of the kind of wine they used, he sprinkled with that hyssop and on all four sides of the fire he performed his ceremonies and sprinkled the coals with it. And then he ordered them to take off his sandals and he went on the bed of hot wood sprinkling, and behind him the whole procession of Indians. And this *alquin* passed over without suffering any injury. (Tozzer 1941:148)

Thus the emphasis in Yucatán, as in Chamula, was on ridding the individual of evil, but from the calamities of the preceding year rather than from the evil of the five "lost days."

In highland Chiapas, Indians express their disdain for Ladinos by making fun of them in ritual humor. However, Landa points out that in the Yucatán Peninsula, at least, the Spaniards themselves encouraged the native buffoon to parody Spanish customs for their entertainment: "These Indians have very agreeable amusements, and especially have players who act with a great deal of wit, so much so that the Spaniards hire them for no other reason than that they may see the jokes of the Spaniards which pass between them and their maid servants, their husbands or their own people upon the manner of serving them well or ill, and afterwards they act this with as much skill as clever Spaniards" (Tozzer 1941:93). Thus, whatever the function of these burlesques is today, it is clear that in the past they served as entertainment for Spaniards as well as Indians.

Some of the dances and dramas which are performed in Mayan communities of the Yucatán Peninsula at the present time probably originated as parodies of the Spaniards. Stephens (1843:65) suggests that the *báyle de dia* which he observed at Ticul in 1841 "was intended to give a picture of life at a hacienda." The performers included men "called fiscales, being the officers attendant upon the ancient cacique, and representing them in their authority over the Indians" (Stephens

1843:II, 65). The *vaquería* of X-Cacal is performed by characters representing the personnel who once lived on the Yucatecan hacienda, such as the owner of the hacienda, his wife, son, daughter, the overseers, cowboys, and swineherds (Villa Rojas 1945:127). The highlight of the *vaquería* is a mock bullfight: "Then the bull fighters entered, followed by the vaqueros [cowboys] who with fierce shouting dragged the struggling 'bull' into the arena and tied him to a post. The 'bull' was simply a man placed inside a framework of vines, wood, and sacking, in the shape of a bull. Freed from the post, the 'bull' charged the fighters who used deerskin as capes. The droll capers of the actors made for a very amusing bullfight" (Villa Rojas 1945:130). Evidently this is a parody of the Spanish bullfight. There are similarities between this *vaquería* and the mock bullfights with reed bulls which I have described elsewhere for Zinacantan during the Christmas–New Year's–Epiphany season and for Chenalhó during the fiesta of Carnaval. In Chan Kom there is no bull framework, but men perform as bulls and girls as bullfighters: ". . . the dance itself is referred to as a *vaquería*: and it always concludes with a special dance (the *torito*) in which the girl, striving to cause the man who dances opposite her to lose his balance and step off the platform, represents the bullfighter, while he is the bull" (Redfield and Villa Rojas 1934:158). At the end of the dance the Cowgirls (*vaqueras*) are whipped to purge them of evil winds (spirits?) (Redfield and Villa Rojas 1934:159). In nearby Tekom the whipping of Cowboys signals the end of the fiesta: "This they do to get rid of the winds that have been around the animals they have been fighting. Then the people say: 'Now you are not a vaquero any more. The fiesta is over'" (Redfield 1941:291). The whipping of Cowboys or Cowgirls serves a purpose similar to that of the Pedrano custom of beating the Carnaval celebrators with monkey-fur headdresses at the end of the fiesta.

Another Yucatecan dance, the Dance of the Mestizas, is probably a parody of Spanish women. The dictionary of Pío Pérez refers to a Dance of the Foreigners (*Dzul okot*) which used to be performed in Tinum (Campeche) (Martí 1961:88). Since the Spaniards were called *dzul* by the Yucatec Maya, it is likely that this dance was still another burlesque of the unfamiliar customs of the Spaniards.

Although no Dance of the Conquest is performed in Mayan towns of the Yucatán Peninsula today, Ponce (1875:403) mentions having seen Indians disguised as Moors at a fiesta in Tinum during his visit to Yucatán in the 1580's. It is unclear whether the Warrior Dance described by Landa could have served as a prototype for such dances, for there is nothing in his description to suggest that it was staged as a sham battle. On the other hand, Molina Solís (1896:234) is of the opinion that the dance called *lolomché* (*Colomché*) by Landa (Tozzer 1941:93–94) was performed as a mock battle. Landa does not describe this dance. Be that as it may, no Dance of the Conquest is performed in this region today. It is possible that the Dance of the Conquest was abandoned during the almost-successful Caste War and nativistic movement of the nineteenth century (Reed 1964) because of its unpleasant connotation of domination by the much hated Ladinos.

Central Highlands

Perhaps the best source on the pre-Columbian ritual humor of the Aztecs and other speakers of the Náhuatl language is Fray Diego Durán's *Historia de las Indias de nueva España e islas de la tierra firme*, written sometime during the sixteenth century. Less detailed sources include Sahagún's *Historia de las cosas de Nueva España* (Anderson and Dibble 1951) and José de Acosta's *Historia natural y moral de las Indias*. All of these sources agree that the chief occasion for ritual humor was the fiesta in honor of Quetzalcóatl on February 3. In the courtyard of the temple of Quetzalcóatl in Cholula there was a small theater, about thirty feet square (Durán 1967:65). The presentation consisted of four comic acts. In the first comedy a buffoon pretended to be afflicted with boils and walked around complaining about the pain he was suffering. Between his complaints he interspersed witty remarks at which his audience laughed. Four men came on the stage for the second act. Two pretended to be completely blind, while the others pretended to be partially blind from cataracts. These four argued among themselves in a witty manner, ridiculing each other, possibly about their infirmities. Act 3 featured a man sick with a cold,

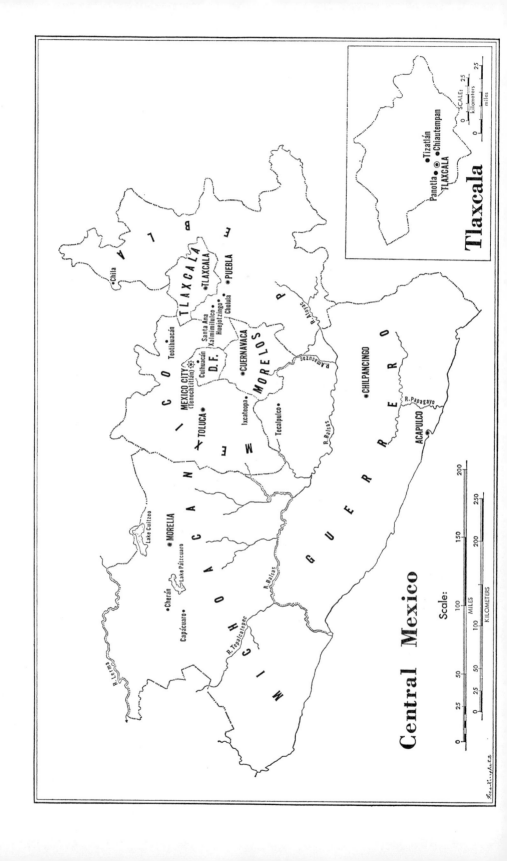

Tlaxcala

Panotla •   • Tizatlán
TLAXCALA ⊛   • Chiautempan

SCALE:
kilometers
0   25
miles
0   25

Central Mexico

Scale:

MILES
0   25   50   100   150   200

KILOMETERS
0   50   100   200   250

R.Lerma

M I C H O A C A N

Lake Cuitzeo

•MORELIA
Lake Pátzcuaro
•Cherán
Capácuaro •

R.Tepalcatepec

R.Balsas

M E X I C O

X TOLUCA

Teotihuacán •

Culhuacán
MEXICO CITY •
(Tenochtitlan)

D. F.

Santa Ana
Xalmimilulco •
Huejotzingo •
Cholula •

• TLAXCALA

T L A X C A L A

• PUEBLA

P   U   E   B   L   A

Chila •

Ixcateopa •

Tecalpulco •

M O R E L O S

• CUERNAVACA

R.Amacuzac

R.Atoyac

R.Balsas

G   U   E   R   R   E   R   O

• CHILPANCINGO

R.Papagayo

ACAPULCO
●

who coughed a lot and pretended to be seriously ill. In act 4, one man impersonated a large fly and another a black beetle. They were dressed in realistic costumes. The "fly" made a buzzing sound and approached some meat and examined it carefully; the other actor behaved just like a beetle as it scampered through some rubbish. The audience responded to all these acts with appreciative laughter (Durán 1967:65). According to the Codex Ramírez, some buffoons pretended to be crippled or maimed at this fiesta, and others impersonated large toads, small lizards, butterflies, and birds (Ramírez 1944:161).

Although the festival of Quetzalcóatl is the only religious holiday for which the chroniclers describe comedies (Durán 1967:65; de Acosta 1963:387–388), there were secular holidays at which humorous dances were performed. In a dance of old men, the participants pretended to be stooped or hunchbacked. The buffoon played the fool in another dance, changing the order of the words said by his master (Durán 1967:30). Durán describes still another dance, called the Dance of Titillation or Desire, which was both "witty and lewd," and at which some of the dancers impersonated women (Durán 1967: 193). López de Gómara (1943:I, 220), writing in the sixteenth century, refers to a dance in which buffoons appeared disguised as people of other tribes, whose speech they imitated. In the same dance other buffoons impersonated old women and pretended to be drunk and crazy, much to the amusement of their audience.

The nobles of Tenochtitlán, Tlaxcala, and Michoacán, and probably of other tribes as well, maintained jesters to amuse them (Anderson and Dibble 1951:VIII, 30; Herrera 1934:175; Torquemada 1943:II, 525). According to Sahagún there were those "who rolled a log with their feet thus bringing pleasure in many ways. Their deeds were laughable and marvellous; for with the soles of his feet one man [lying] below this did—he made a thick, round log dance with the soles of his feet [while] he lay upon his back and cast the log upward. With only the soles of his feet he did this" (Anderson and Dibble 1951:VIII, 30). In Montezuma's palace, while the monarch was eating dinner, "there entered certain Indians, hump-backed, very deformed, and ugly, who played tricks of buffoonery, and others who they said were jesters. There was also a company of singers and dancers, who afforded Montezuma much entertainment" (Díaz del Castillo 1927:172).

It is clear that pre-Columbian Aztec humor belonged to the same tradition as that of the Maya. Aztec buffoons impersonated animals as well as people. The people whom they impersonated were foreigners and those afflicted with blemishes and deformities, just the types of people most apt to be the butt of ridicule in Mayan communities of highland Chiapas.

As late as the eighteenth century, some Náhuatl-speaking Indians were producing a farce which resembled the pre-Hispanic perform- ances in several respects (Paso y Troncoso 1902:313). One of the characters, a stooped or hunchbacked old woman, pretends to be preg- nant. Her grandson imitates coyotes and dogs. The farce begins with the deformed old woman announcing her craving for agave sap, which she carries in a gourd: "I have a desire, a longing, a craving for thick [agave] sap . . . which will prevent me from having a miscarriage" (Paso y Troncoso 1902:314; my translation).

She does not want her grandson, Peter, to drink the juice, so she tells him that the gourd contains poison for dogs. Having told him this, she leaves the stage, groaning with pain: "Look, I should think first of the child that I have conceived. I have very sharp pains in my hips. Perhaps I am going to have a miscarriage" (Paso y Troncoso 1902:315; my translation).

Peter cannot resist tasting the bowl of juice she has left behind, and he likes it so much that he drinks it all: "Ah, ah, is that ever good and sweet! That is why dogs like to eat it, and that is why they die. God will it that I do not transform myself into a dog. Here is a truly sweet death. This is the end. Let's scrape the bowl" (Paso y Troncoso 1902: 315; my translation).

Then he thinks he is dying: "I have sought for myself a violent death! Oh! How unfortunate I am! It is my gluttony which carries me away. Please God, that I may still live on earth! It seems to me that I am already getting numb, that my eyes are clouding over . . . I am dying, I am already dying" (Paso y Troncoso 1902:315; my trans- lation).

Peter's grandmother returns and asks where he is. Peter replies,

"Grandmother, I am only holding onto my soul by the skin of my teeth: I am already dying" (Paso y Troncoso 1902:316; my translation).

The old woman asks what happened to him, and Peter lies: "Grandmother! Twelve hundred dogs came. They began to eat the poison which you left down there; because the food seemed to be so very tasty, I immediately wished to taste a little bit of it" (Paso y Troncoso 1902:316; my translation).

The old woman scolds him: "Imbecile, scamp, glutton! You have eaten the thick sap that I crave! Now if I feel the craving of a pregnant woman, what will I eat?" (Paso y Troncoso 1902:316; my translation). And she hits him with her stick. The act ends with the old woman chasing her grandson around the stage.

This farce is similar to some modern *loas* of the Valley of Teotihuacán, texts of which Gamio collected and published in 1922 (Gamio 1922:II, 362–374). Gamio describes the *loa* as a short dramatic piece in honor of the virtues of some Christian saint, preceded or followed by a dialogue or humorous discourse characterized by incidents of daily life in the region (1922:II, 294). He says that a farcical interlude called "Los Serranos" is of the same genre (1922:II, 294). The titles of some of the *loas* are as follows: "*Loa* about a Tailor and his Apprentice," "*Loa* about a *Fiscal* and an Indian," "*Loa* about a Cambric Vendor," "A Humorous *Loa* about a 'Tomato' and Lady Onion." The theme of the last-mentioned *loa* is reminiscent of the farce about the old woman and her grandson. The scene opens with Mr. Tomato's monologue extolling the pleasures of eating:

> Well, sir, one cannot doubt it;
> No one has convinced me
> that the greatest enjoyment
> is other than eating . . .
> Ay, Tomato friend!
> It is time to profit,
> For now you are all alone.
>
> · · · · · · · · · · · · ·
>
> I will eat with gusto
> everything which it [the pot] contains.

> Of chicken, here is a thigh,
> sardines and sausages,
> a larded chicken,
> and a piece of ham.
> No, there is nothing in the world to equal the
> delight of eating;
> away with the dance
> and even farther the woman.
>
>   (Gamio 1922:II, 372–373; my translation)

Unfortunately for him, at this point Lady Onion arrives and asks Mr. Tomato what is in his pot. In order to get rid of her quickly, he replies that it contains rat poison, which he claims is effective within an hour after being consumed. Lady Onion decides that she wants to die and eats the contents of the pot. Thinking she is poisoned, she calls out in words similar to those of the boy who drank the agave sap:

> Oh, my God! I feel like I am dying!
> Defend me, Saint Anthony!
> Who ordered me to try what
> was in the pot?
>
>   (Gamio 1922:II, 373; my translation)

Mr. Tomato's response is sarcastic:

> She ate the crumbs,
> And now she believes that she is poisoned.
>
>   (Gamio 1922:II, 373; my translation)

He offers her a bottle of liquid, which he says is an antidote for the poison, and all ends happily with panegyrics to the Virgin Mary (Gamio 1922:II, 373–374).

In their form and content *loas* resemble the farces of the pre-Columbian Aztecs and the Mayas. The titles of some *loas* call to mind those of the Maya farces cited in the Motul dictionary: compare "The *Loa* of the Cambric Vendor" with "The Pot Vendor" and "The Chili Pepper Vendor" of the Maya. Pre-Columbian Aztec comedies also concerned such incidents of daily life as illness and drunkenness (Durán 1967:65–66, 194).

In place of the religious dances and rituals which the Aztecs had performed for their gods, the Spanish friars introduced religious morality and mystery plays as a means of instructing the Indians in the teachings of the Bible and Catholicism. Motolinía (Fray Toribio de Benavente) describes a mystery play, representing the Fall of Adam and Eve, which he observed being performed in Tlaxcala in 1538 in the Náhuatl language (Steck 1951:157–159). In this play there were human impersonators of animals: "There were other artificial animals, all well simulated, with some boys inside them. These acted as if they were domesticated and Adam and Eve teased and laughed at them . . . On the rocks there were animals; some of them were real, others were artificial. One of the artificial animals was a boy dressed like a lion. He was tearing to pieces and devouring a deer that he had killed. The deer was real and lay on a crag which was made between two rocks" (Steck 1951:158).

Other plays introduced during the sixteenth century include the Final Judgment, the Passion of Christ, the Shepherds, and the Adoration of the Kings (Ravicz 1970:49, 64–65). The last two are Nativity plays. I suspect that the angel impersonators of Zinacantan once performed in a Nativity play, because, according to a Zinacanteco myth, they were present at the birth of the Christ Child (Early 1965:317). Elements of the Passion play are found in Zinacantan, Chamula, and Chenalhó.

One of the humorous themes common to Chamula, Chenalhó, and Zinacantan is that of war and conquest. In one of their fiestas the Aztecs made their sacrificial victims fight in a mock battle, and, using "tortillas of ground corn which had not been softened in lime [as mock hearts], they thus cut their hearts out" (Anderson and Dibble 1951: II, 44). At the festival of Pauquetzalitzi in the month of Atemoztli, there occurred an event called the Mock Fight of the Chonchayotl. The priests and warriors formed two sides and struck each other with fir branches, canes, or reeds. If, in the course of the battle, the warriors caught a priest, "they rubbed him with [powdered] *maguey* leaves; sorely he burned and itched; [it was] as if his flesh crept. And if one of the young warriors was caught, the priests bled his ears with a [maguey] thorn, and his arms, his breast, and his thighs, [so that] he cried out loud . . . In the course of these skirmishes they looted each other's strongholds, the royal palace and the priests' quarters" (Anderson and Dibble 1951:II, 138).

The Spanish friars easily adapted the mock battles of the Aztecs into representations of combats important in Christian history. On June 18, 1539, the emperor of Spain and the king of France signed a peace treaty. To commemorate this event, the Indians and Spaniards of Mexico City staged the conquest of Rhodes. The Tlaxcalans, not to be outdone, staged the conquest of Jerusalem (Steck 1951:158). This was perhaps the first performance of the religious play commonly known as the Battle (or Dance) of the Moors and Christians, of which the struggles between Indians and Ladinos, Blackmen and Whitemen, Monkeys and Passions characteristic of the fiesta of Carnaval in highland Chiapas are but variants, as are the Dances of Conquest of highland Guatemala. In the Tlaxcalan version, the holy army included troops representing Castile and León, Toledo, Aragon, Galicia, Granada, Bizcaya, Navarre, Germany, Rome, Italy, the Huaxtecs, the Zempoaltecas, the Mixtecas, the Colhuaques, the Tarascans, and the Guatemalans (Steck 1951:160–161). "In point of uniforms, there was little difference among the men of the army because, not having seen European soldiers, the Indians do not know how each group dresses, and hence they are not wont to differentiate. This explains why all entered as Spanish soldiers with trumpets, simulating those of Spain, and with drums and fifes" (Steck 1951:160). On the other side were the Moors or Turks, and soldiers from Galilee, Judea, Samaria, Damascus, and Syria. Here then was the first association of Blackmen (Moors) with Jews and Turks, villains of the fiesta of Carnaval in Zinacantan, Chamula, and Chenalhó. In the conquest of Rhodes staged in Mexico City in 1538, those representing the Turks were painted black (Díaz del Castillo 1904:420).

Robert Ricard has pointed out that there are many variants of the dances of Moors and Christians in Middle America (Ricard 1932:64). Even a dance performed in Michoacán in 1643, entitled Christians and Chichimecs, would belong to this genre because "the theme was exactly the same" (Ricard 1932:65). Gillmor shows "how the fighting pattern of the *Moors and Christians* turns easily into battles between Spaniards and Aztecs and between French and Mexicans" (1943:17). Only the names distinguish Santiago from Cortés and the Moorish king from Montezuma (Gillmor 1943:20–21). The fiesta of the Holy Cross celebrated on May 7, 1651, included impersonators of Indians, Montezuma, Cortés, the Moors, and the Grand Turk (Rangel 1924:87–88). Certainly, for the Indians of highland Chiapas it makes no difference whether a Dance of the Conquest features as protagonists Moors vs. Christians, Spaniards vs. Indians, Montezuma vs. Cortés, Christians vs. Chichimecs, Indians vs. Ladinos, Blackmen vs. Humans, Animals vs. People, Mexicans vs. French, or Mexicans vs. Guatemalans. The theme is always the same. And the triumph of good over evil is always humorous.

The Dance of the Moors is performed today in many communities of the Náhuatl area (Redfield 1930:117, 120; Madsen 1960:155; Gillmor 1943:12; Gamio 1922:II, 230–231; Kurath 1949; Parsons 1932: 330–333; Vázquez Santana 1940:359–362; Vázquez Santana and Dávila Garibi 1931:49, 50, 111; plate 33). In Culhuacán, a buffoon dressed as the devil "mocked the Moorish king and the Christians and leered at the bystanders" (Gillmor 1943:12). In the Valley of Teotihuacán, clowns called *achileos* ("Jews") carry dried squirrels, which they hurl at spectators, provoking shouts and protests from the women and noisy laughter from the men (Gamio 1922:II, 233). At one point, an *achileo* goes up to Pilate and pretends to eat, with great gusto, the imaginary lice which he has succeeded in catching (Gamio 1922:II, 234). Buffoons are also known to carry dried squirrels at fiestas in Chila (Puebla) and Tecalpulco (Guerrero) (Kurath 1949:87, 89).

A variant of the Dance of the Christians and Moors, called "Agustín Lorenzo," is performed in Huejotzingo (Puebla) and Santa Ana Xalmimilulco (Puebla) during the fiesta of Carnaval. In Santa Ana "there are groups of soldiers—Zacapuastlas [mountain Indians], Zapadores [sappers], Franceses [Frenchmen], and Turcos [Turks], all carrying guns or swords or both, also groups of Serranos [mountain people] and Riris who do some clowning together with the Diablos [devils], and of mounted Bandidos [bandits], including their chief, Agustín Lorenzo, and his bride, the Novia (or the Dama, the Lady)" (Parsons 1932:320). This dance dates from the epoch of the French interven-

tion and the period when the highway robber, Agustín Lorenzo, ter-
rorized travelers on the road between Mexico City and Veracruz (Vázquez and Dávila 1931:54). The dance symbolizes two conflicts: (*a*)
wealthy Mexicans against bandits and (*b*) the French against the Indians. The Zacapuastlas were Indians of the mountains to the north of
Puebla who fought heroically against the French in the 1860's (Toor
1929:19). The Serranos, who represent poor mountain people, are
buffoons who carry stuffed animals: "They carry bow and arrow or
machete or gun and at Santa Ana they had a small cannon which they
raced about with and fired off every hour or so with a terrific explosion.
At Huejotzinco [*sic*] the serranos went about singly or in couples,
gathering crowds, with whom they joked. The chief joke of one of
them was raising his little animal's tail to defecate [animal abuse!]"
(Parsons 1932:322). The French are represented in caricature with
Zouave costumes, "pink face mask with enormous black beard or
moustache and many with short stemmed wooden pipe in mouth"
(Toor 1929:20). The Turks wear the same mask as the French do,
but painted black (Toor 1929:20).

The Bandits abduct the Lady, and their leader marries her in a
mock wedding. One of the men impersonates a priest and says, "En el
nombre des Pashcle y del Hishcley y del Espíritu Shashcle. Amén," a
parody on the Spanish "En el nombre del Padre y del Hijo y del Espíritu Santo" for "In the name of the Father and the Son and the Holy
Ghost" (Parsons 1932:325). Then the Indians appear and set fire to
the hut in which the "marriage" took place and recapture the Lady
(Vázquez and Dávila 1931:55).

At one point the Bandits go on a looting spree in the village: "They
visit the stores. 'What['s for] sale today? ¿Qué venta hoy?' they ask
and are given biscuits, etc. by the storekeeper" (Parsons 1932:45). In
their character and activities the Bandits of Huejotzingo and Santa
Ana Xalmimilulco resemble the Monkeys of Chamula and the Blackmen of Zinacantan and Chenalhó.

A female impersonator called La Tristeza ("The Sad One") sometimes accompanies the Serranos (Parsons 1932:322 n., 325). She represents Agustín Lorenzo's mistress, whom the Bandit would seal in a
cave with enough food until his return. "But in the end, after many

raids, Agustín fell into the hands of the rural guards, horsemen as skillful as he himself, and then the woman died captive in the depths of the cavern, whose rocks did not tremble at her cries of agony nor soften under the flow of her tears" (Toor 1929:27). La Tristeza is given a mock funeral at the end of the fiesta (Parsons 1932:325), which probably represents her entombment after her lover's death.

In Panotla and Tizatlán, two communities in the state of Tlaxcala, groups of men impersonating bandits called *camadas* roam the streets during the fiesta of Carnaval, cracking jokes and making witty remarks for the benefit of the spectators (Vázquez and Dávila 1931:52–53, 46–48). One of the Bandits in Tizatlán is costumed as a woman (Vázquez and Dávila 1931:47).

In Ixcateopa (Mexico) and Panotla (Tlaxcala), buffoons called *huehuenches* impersonate old men. Vázquez Santana (1940) says that in the state of Guerrero, the dance company includes twelve Old Men, an Old Woman, four Buzzards, a Jaguar, a Deer, a Dog, a Mule, a Doctor, and a Hunter. The Old Woman carries a fox in her hand. In the course of their dance the Old Men pretend to capture the Jaguar, whom they ridicule and then kill. The Buzzards approach the carcass and pretend to devour it while the Dog "barks" (Vázquez Santana 1940:177–180). The prototype for the Old Men is clearly pre-Columbian in origin, because the *huehuenche* dance has affinities with the Aztec dance of hunchbacked old men (Durán 1967:30). Variants of this dance are found all over Middle America: among the Mixes (Parsons 1936:258; Beals 1951:74, 80–81), Zapotecs (Parsons 1936:259, 262–263), Tarascans (Beals 1946:133), Totonacs (Ichon 1969:373–377), Yaquis and Mayos (Parsons and Beals 1934:508), and, of course, the Zinacantecos of highland Chiapas (i.e., the Grandfather clowns who perform during Christmas, New Year's, and Epiphany). The dance seems to have followed the spread of the Náhuatl language southward into Nicaragua (Brinton 1883:xliv) and appears in the north among the Pueblo and Navaho Indians (Parsons and Beals 1934:508; Haile 1946).

Of much more recent origin, but probably conforming to an old pattern of social satire, is the Dance of the City Slickers, which is performed in Chiautempan (Tlaxcala) during the fiesta of Carnaval. The word *catrín* indicates "a person of the city, or with city habits and dress" (Foster 1948:33 n.). The dancers wear shoes, tailored suits, white dress shirts, neckties, and top hats or dresses. All carry umbrellas (Vázquez and Dávila 1931:fig. 21). They make the following satirical remarks:

> Even though the monkey wears silk,
> she's still a monkey.
>
> Why do you paint yourself,
> if you are not a cathedral?
>
> You used to be an affected old woman;
> now you are an abandoned hen.
>
> Ay, how plump Athanasia is,
> just like a tender head of lettuce.
> (Vázquez and Dávila 1931:51–52; my translation)

The humor of two of these remarks is based on animal abuse—the equation of a condescending woman of the city with a hen too old to lay eggs any more and that of a fashionable woman with a monkey.

The above examples show that even today animal symbolism is an essential ingredient of ritual humor among the Indians of the Central Highlands. But in contrast to the situation among the Maya of highland Chiapas, Guatemala, and the Yucatán Peninsula, here no one animal species is a focal symbol of humor. In this and adjacent regions the stage is dominated by buffoons who pretend to be old men, rather than by impersonators of monkeys or coatis as is the case among the Maya.

Oaxaca

Several variants of the Dance of the Conquest are performed in Zapotec towns. In Yalalag the opposing sides are called Soldiers and Indians (de la Fuente 1949:283). The principal dancers in the Dance of the Plumes of Santa Ana del Valle and Avasolo are called Montezuma, Cortés, and Malinche (Parsons 1936:250–252). A dance called the Dance of the Conquest was performed in Mitla as late as 1932 (Parsons 1936:261–263). The Dance of the Conquest is per-

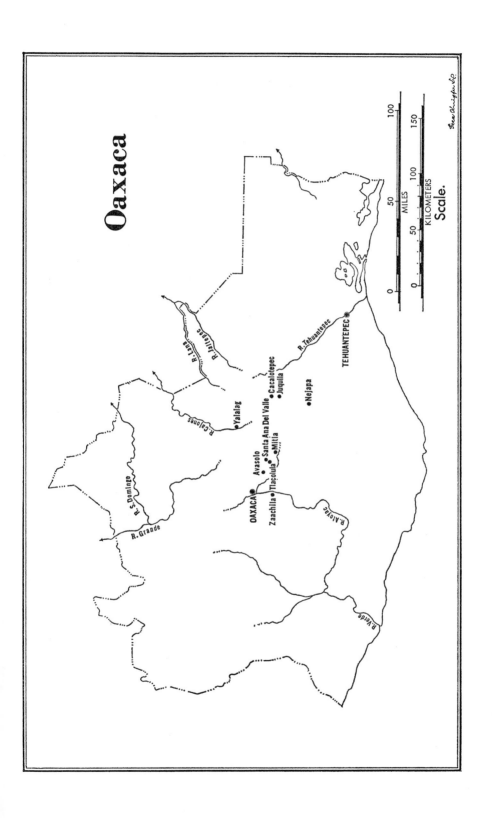

Oaxaca

formed in the Mixe towns of Cacalotepec and Juquila (Beals 1951: 81–82; Starr 1908:30).

In the state of Oaxaca two kinds of clowns burlesque the Dance of the Conquest: Blackmen and Old Men. In Avasolo the Dance of the Blackmen is performed at the same time as the Dance of the Plumes. The two Blackmen pretend to be Montezuma's servants. They are clearly a syncretism of the dark-skinned Moors and Indians. At times the Blackmen parody the Dance of the Plumes: "The Negritos [Blackmen] are lively clowns. One dances a burlesque step behind Montezuma, up and down the lines, while the other lolls over Cortés' chair" (Parsons 1936:252). The Bad Old Men of Zaachila, who appear on Ash Wednesday, "say nothing because they are supposed to be dumb but they make expressive gestures to Montezuma as well as to onlookers, holding their right hand over their eyes, as if peering underneath, cocking their head to one side, carrying thumb and index finger to their mouth in the familiar sign for drinking, holding their hand to their heart, the lover's gesture, etc." (Parsons 1936:262– 263). Parsons describes the Old Men pretending to delouse a little boy and imitating the anthropologist, "resting his face in his hand, as she happens to be doing, or, as she smokes, holding up his lance to his mouth as a cigarette" (Parsons 1936:263). In Tlacolula, a group of Old Men "go from house to house and are given food and drink and money. One masquerades as a woman, and others as her children representing a family. At Nejapa, *Mal Viejos*, Bad Old Men, some impersonating women, drag about a stuffed *tigre*, a wild cat, which they pretend to shoot" (Parsons 1936:259).

Among the Western Mixe, groups of Blackmen and Old Men perform together: the Old Men burlesque the activities of the Blackmen (Parsons 1936:258; Beals 1951:74). "The *viejo* [Old Man], acting like a feeble old man, imitates the Negrito dance. He dances around the performers in a clockwise circuit, pushes back spectators and jests with them, particularly with old Tata Le, whose beard is strikingly like that of the *viejo*. . . . There were a few obscene gestures with the *tiznado* [Blackman] or others, mostly making grabbing motions at the sexual organs. Later a man dressed as a woman joined the group. The *viejo* pretended she was his wife" (Beals 1951:80–81). The Old Men of the Mixe and the Zapotec are probably related to the *huehuenches* of Ixcateopa (Mexico) and Panotla (Tlaxcala).

There are also impersonators of women, whose chests are "padded to resemble breasts, at which the *viejo* pretended to suckle. Later the *viejos* and *tiznados* and the men dressed as women burlesqued the Negrito dancers" (Beals 1951:74–75).

Other masked figures in Zaachila include a lion impersonator who uses a chicken foot as a claw, Devils, and Priests. The Priests "carry crosses of all kinds (one is a very large cross made of rough branches) and mock prayer-books, and three or four of them will gather around a passer-by and read to him. One carries a pitcher of water and a corn husk as aspergill" (Parsons 1936:264). Parsons (1936:264) points out that, as late as 1841, priest impersonators appeared on the streets of Mexico City during Carnaval. She quotes the indignant words of Bustamante: "We are amazed that in Mexico the government author-izes carnival maskers who come out in a mummery dressed as popes, bishops, cardinals and friars making monkeys of themselves to mock most indecently the dignitaries of the Church, parading through the streets and the cemetery of the cathedral—and they say we are Catho-lics!" (Bustamante 1841:I, 335 n.). This custom survives today only in Indian villages like Zaachila (Parsons 1936:264).

Michoacán

The Tarascans share with other Indian groups of Mexico the Dance of the Conquest (Beals 1946:144; Brand 1951:204; Carrasco 1952: 25; Foster 1948:208; Toor 1925) and ceremonial buffoons disguised as Blackmen and Old Men (Beals 1946:133, 144–145; Carrasco 1952:25). Before the arrival of the Spaniards, the Chichimecs and Otomies were the chief enemies of the Tarascans (*Relación de Michoa-cán* 1903:30). Fray Alonso Ponce, visiting Michoacán between 1584 and 1588, described dancers in many Tarascan towns who were dis-guised as armed Chichimecs (Ponce 1875:4, 8, 525). Much more im-portant today are the dances of the Moors and Christians.

The Old Men (plate 34) are of special interest for this study because their performance closely resembles that of the Grandfathers and Grandmothers of Zinacantan and of the masked figures of Chenalhó. The Old Men of Cherán mock the change-of-office ceremony of the *kéŋi*, an official "who cares for the church property and the stores of the priest, rings the churchbells every noon, runs errands for the *colector*, and does any odd jobs he may be assigned" (Beals 1946:133). For the change-of-office on December 8, "both the old kéŋi and the new provide themselves with "old men" or *viejos*. These are men dressed in an overcoat and with a cane. They carry a little bell adorned with flowers, wear a small hat, and a wooden *viejo* mask (a wooden mask carved to represent an old man with a long white beard). These are the speakers for the two kéŋi" (Beals 1946:133). The Old Men attack each other verbally: "the *viejo* representing the incoming kéŋi makes a long speech, criticizing the administration of the outgoing kéŋi. The other *viejo* then responds, defending the outgoing kéŋi and explaining all the good things he has done" (Beals 1946:133). Thus, like the Grandfathers and Grandmothers of Zinacantan and the masked figures of Chenalhó, the Old Men of Cherán burlesque the change-of-office ceremony of public officials. Also, like the Blackmen of Zinacantan, they chastise the retiring public official for neglecting his duties, thereby instructing the new official in the proper execution of his role.

Another group of Old Men, sometimes called Europeans, appear in Cherán on January 6 and in Capácuaro on December 25. In Cherán one of the dancers "said he was very old, so old he couldn't walk on level ground. If he couldn't walk on level ground, how was he going to walk downhill? Nevertheless he was going to the place of the Holy Child anyway. Another said that if he got tired walking, he would go on his knees to visit the child, even though they were scratched. Yet another complained of his high squeaky voice, but even if his voice gave out, he would still go to the Holy Child" (Beals 1946:152–153). These old men closely resemble the *huehuenches* of the Náhuatl-speaking areas of Mexico.

On other occasions buffoons impersonate Spaniards and Ladinos. Especially humorous are those called Hermits, who are disguised as friars in gray robes and conical caps (Beals 1946:154). "One was seen 'praying' before the church with his hands together but with both thumbs to his nose" (Beals 1946:155). They are similar to the priest impersonators of Zaachila (Oaxaca) in expressing their contempt for Ladino customs.

Gulf Coast

The Totonacs perform a variety of dance dramas which have war and conquest as their theme. They include the Dance of Moors and Spaniards, the Santiagueros, and the Tocotín Dance, which commemorates the conquest of Mexico by Cortés. Malinche, Cortés's mistress, appears in all these dances, which suggests that they are simply variants on a common theme. Malinche is always a comic figure (Ichon 1969: 349).

Malinche also plays an important role in a Dance of Blackmen, but in this case the Blackmen are Negro slaves who were imported from Africa during the sixteenth and seventeenth centuries (Aguirre Beltrán 1946). The setting of the dance is a sugar-cane plantation. The principal figures are the Owner of the plantation, his wife (Malinche), and an Overseer. Some Negroes working in the fields tell the Overseer that they have seen a snake. He pooh-poohs them, saying that it is only a vine, or a root, or a squash. Even when one of the Negroes exhibits a snakebite, the Overseer laughs at him and tells him that it was only a fly or a mosquito bite (Ichon 1969:359).

Two dance groups perform during the fiesta of Carnaval: the Old Men (*huehues*) and the Mulattoes. The term for Old Men is a Náhuatl word, which implies that the dance is related to dances of that name in other regions of Mexico. The Mulatto group includes Mulattoes in blackface, the ubiquitous Malinche, Cats or Jaguars, and Bulls. The highlight of their performance is a mock bullfight. On the last day of the fiesta the Mulattoes lasso and shoot the Bull with a wooden gun and, as in Zinacantan, they drink the Bull's "blood" (rum) (Ichon 1969:373–379).

Northern Mexico

Among the Mayo and the Yaqui of Sonora there are two kinds of ritual humorists: the *pascola* dancers and the Pharisees or *chapayekas*.

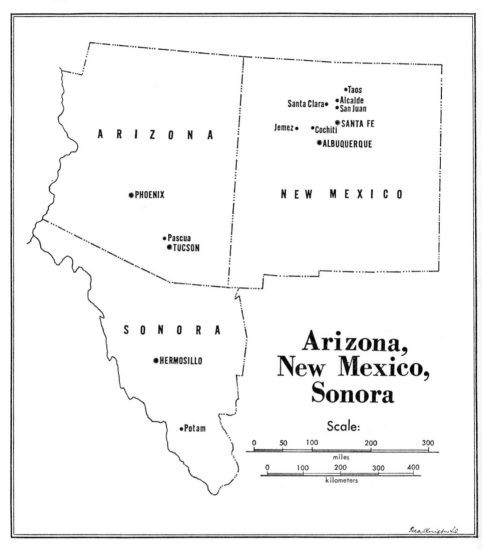

Pascola is the hispanicized form of the Yaqui word *pahko?ola*, meaning "old man of the fiesta" (Spicer 1954:75). *Pascola* dancers play the
same role in Yaqui and Mayo fiestas as do the Grandfathers and
Grandmothers in Zinacantan and the masked figures in Chenalhó. They

parody the Deer Dancer and the Matachini Dancers. The Deer Dance traditionally consisted of a mock deer hunt "which took place at dawn or shortly after, in which the *pascolas* acted as hunters and went through an elaborate hunting scene, eventually catching the deer-dancer, pretending to skin him, and carrying him home to their wives" (Spicer 1940:196). While he dances, "the deer-dancer is the constant butt of the *pascolas'* jokes. It is a customary part of the *pascolas'* activities to stumble over the deer-dancer, interfere with his dance, imitate all his movements, and attempt to make him laugh" (Spicer 1940: 195). When the *pascolas* are not mocking the Deer Dancer, they perform their own dances in which they impersonate such animals as badgers, wolves, canaries, and turtles. When performing as badgers the *pascolas* dance on all fours, in imitation of the animal (Spicer 1940: 181). Like the men who "cure" the Grandfathers and Grandmothers in Zinacantan, the *pascola* recites mock prayers in which he appeals to animals instead of the saints. "He addresses each one as 'saint,' such as *'santo 'vovok* ('Saint Frog')" (Spicer 1940:192). Yaqui *pascolas* pretend sexual intercourse with each other or masturbation (Parsons and Beals 1934:504).

Between dances the *pascolas* tell humorous stories and joke with the spectators. "If the dancer hears someone say that he had danced well, he will retort to the speaker, 'That is because I slept with your wife last night.' When he sees someone he knows, he may say, 'How is my wife, ———?' or 'How is my daughter, ———?' naming the person's wife or daughter. He also addresses men and women by relationship terms as son, brother, wife, daughter, or mother-in-law. 'See the lazy one,' he will say of some woman, 'she does not give me food, she, my daughter, she left everything home' " (Beals 1945:121). Unlike the ritual humorists of highland Chiapas, the *pascolas* perform at many fiestas during the year—they were active in twenty-five ceremonies during 1936–1937 (Spicer 1940:194). In fact, "Pascolas formally open all fiestas" (Beals 1945:125). They also participate in weddings (Spicer 1940: 188–189) and funerals (Holden et al. 1936:62), at which they mock the ceremonies. At a Yaqui wedding in Pascua (Arizona)[4]:

[4] The Yaqui of Pascua recently migrated from Northern Mexico to Arizona (Spicer 1940).

there are two *pascolas*, one who represents the bride and one who represents the groom. While the serious ceremony of marriage is taking place on one side of the household *ramada* [arbor], the two *pascolas* carry on an absurd burlesque of the marriage ceremony and the marriage relationship. The burlesque is charged with obscenity at times, but consists mainly of a simple farce. The *pascola* representing the groom places a comb in the other *pascola*'s hair and puts a necklace about his neck. The man's *pascola* sits on a blanket and the bride's *pascola* sits on his lap. They talk at length, after a little obscene horseplay. The bride's *pascola* points out all the faults in the house and *patio* and says that she will clean it up and make things look better. Then she intimates that the well is dirty and that the drinking water is full of mud. The groom's *pascola* insists that it is not and says that he will prove it. He pretends to be getting water but actually fills a glass with whiskey and hands it to the bride's *pascola*. The latter looks for dirt in it, holding it up to the light and then drinks it. (Spicer 1940:188–189)

Pharisees appear during the Easter ceremonial season in Pascua, at which time a version of the Dance of Christians and Moors is performed. There are two kinds of Pharisees, a masked clown group called *chapayekas* and another group who represent the " 'soldiers of Rome,' a title which refers to the part they play in the ceremonies during Holy Week as persecutors of Christ" (Spicer 1940:125). They thus perform the same role in these communities as do the Blackmen and Monkeys in highland Chiapas. In Potam, a Yaqui community in Sonora, the Dance of the Christians and Moors takes place at the time of the Holy Trinity in late May or early June (Spicer 1954:142–143). There "the ceremonial society that corresponds closely to the Arizona *Fariseos* [Pharisees] is most often spoken of as *hurasim* (the Yaqui form of the Spanish term for Judas)" (Spicer 1954:89).

Among the Mayo the Pharisees "are masked and usually are dressed to some extent to burlesque the pascola dancer" (Beals 1945:101). Some of the Pharisees are called Old Men or Grandfathers (Parsons and Beals 1934:502).

Fariseo actions are at all times intended to be ludicrous and are frequently obscene. Perhaps the most common behavior of this latter type is repeatedly treating the sword as a bottle, which is first filled in pantomime from the excretory organs of any convenient subject, animal or human, and then passed about the group of fariseos, who pretend to drink with great relish. They also pretend to be hurt, limp, fall down, stage mock fights, mount their spears as horses and shy from various objects as they gallop about, burlesque onlookers, and in the past were said frequently to become annoying by spilling water when they found someone carrying it or by indulging in other practical jokes. (Beals 1945:102)

The Pharisees use squirrel skins to imitate the foxskin bags of the fiesta sponsors. The squirrel skins "are often wiped in dust or even filth, then rubbed over the faces of unwary bystanders" (Beals 1945:103).

The Opata and Tarahumara are tribes in northern Mexico related to the Mayo and the Yaqui. Among both peoples the Dance of the Christians and Moors is performed (Bennett and Zingg 1935:314–315; Johnson 1950:39–40). The Pharisees of the Opata are similar to those of the Yaqui (Johnson 1950:39). Bennett and Zingg do not state whether the Pharisees of the Tarahumaras are clowns, but Lumholtz, who passed through the region in about 1900, reports that "the so-called *matachines* paint their faces and carry on their backs stuffed animals, such as the grey fox, squirrel, or opposum, while dancing to the music of the violin. They jokingly call the skins their *muchachitos* [little boys], and hold them as women carry their babies" (Lumholtz 1902:I, 354). According to Bennett and Zingg (1935:302) the *matachines* of the Tarahumaras are not, at present, clowns.

Southwestern United States

Beals and Parsons (1934:508) have suggested a possible historical connection between the *chapayeka* clowns of the Mayo and the Yaqui and the Grandfather or *k'apyo* clowns of the Pueblos. The names for these clowns may be cognates (Bennett and Zingg 1935:302). Moreover, some of the *chapayekas* among the Mayo are referred to as Old Ones or Grandfathers (Parsons and Beals 1934:502). On the other hand, the clowning activities of the *chapayeka* clowns are quite different from those of the *k'apyo*. If, however, we compare all clown behavior characteristic of the Indians of the American Southwest with that of the *pascolas* and *chapayekas* of the Mayo and the Yaqui, irrespective of which clowns perform it, then close parallels in their ritual humor emerge.

In 1880 and 1882 Adolf F. Bandelier observed the clowning of *koshare* clowns in the Cochiti pueblo (New Mexico), which strongly resembles some of the ritual humor of the *pascolas* and Pharisees of Northern Mexico, and of the Blackmen of Chenalhó: "Sodomy, coitus, masturbation, etc., was performed to greatest perfection, men accoupling with each other on the ground or standing. . . . The whole is a filthy, obscene affair. Drinking Urine out of bowls and Jars used as Privies on the house-tops, eating excrements and dirt, ashes and clay, washing each others' faces with Urine and with every imaginable dirt, imitating cohabitation and Sodomy, were the principal 'jokes' of the abominable leaders of the 'Qoshare' " (Lange 1959:303, 304). Among the Hopi, clowns whom Stephen (1936) labels as Grotesques put on a marriage burlesque. The men who impersonate female wedding guests place on the ground a sheepskin, on which they place another Grotesque disguised as the bride. After the "groom" joins her on the sheepskin, the wedding guests cover them with a ragged blanket. "The bride and groom pretend dalliance under the mantle and soon he surmounts her, then some of the Chükü run up and snatch away the mantle that had been covering them, shouting to them to go ahead but that everyone wanted to see the act. Then, it is plain to be seen, the bride exhibits a false vulva and the groom a false penis, these secured in place with strings, and they explicitly perform the simulated act of copulation, and the throng of spectators rend the air with their hilarious shouts" (Stephen 1936:331).

The Navaho have greatly elaborated upon the Grandfather theme, which is barely hinted at among the Mayo and Yaqui. There are both Grandfather and Grandmother clowns who perform during the Navaho Fire Dance or Corral Dance (Haile 1946). They resemble the clowns of the same name who perform in Zinacantan between Christmas and Epiphany. Among the Navaho, Grandfather pretends to be old, nearsighted, and stupid. He tries to seize a yucca fruit, but only succeeds in impaling himself on the sharp blades of the plant. He then pretends to be terribly bruised. The role of Grandmother, on the other hand, is played by a tall strapping young man who pretends to be stooped and disfigured like an old granny. She helps the old man pluck his fruit (Haile 1946:46–47). This piece is similar to the farces of the Aztecs in which infirmities were mocked and to the dances of Old Men characteristic of the Mixe, Zapotec, Tarascans, and Indians of the central Mexican highlands. Like the *loas* of the Valley of Teoti- huacán, this performance concerns a simple theme of everyday life. Impersonations of grandmothers and grandfathers are widespread in the Southwest, occurring in the Tewa pueblos of Alcalde, San Juan, Taos, and Jemez, in some of the Keresan pueblos and Zuñi towns, and among the Hopi, as well as among the Navaho (Parsons 1930:582– 583; Stephen 1936:114–115, 323, 324, 328, 329, 385).

In the Tewa town of Santa Clara, men masquerade as women and women disguise themselves as men:

> Women dress as men, and men as women, some of them making up as pregnant women, and these sing, "Some of those boys made me pregnant." The men in masquerade do women's work, fetch- ing water, baking bread outdoors in the ovens on street or roof, and carrying dinner to the dancers. The women masqueraders with cloths in their hands to clean the ovens go from door to door and sing, "I am scared, let's run away." People give them bread. "You are lazy. You don't bring us wood, you don't hunt deer, you bring nothing to us," the men say to the women. (Parsons 1929:212)

They make fun of how poorly they are able to execute the roles they are pretending to fill, much as the Grandmothers of Zinacantan mock women who try to behave like men.

Animal symbolism is prevalent in the ritual humor of several Tewa towns. In the Dog Dance, the dog impersonator snaps at people who approach him. "The woman holding him in leash would say, 'This dog is hungry.' People brought him food. The performance was to make happy our Lord on the cross. As he suffered, the dog also suffered, from hunger" (Parsons 1929:223). A Navaho buffoon "carries a fox-skin; drops it on the ground; walks away as if unconscious of his loss; pretends to become aware of his loss; . . . imitates in various exaggerated ways the acts of Indian hunters; pretends, at length, to find the lost skin; jumps on it as if it were a live animal he was killing; shoulders it and carries it off as if it were a heavy burden; staggers and falls under it" (Matthews 1902:150–151). Here the humor arises from the fact that the clown pretends that the fox is a large animal, rather than that it represents a human being. But among the Zuñi, clowns sometimes chase and kill dogs whom they refer to as Navahos (Parsons and Beals 1934:498). And the Hopi pig impersonator "comes in waddling and grovelling, imitating the motions of a fat hog, and lies down under a tree, lays his head flat on the ground, a faithful imitation of a wallowing swine" (Stephen 1936:455). The porcine traits chosen for ridicule are obesity and gluttony (Stephen 1936: 455–456).

The ridicule of outsiders is common among the Pueblos. They ridicule "the Navaho Shaman, the Mexican bullfighter or the American tourist" (Parsons and Beals 1934:500).

> A characteristic Santo Domingo theme is the "bull and horse" ceremony, which depicts the first arrival of the white men, missionaries and traders, in ludicrously ragged costumes. A mock bull fight is held, followed by songs of "London Bridge is falling down" and "Good Night Ladies." At the end the "traders" produce a suitcase and the Indians buy from them with paper money. A Santa Clara fiesta enacts the arrival of the United States soldiers in a covered wagon, their drunkenness, and finally their fight with the Navajo, in which they are worsted until Utes come to the rescue. A Hopi Powamu ceremony of 1928 caricatured American white girls. The *"Kachina* girls," impersonated by men, were dressed in an incongruous attire of skirts, riding boots, sombreros and six-shooters, and they carried vanity-boxes. (Steward 1931: 197)

Hopi clowns impersonate American schoolteachers and storekeepers, Navaho horsemen and medicine men, Mexicans, Apaches, and Paiutes (Stephen 1936:330, 367–368, 383, 385, 456, 920, 932–934). The *kossa* clowns of the Tewa town of San Juan burlesque the Catholic mass. The priest reads from an American trade journal instead of a Bible, and asperges with a broom dipped in a white porcelain bowl (Parsons 1929:183).

Thus the Indians of the American Southwest share many themes of ritual humor with their Mexican neighbors to the south. Most important for the study of the ritual humor of highland Chiapas is the tradition of Grandmother and Grandfather clowns, the ridicule of foreigners, animal abuse, and realistic representations of deviant sexual behavior. The burlesques of Catholic priests and of marriage are further proof that, as far as ritual humor is concerned, the American Southwest belongs to the Middle American culture area and deserves to be included in a comparative study of the ritual humor of this area.

Conclusions

The themes of ritual humor which enjoy the broadest distribution in both space and time include mocking old age and the infirmities associated with it, masquerading as women, and ridiculing the customs of foreigners. Of the three themes, only the first is universally presented in terms of the same symbols: white hair, stooped posture, hobbling gait, and high-pitched cracked voice. The other themes are defined in terms of the local situation. In a few cases female impersonators mock the deviant behavior of women within the community, but more often they make fun of foreign women. In Mexico some favorite targets of ridicule are snobbish city women or condescending local Ladino women. The Indians of the American Southwest delight in the burlesque of American girls, not Mexican (i.e., Ladino) women. There is similar regional variation in the humorous characterization of men who are not members of the community, ranging from the stereotype of the hacienda owner in the Mayan area to those of the storekeeper, schoolmaster, and Catholic priest in the American Southwest. Both the costumes and the realistic behavior of the performers reveal the traits considered most ridiculous and render the identity of the target unmistakable.

In no region of Middle America is animal symbolism lacking as an ingredient of ritual humor. Animal traits chosen for representation in humor are, however, not peculiar to animals. They are exhibited by human beings who are incapable of exerting self-control. Thus, while some animals are by nature gluttonous or sexually promiscuous, human beings are endowed with the capacity for controlling these tendencies. In general the mammalian species are most frequently the subject of ritual humor, probably because their habits are most similar to those of people and therefore lend themselves more easily to anthropomorphic symbolism than those of other animals.

On the whole the Indians of Middle America ridicule behavior and dress which deviate from the norms of the community. Outsiders, by definition, behave and dress differently from insiders and therefore are obvious targets of humor. Within the community, sexual promiscuity, gluttony, and social irresponsibility are universally discouraged and are universally the butt of ridicule. What the community defines as humorous depends on its criteria of what is normative and what is deviant.

The descriptions of comic performances made by Durán, López de Gómara, Landa, and others not long after the Spaniards first arrived in Middle America suggest that the humorous themes in question were native to the New World. Most of Middle America was subjected to influences from Central Mexico at one time or another. The Indians of the American Southwest were in contact with the cultures of Central Mexico between A.D. 500 and 1200 (Willey 1966:225–227); invaders from Central Mexico became the ruling families of the Yucatán Peninsula and the highlands of Chiapas and Guatemala, beginning in about A.D. 950 (Tozzer 1957:30; Calnek 1962:24–25; Edmonson 1971). By the time of the Spanish conquest many areas of Middle America were paying tribute to the Aztecs (Barlow 1949). It is not surprising, then, that a common tradition of ritual humor was distributed over such a large area.

Europeans are not without their own tradition of ritual humor, which is similar in many respects to what I have described for Middle America. Animal symbolism, animal impersonation, and female impersonation are characteristic of ritual humor in Spain and in other European countries. For example, in the town of Sobrado, Portugal, on St. John's Day, "The *Mouriscos*, in white trousers and shirts and high ornamental *shakos*, file in two columns and decorous longways to a monotone drumbeat. A clown in overalls apes their king. They are challenged by an unruly horde of *Bugios* (clowns or monkeys), in grotesque animal masks, tattered finery, paper streamers, and with agricultural implements. Their king, in church vestments, conducts them like a necromancer, as they leap and cower and attack. Their king is captured and led off amid lament. Suddenly a *bicha* or dragon routs the *Mouriscos* and restores the prisoner" (Kurath 1949:95). Bernal Díaz del Castillo (1927:175) notes the similarity between some Aztec dances and the *matachini* dances of Italy. Kurath (1949) says that "in the Middle Ages the *Matachini* were masked buffoons in motley and bells; they cut capers and struck each other with their swords or air-filled bladders. The name is derived from the Arabic 'mudawajjihin,' Pl. 'mudawajjihen,' which can mean 'those who put on a face' or else 'those who face each other,' . . . They entertained at private secular *entremets* and developed into the Court Masques, as the *mataciino* of Italy and the German Carnival plays of the fifteenth century, the Moriskentänze" (Kurath 1949:97). In one dance of Rumania, "a masked fool carries a phallos. Formerly a man-woman talked in falsetto" (Kurath 1949:98).

Even the social satire characteristic of Mayan ritual humor is found in Spain:

> In relation to the moral sanctions of the pueblo, the songs of *Carnaval*, sung by the bands of masked people, possessed particular importance. A certain shamelessness must needs be authorized for them to be sung, for they represented the public exposition of the year's harvest of gossip. For weeks before the arrival of *Carnaval* those who had talents of that order spent their evenings composing these songs, and into them put all the scurrilous events of the year. Things which had been kept dark for many months came out in a couplet in *Carnaval* sung hilariously by the masked figures as they danced down the street. Shopkeepers who had used false scales, municipal employees who abused their position found themselves lampooned, but most of all the couplets were intended to reveal illicit relationships between the sexes. Through the

masked voice of the pueblo the *novio* [fiancé] whose *novia*
[fiancée] had deceived him while he was away was warned of his
plight and exhorted to put off his horns. (Pitt-Rivers 1961:176–
177)

The native performances of ritual humor struck a responsive chord
in the hearts of the conquering Spaniards, who saw in them similarities with their own tradition. The Spaniards encouraged Mayan ceremonial buffoons of the Yucatán Peninsula to include Spanish customs
in their social satire (Tozzer 1941:93) and in this way were instru-
mental in bringing about a syncretism of the two traditions of humor.
The Spaniards also introduced morality plays to aid in the process of
conversion to Catholicism, and these in time were syncretized with
pre-Columbian themes of battle and conquest. Thus the unity of the
tradition of ritual humor in Middle America results not only from
cultural diffusion from Central Mexico at various times, but also from
contact with Spanish culture. The Spaniards were the first Europeans
to visit all the regions of Middle America that I have covered in this
chapter, and they have influenced the development of ritual humor in
this culture area.

10. The Social Meaning of Ritual Humor

The Indians of highland Chiapas stress the entertainment function of ritual humor when they describe the fiestas which provide its setting. Zinacantecos call the ritual humorists of the fiesta of San Sebastián "entertainers" (*htoyk'inetik*), Pedranos describe the performances of Carnaval ritual humorists as entertainment (*ta šak'be h-beh ʔelov*), and the name of the fiesta of Carnaval in all three communities is the Fiesta of Games (*k'in tahimoltik*). However, the fact that ritual humor is so often concerned with the contrast between normative and deviant behavior suggests the possibility that it may serve another, more important function, namely that of social control.

The term "social control" has been used with several meanings. "In its wider sense the term social control describes any influence exerted by society upon the individual" (Everett 1931:344). Slotkin uses a more anthropological definition which refers specifically to customs and culture: "the social controls found in a culture . . . are a body of customs by which the behaviour of the participants is regulated so that they conform to the culture" (1950:525). The functional anthropologists Malinowski (1926) and Radcliffe-Brown (1934) discuss social control in terms of rules (norms) backed by sanctions. Radcliffe-Brown defines a sanction as "a reaction on the part of a society or of a considerable number of its members to a mode of behaviour which is thereby approved (positive sanctions) or disapproved (negative sanctions)" (1934:531). By "reaction" he means physical force (legal sanctions) and such informal sanctions as ridicule, gossip, slander, and scolding.

The type of humor which is most likely to serve as a mechanism of social control is ridicule, and ridicule is certainly an important ingredient of ritual humor. No Zinacanteco, Chamula, or Pedrano likes to be the butt of ridicule. It would be logical to conclude, then, that, when Zinacantecos, Chamulas, and Pedranos see deviant members of their community being ridiculed in public at fiestas, they are deterred from behaving deviantly themselves for fear of receiving the same treatment.

This functional explanation of ridicule is attractive because it is logically coherent, that is, it seems to make sense. Parsons and Beals suggest it as an explanation for the behavior of the sacred clowns of the Pueblo and Mayo-Yaqui Indians to whom I refer in chapter 9. They note that "in general the clowns have a punitive and policing function in ceremonial matters and through their license in speech and song a somewhat similar function in domestic matters, ridicule being a strong weapon among the Pueblos" (1934:499). Hammond sees social control as a basic process in humor: "As a means of control, the public nature of most joking serves to shame the object of the jocular offensive, to invoke social pressure for his conformity, and to elicit support for the complainant" (1964:264).

My best data on this subject come from Zinacantan, where I made an ethnographic study of all humor, and not just ritual humor (Bricker 1968). Zinacantecos seem to be consciously aware of the intimate relationship among norms, ridicule, and shame, as the following description of a humorous incident suggests: "My foot slipped and I fell down in the mud. All the people who saw what had happened laughed at me. I was very ashamed and ran away." If a Zinacanteco man is asked why he does not wear Ladino clothes, or appear in public without shoes, purse, or hat, or have more than one wife, his typical response is that he is ashamed to do so because other people would ridicule him. Zinacanteco women likewise cite shame and ridicule as reasons for not wearing Ladino clothes or singing and dancing in public. This implies that Zinacantecos view ridicule as a sanction for deviant behavior.

I have argued, in chapters 7 and 8, that ritual humorists are preoccupied with morality and that cultural norms are implicit in all ritual humor. Sometimes the ritual humorists explicitly state what the norms are:

Host: Now, don't do that again. Don't get on horses. It's not for you. It's only for men— only *they* may mount horses.

More often the norms must be inferred from what the ritual humorists say and do:

First Blackman: Look, ladies and gentlemen! See how long the neck ribbons of Lol ʔUč's wife are. They just buy for themselves, but they don't pay for his *cargo*.

It is clear that in both cases ritual humor appeals to rules.

Ritual humor employs two types of informal sanctions. Ridicule (*labanvaneh*) is the most common type, but scolding (*ʔut bail*) also occurs. Below I present two examples of scolding speech in ritual humor. The first example comes from the mock trial of the grandfather impersonators on New Year's Day in Zinacantan:

Presidente: You know that it is wrong! You don't have the correct receipt. You stole it and the two horses.

The second example comes from the fiesta of Carnaval in Chenalhó, when the Blackmen berate Andrés Luis Turkey Belly for his licentious behavior:

> Why didn't you grow up?
> Why didn't you mature?
> Why did you look for trouble?
> Why did you seek out evil?
> Why did you do all that,
>   Andrés Luis Turkey Belly?

Both ridicule and scolding speech are sprinkled with such negative terms of evaluation as "bad," "evil," "wrong," "sin," and "shameless." Therefore they correspond to Radcliffe-Brown's definition of "negative sanction."

In one sense the functional definition of social control is unsatisfactory, because it does not use *effectiveness* as a criterion for evaluating formal or informal sanctions as mechanisms of social control. It is easy enough to show that sanctions are *intended* as mechanisms of social control and that they are *regarded* as such by the members of a community; it is much more difficult to show that ritual humor *enforces* rules, that it is an effective deterrent to deviant behavior. The term "social control" implies some quantitatively measurable degree of effectiveness in controlling behavior; that is, that there is a demonstrable cause-and-effect relationship between ridicule and the incidence of deviance in a society. This relationship has never been proved. Proof would entail showing both (*a*) that societies which ridicule certain types of behavior have a lower incidence of those behaviors than societies which do not ridicule them and (*b*) that the lower incidence of ridiculed behavior in the first group of societies is motivated by the fear of being ridiculed and not by some other factor, such as the fear of supernatural sanctions or the fear of legal punishment.

My data do not permit me either to prove or disprove the causal relationship. Even if I had collected information about the frequency of deviant behavior in Zinacantan, Chamula, and Chenalhó, my sample of societies would be too small to make a statistical analysis feasible. My data fit the weak definition of "social control" accepted by sociologists and anthropologists, but they are insufficient for the task of evaluating the effectiveness of ridicule in regulating social behavior.

The principal kinds of deviant behavior ridiculed by Zinacanteco ritual humorists are (*a*) behavior unbecoming for women, (*b*) poor performance of religious officials, and (*c*) Ladino behavior. The first kind of ritual humor has an explicitly didactic function: the grandmother impersonators announce that they are going to teach women how to spin and get along with their husbands:

> Look, girls, and look, women!
> This is how you should spin . . .
> Girls!
> If you are looking for husbands,
> then you should be able to make clothes for them,
> just as we are making clothes for our husbands.

Furthermore, much of the ritual humorists' dialogue during the fiestas of the Christmas-Epiphany season is concerned with what is and what is not acceptable behavior for women. The Host's admonition to the grandmother impersonators which is quoted above is an example of conscious teaching. However, the fact that the Host makes an explicit effort to instruct does not necessarily mean that Zinacanteco women actually learn how to behave appropriately from observing and listening to ritual humor. It means only that, should they be receptive to instruction in this context, the instruction is available.

A didactic motive is also evident in the junior entertainers' ridicule of delinquent religious officials when they moralize about how the officials ought to have behaved. An example of a Blackman's moralizing in this context also appears above. Here again a ritual humorist defines the limits of normative behavior in a way that attracts the audience's attention.

The Blackmen of Chenalhó are also playing the role of teacher when they explain why Andrés Luis Turkey Belly died:

> Don't be embarrassed!
>   Look!
> One of our people died—
>   Andrés Luis Turkey Belly!

> Because he was so tricky;
>   Because he was so unruly—
> He is dead.

They instruct the spectators not to follow in his footsteps:

> Look, you-all!
> Don't learn how to be tricky!
>   Don't learn how to steal!
> He has sinned.
>   His head is broken off here.
> It doesn't pay to sin!
>   It doesn't pay to steal!
> Because Andrés Luis Turkey Belly is very tricky.

The third kind of ritual humor serves a didactic function in a negative sense by pointing out the ways in which Ladino behavior differs from Indian behavior (rather than by describing normative Indian behavior). When ritual humorists ridicule Ladinos, they focus on those aspects of Ladino behavior which conflict most sharply with Indian norms. In chapter 8, I explained how the people of Zinacantan, Chamula, and Chenalhó maintain strong ethnic boundaries which set them off from Ladinos as well as from each other and other Indian groups. By emphasizing cultural differences, the ritual humorists remind Indians of the ways in which they differ from Ladinos, thereby helping to keep their sense of ethnic distinctiveness alive.

It is clear that whatever social significance the ritual humor of highland Chiapas has is derived from its preoccupation with morality. The functional explanations that have been considered in this chapter—social control, social sanctions, and socialization—are all attempts to explain this emphasis on normative and deviant behavior. But there is another, equally valid functional explanation of this phenomenon. The emphasis on morality is consistent with its salience in every other sphere of Indian culture. Morality is a pervasive theme in the culture of the Indians of highland Chiapas. In Zinacantan and Chamula it even influences the classification of speech genres (Bricker 1968:33; Gossen 1970:204). Thus, in stressing morality, ritual humor is thematically congruent with other sectors of Indian life in highland Chiapas.

BIBLIOGRAPHY

Acosta, P. José de
  1963 *The natural and moral history of the Indies*. Translated by Edward Grimston. [First published in English in 1604.] London: Hakluyt Society.
Aguirre Beltrán, Gonzalo
  1946 *La población negra de México 1519–1810*. Mexico City: Ediciones Fuente Cultural.
Alemany y Selfa, Bernardo
  1930 *Vocabulario de las obras de Don Luis de Góngora y Argote*. Madrid: Tip. de la "Revista de Archivos, Biblioteca, y Museos."
Alston, G. Cyprian
  1912 Way of the cross. In *The Catholic encyclopedia*, XV, 569–571. New York: The Encyclopedia Press, Inc.
Anderson, Arthur J. O., and Charles E. Dibble, trans.
  1951 *General history of the things of New Spain; Florentine codex*, by Fray Bernardino de Sahagún. Santa Fe, N.M.: School of American Research.
Baluarte de la libertad, El
  1867–1870 [Two-sheet weekly newspaper, published in Chiapa de Corzo, of which the Latin American Library of Tulane University has an incomplete file from July 6, 1867, to September 22, 1870.]
Barlow, Robert H.
  1949 *The extent of the empire of the Culhua Mexica*. Ibero-Americana 28. Berkeley: University of California Press.

Barrera Vázquez, Alfredo

1965   *El libro de los cantares de Dzitbalché.* Instituto Nacional de Antropología e Historia Serie Investigaciones 9. Mexico City.

Beals, Ralph L.

1945   *The contemporary culture of the Cáhita Indians.* Bureau of American Ethnology Bulletin 142. Washington, D.C.

1946   *Cherán: A sierra Tarascan village.* Smithsonian Institution, Institute of Social Anthropology Publication 2. Washington, D.C.

1951   *Ethnology of the western Mixe.* University of California Publications in American Archaeology and Ethnology 42. Berkeley.

Bennett, Wendell C., and Robert M. Zingg

1935   *The Tarahumara: An Indian tribe of northern Mexico.* Chicago: University of Chicago Press.

Blom, Frans F.

1956   Vida precortesiana del indio Chiapaneco de hoy. In *Estudios antropológicos publicados en homenaje al Doctor Manuel Gamio,* pp. 277–285. Mexico City: Universidad Nacional Autónoma de México.

Bode, Barbara

1961   *The dance of the conquest of Guatemala,* pp. 209–292. Middle American Research Institute Publication 27. New Orleans.

Bork, Albert W.

1949   *Versos del sombrero blanco.* University of Arizona Bulletin 20(2). Tucson.

Brand, Donald D.

1951   *Quiroga: A Mexican municipio.* Smithsonian Institution, Institute of Social Anthropology Publication 11. Washington, D.C.

Brasseur de Bourbourg, Charles E.

1862   *Rabinal-Achi ou le drame-ballet de tun.* Paris: Arthus Bertrand.

Bricker, Victoria R.

n.d.*a*   The ethnographic context of some traditional Mayan speech genres. In *Explorations in the ethnography of speaking,* edited by R. Bauman and J. Sherzer. Cambridge: Cambridge University Press (in press).

n.d.*b*   A Maya passion. Unpublished manuscript.

1968   The meaning of laughter in Zinacantan: An analysis of the humor of a highland Maya community. Ph.D. dissertation, Harvard University.

Brinton, Daniel G.
1883 *The güegüence: A comedy ballet in the Nahuatl-Spanish dialect of Nicaragua.* Brinton's Library of Aboriginal American Literature, no. 3. Philadelphia: D. G. Brinton.

Bunzel, Ruth
1952 *Chichicastenango: A Guatemalan village.* Publications of the American Ethnological Society 12. Locust Valley, N.Y.: J. S. Augustin.

Bustamante, Carlos María
1841 *Historia de la compañía de Jesús en Nueva-España, que estaba escribiendo el P. Francisco Javier Alegre al tiempo de su expulsion.* 3 vols. Mexico City: Imp. de J. M. Lara.

Cáceres López, Carlos
1946 *Chiapas: Síntesis geográfica e historica.* Mexico City: Editorial Forum.
1962 *Chiapas y su aportación a la república durante la reforma e intervención Francesa 1858–1864.* Colección del Congreso Nacional de Historia para el estudio de la Guerra de Intervención 4. Mexico City.

Calnek, Edward E.
1962 Highland Chiapas before the Spanish conquest. Ph.D. dissertation, University of Chicago.

Cámara Barbachano, Fernando
1966 *Persistencia y cambio cultural entre Tzeltales de los altos de Chiapas.* Escuela Nacional de Antropología e Historia Sociedad de Alumnos: Acta Anthropológica [*sic*] Epoca 2a, 3(1). Mexico City.

Cancian, Frank
1965 *Economics and prestige in a Maya community: The religious cargo system in Zinacantan.* Stanford: Stanford University Press.

Carrasco, Pedro
1952 *Tarascan folk religion: An analysis of economic, social, and religious interactions,* pp. 1–64. Middle American Research Institute Publication 17. New Orleans.

Castro, Carlo Antonio
1962 Una relación Tzeltal del Carnaval de Oxchuc. *Estudios de Cultura Maya* 2:37–44.

Clavigero, Francesco Saverio
   1787   *The history of Mexico.* Translated by Charles Cullen. London:
          G. G. J. and J. Robinson.
Codex Ramírez.
   See Ramírez, Codex.
Coe, Michael D.
   1965   A model of ancient community structure in the Maya lowlands.
          Southwestern Journal of Anthropology 21:97–114.
Corzo, Angel M.
   1943   *Historia de Chiapas: La leyenda de la patria.* Mexico City: Edi-
          torial "Protos."
Cuyás, Arturo
   1904   *Appleton's new Spanish-English and English-Spanish dictionary.*
          New York: D. Appleton and Company.
Dabbs, Jack Autrey
   1963   *The French army in Mexico, 1861–1867: A study in military gov-
          ernment.* The Hague: Mouton and Co.
de la Fuente, Julio
   1949   *Yalalag: Una villa Zapoteca serrana.* Mexico City: Museo Na-
          cional de Antropología.
Díaz del Castillo, Bernal
   1904   *Historia verdadera de la conquista de nueva España.* Genaro García
          edition. 2 vols. Mexico City: Oficina Tip. de la Secretaría de
          Fomento.
   1927   *The true history of the conquest of Mexico.* Translated by Maurice
          Keatinge. New York: Robert McBride and Co.
Durán, Fray Diego
   1967   *Historia de las Indias de nueva España e islas de la tierra firme,*
          edited by Angel María Garibay. 2 vols. Mexico City: Editorial
          Porrua.
Early, John D.
   1965   The sons of San Lorenzo in Zinacantan. Ph.D. dissertation, Har-
          vard University.
Edmonson, Munro S.
   1952   Los manitos: Patterns of humor in relation to cultural values.
          Ph.D. dissertation, Harvard University.
   1971   *The book of counsel: Popol vuh.* Middle American Research In-
          stitute Publication 35. New Orleans.

Espinosa, Aurelio M.

1935   New Mexican Spanish *coplas populares*. *Hispania* 18(1):135–150.

Everett, Helen

1931   Social control. In *Encyclopaedia of the social sciences*, edited by E. R. A. Seligman and Alvin Johnson, IV, 344–348. New York: Macmillan.

Flores Ruíz, Timoteo

1939[?]   *La guerra de castas en el año de 1869.* [In Latin American Library, Tulane University.]

Foster, George M.

1948   *Empire's children: The people of Tzintzuntzan.* Smithsonian Institution, Institute of Social Anthropology Publication 6. Washington, D.C.

Fuentes y Guzmán, Francisco Antonio

1882   *Historia de Guatemala; ó, Recordación florida; escrita el siglo XVII por el Capitán D. Francisco Antonio de Fuentes y Guzmán.* Madrid: Luis Navarro.

Gamio, Manuel

1922   *La población del valle de Teotihuacán, el medio en que se ha desarrollado; su evolución étnica y social; iniciativa para procurar su mejoramiento.* Mexico City: Dirección de Talleres Gráficos, Secretaría de Educación Pública.

Gillmor, Frances

1942   *Spanish texts of three dance dramas from Mexican villages.* University of Arizona Bulletin 13(4). Tucson.

1943   *The dance dramas of Mexican villages.* University of Arizona Bulletin 14(2). Tucson.

Goffman, Erving

1956   The nature of deference and demeanor. *American Anthropologist* 58:473–502.

1959   *The presentation of self in everyday life.* New York: Doubleday Anchor.

Gossen, Gary H.

n.d.   Chamula folktale texts. Manuscript.

1970   Time and space in Chamula oral tradition. Ph.D. dissertation, Harvard University.

Greenleaf, Richard E.

1965   The inquisition and the Indians of New Spain: A study in jurisdictional confusion. *The Americas: A Quarterly Review of Inter-American Cultural History* 22:138–166.

1969 *The Mexican inquisition of the sixteenth century.* Albuquerque: University of New Mexico Press.

Guiteras-Holmes, Calixta

1946 *Informe de San Pedro Chenalhó.* Manuscripts on Middle American Cultural Anthropology, no. 14. The University of Chicago Library.

1961 *Perils of the soul: The world view of a Tzotzil Indian.* New York: Free Press of Glencoe.

Haile, Berard

1946 *The Navaho fire dance or corral dance: A brief account of its practice and meaning.* St. Michaels, Arizona: St. Michaels Press.

Hammond, Peter B.

1964 Mossi joking. *Ethnology* 3:259–267.

Herrera, Antonio

1934 *Historia general de los hechos de los Castellanos en las islas y tierra firme del mar océano.* Madrid: Tip. de Archivos.

Holden, W. C.; C. C. Seltzer; R. A. Studhalter; C. T. Wagner; and W. G. McMillan

1936 *Studies of the Yaqui Indians of Sonora, Mexico.* Texas Technological Bulletin, Scientific Series no. 2, 12(1). Lubbock.

Holland, William

1963 *Medicina Maya en los altos de Chiapas: Un estudio del cambio socio-cultural.* Instituto Nacional Indigenista: Colección de Antropología Social 2. Mexico City.

Ichon, Alain

1969 *La religion des Totonaques de la sierra.* Paris: Centre National de la Recherche Scientifique.

Jijena Sánchez, Rafael, and Arturo López Peña

1965 *Cancionero de coplas: Antología de la copla en América.* Buenos Aires: Librería Huemul.

Johnson, Jean B.

1950 *The Opata: An inland tribe of Sonora.* Albuquerque: University of New Mexico Press.

Kurath, Gertrude Prokosch

1949 Mexican moriscas: A problem in dance acculturation. *Journal of American Folklore* 62:87–106.

La Farge, Oliver

    1947   *Santa Eulalia.* Chicago: University of Chicago Press.

————, and Douglas Byers

    1931   *The year bearer's people.* Middle American Research Institute Publication 3. New Orleans.

Lange, Charles H.

    1959   *Cochiti: A New Mexico pueblo, past and present.* Austin: University of Texas Press.

Las Casas, Fray Bartolomé de

    1967   *Apologética historia sumaria.* 2 vols. Universidad Nacional Autónoma de México, Instituto de Investigaciones Históricas. Mexico City.

Laughlin, Robert M.

    n.d.   Zinacanteco folktale texts. Manuscript.

    1960   Cultural symbols in the oral literature of Zinacantan. Manuscript.

    1962   El símbolo de la flor en la religión de Zinacantán. *Estudios de Cultura Maya* 2:123–139.

    1973   *The great Tzotzil dictionary of San Lorenzo Zinacantan.* Smithsonian Institution: Smithsonian Contributions to Anthropology. Washington, D.C.

Leach, Edmund R.

    1964   Anthropological aspects of language: Animal categories and verbal abuse. In *New directions in the study of language,* edited by Eric H. Lenneberg. Cambridge: M.I.T. Press.

León Portilla, Miguel

    1969   *Pre-Columbian literatures of Mexico.* Norman: University of Oklahoma Press.

Lévi-Strauss, Claude

    1966   *The savage mind.* Chicago: University of Chicago Press.

Lizana, Fray Bernardo de

    1893   *Historia de Yucatán.* Mexico City: Imp. del Museo Nacional. [Originally published in 1633.]

López de Gómara, Francisco

    1943   *Historia de la conquista de México.* 2 vols. Mexico City: Editorial Pedro Robredo.

López Gutiérrez, Gustavo

    1963   Chiapas en defensa de la patria: Su participación ante la intervención francesa. In *Linares, Sinaloa, Durango, Tabasco, y Chiapas en la guerra de intervención,* pp. 131–228. Colección de Congreso Nacional de la guerra de Intervención 27. Mexico City.

Lothrop, Samuel K.
   1929   Further notes on Indian ceremonies in Guatemala. *Indian Notes* 6(1):1–25.

Lumholtz, Carl
   1902   *Unknown Mexico.* 2 vols. New York: Charles Scribner and Sons.

Madsen, William
   1960   *The Virgin's children: Life in an Aztec village today.* Austin: University of Texas Press.

Malinowski, Bronislaw
   1926   *Crime and custom in savage society.* London: Routledge and Kegan Paul.

Martí, Samuel
   1961   *Canto, danza y música precortesianos.* Mexico City: Fondo de Cultura Económica.

Martin, Paul
   1963   *Le costume militaire. Military costume: A short history. Der bunte Rock.* Stuttgart: Franckh'sche Verlagshandlung.

Matthews, Washington
   1902   *The night chant.* Memoirs of the American Museum of Natural History 6. New York.

Means, Philip Ainsworth
   1917   *History of the Spanish conquest of Yucatan and of the Itzas.* Papers of the Peabody Museum of American Archaeology and Ethnology, Harvard University 7. Cambridge, Mass.

Metzger, Barbara
   n.d.   Notes on the history of Indian-Ladino relations in Chiapas. Unpublished manuscript.

Michoacán, Relación de.
   See Relación de Michoacán.

Miller, Frank C.
   n.d.   Huistán field notes.

Molina, Cristóbal
   1934   *War of the castes: Indian uprisings in Chiapas, 1867–70.* Translated by Ernest Noyes and Dolores Morgadanes. Middle American Research Institute Publication 5, no. 8. New Orleans.

Molina Solís, Juan Francisco
    1896   *Historia del descubrimiento y conquista de Yucatán.* Merida: Imp. E. Caballero.

Morley, Sylvanus G.
    1946   *The ancient Maya.* Stanford: Stanford University Press.

Nash, June
    1970   *In the eyes of the ancestors: Belief and behavior in a Maya community.* New Haven: Yale University Press.

Nuñez de la Vega, Fray Francisco
    1692   *Constituciones diocesanas del obispado de Chiappa.* Rome: Caietano Zenobi.

Orantes, Teofilo H.
    1960   *Síntesis de hechos históricos del estado de Chiapas.* Mexico City.

Pacheco Cruz, Santiago
    1947   *Usos, costumbres, religión i supersticiones de los Mayas.* Merida.

Paniagua, F. A.
    1870   *Una rosa y dos espinas: Memorias del imperio en Chiapas.* San Cristobal: Porvenir.

Parsons, Elsie Clews
    1929   *The social organization of the Tewa of New Mexico.* Memoirs of the American Anthropological Association 36. Menasha, Wisc.

    1930   Spanish elements in the Kachina cult of the Pueblos. In *Proceedings of the twenty-third International Congress of Americanists, New York, 1928,* pp. 582–603. New York.

    1932   Folklore from Santa Ana Xalmimilulco, Puebla, Mexico. *Journal of American Folklore* 45:318–362.

    1936   *Mitla, town of the souls.* Chicago: University of Chicago Press.

————, and Ralph L. Beals
    1934   The sacred clowns of the Pueblo and Mayo-Yaqui Indians. *American Anthropologist* 36:491–514.

Paso y Troncoso, Francisco del
    1902   Comédies en langue naualt. *Compte rendu du Congrès International des Américanistes, XIIIᵉ session, Paris 1900,* pp. 309–316. Paris.

Pineda, Vicente
    1888   *Historia de las sublevaciones indígenas habidas en el estado de Chiapas.* Chiapas: Tip. del Gobierno.

Pitt-Rivers, Julian
    1961   *The people of the sierra.* Chicago: University of Chicago Press.

Ponce, Fray Alonso

1875   *Relación breve y verdadera de algunas cosas de las muchas que sucedieron en las provincias de Nueva España, siendo comisario general de aquellas partes (1584–1588)*. Madrid: Imp. de la Vda. de Calero.

Pozas, Ricardo

1959   *Chamula, un pueblo indio de los altos de Chiapas*. Memorias del Instituto Nacional Indigenista 8. Mexico City.

Radcliffe-Brown, A. R.

1934   Social sanctions. In *Encyclopaedia of the social sciences*, edited by E. R. A. Seligman and Alvin Johnson, XIII, 513–534. New York: Macmillan.

Ramírez, Codex

1944   *Relación del origen de los indios que habitan esta Nueva España según sus historias*. Mexico City: Editorial Leyenda.

Rangel, Nicolás

1924   *Historia del toreo en México, época colonial* [*1529–1821*]. Mexico City: Imp. M. L. Sánchez.

Ravicz, Marilyn Ekdahl

1970   *Early colonial religious drama in Mexico: From Tzompantli to Golgotha*. Washington, D.C.: The Catholic University of America Press.

Redfield, Robert

1930   *Tepoztlán, a Mexican village*. Chicago: University of Chicago Press.

1936   The coati and the ceiba. *Maya Research* 3:231–243.

1941   *The folk culture of Yucatan*. Chicago: University of Chicago Press.

————, and Alfonso Villa Rojas

1934   *Chan Kom: A Maya village*. Carnegie Institution of Washington Publication 448. Washington, D.C.

1939   Notes on the ethnography of Tzeltal communities of Chiapas. In *Contributions to American Anthropology and History* no. 28, pp. 105–119. Carnegie Institution of Washington Publication 509. Washington, D.C.

Reed, Nelson

1964   *The caste war of Yucatan*. Stanford: Stanford University Press.

Relación de Michoacán

1903 *Relación de las ceremonias y ritos y gobernación de los indios de la provincia de Mechuacan.* Morelia: Tip. de Alfonso Aragon. [Originally published in 1541.]

Remesal, Fray Antonio de

1932 *Historia general de las Indias occidentales y particular de la gobernación de Chiapa y Guatemala.* Biblioteca Goathemala, vols. 4 and 5. Guatemala City.

Reynolds, Dorothy

1956 Guatemalan dances at colorful highland festivals. *Américas* 8(1): 31–35.

Ricard, Robert

1932 Contribution à l'étude des fêtes de "Moros y Cristianos" au Mexique. *Journal de la Société des Américanistes* n.s.24:51–84.

Rodríguez Marín, Francisco

1882 *Cantos populares españoles.* 5 vols. Sevilla.

1927 *Miscelánea de Andalucía.* Biblioteca Giralda. Madrid: Editorial Páez.

Roys, Ralph L.

1933 *Chilam Balam of Chumayel.* Carnegie Institution of Washington Publication 438. Washington, D.C.

1943 *The Indian background of colonial Yucatan.* Carnegie Institution of Washington Publication 548. Washington, D.C.

Sahagún, Fray Bernardino de

See Anderson, J. O., and Charles E. Dibble, trans.

Sapper, Carl

1897 *Das nördliche Mittel-Amerika nebst einem Ausflug nach dem Hochland von Anahuac: Reisen und Studien aus den Jahren 1888–1895.* Braunschweig: Friedrich Vieweg und Sohn.

Siverts, Hennig

1969 Ethnic stability and boundary dynamics in southern Mexico. In *Ethnic groups and boundaries,* edited by Fredrik Barth, pp. 101–116. Boston: Little, Brown and Company.

Slotkin, J. S.

1950 *Social anthropology.* New York: Macmillan.

Spicer, Edward H.

1940 *Pascua: A Yaqui village in Arizona.* Chicago: University of Chicago Press.

1954   *Potam: A Yaqui village in Sonora.* Memoirs of the American Anthropological Association 77. Menasha, Wisc.

Starr, Frederick
1908   *In Indian Mexico: A narrative of travel and labor.* Chicago: Forbes and Company.

Steck, Francis Borgia
1951   *Motolinia's history of the Indians of New Spain.* Washington: Academy of American Franciscan History.

Stephen, Alexander M.
1936   *Hopi journal.* Columbia University Contributions in Anthropology 23. New York.

Stephens, John L.
1843   *Incidents of travel in Yucatan.* 2 vols. New York: Harper and Brothers.

Steward, Julian
1931   The ceremonial buffoon of the American Indian. *Papers of the Michigan Academy of Science, Arts and Letters* 14:187–207.

Termer, Franz
1930   Zur Ethnologie und Ethnographie des nördlichen Mittelamerika. *Ibero-amerikanisches Archiv* 4(3):303–492.

Thompson, J. Eric S.
1930   *Ethnology of the Mayas of southern and central British Honduras.* Field Museum of Natural History Anthropological Series 17(2). Chicago.

1970   *Maya history and religion.* Norman: University of Oklahoma Press.

Toor, Frances
1925   The passion play at Tzintzuntzan. *Mexican Folkways* 1(1):21–25.
1929   Carnavales en los pueblos. *Mexican Folkways* 5(1):10–27.

Torquemada, Fray Juan de
1943   *Monarquía indiana.* 3 vols. Mexico City: S. Chávez Hayhoe.

Tozzer, Alfred M.
1941   *Landa's relación de las cosas de Yucatan.* Papers of the Peabody Museum of American Archaeology and Ethnology, Harvard University 18. Cambridge, Mass.

1957   *Chichen Itza and its cenote of sacrifice.* Memoirs of the Peabody Museum of Archaeology and Ethnology, Harvard University 11, 12. Cambridge, Mass.

Vázquez Santana, Higinio
1940 *Fiestas y costumbres mexicanas.* Mexico City: Ediciones Botas.
——, and J. Ignacio Dávila Garibi
1931 *El carnaval.* Mexico City: Talleres Gráficos de la Nación.
Villagutierre Soto-Mayor, Juan de
1933 *Historia de la conquista de la provincia de el Itzá reducción, y progresos de la de el Lacandon, y otras naciones de indios bárbaros, de la mediaciones de el reyno de Guatimala, a las provincias de Yucatán, en la América septentrional.* 2d ed. Guatemala: Biblioteca "Goathemala" de la Sociedad de Geografía e Historia. [Originally published in 1701.]
Villa Rojas, Alfonso
1945 *The Maya of east central Quintana Roo.* Carnegie Institution of Washington Publication 559. Washington, D.C.
Vogt, Evon Z.
1965 Zinacanteco "souls." *Man* 29:33–35.
1969 *Zinacantan: A Maya community in the highlands of Chiapas.* Cambridge: Belknap Press.
Wagley, Charles
1949 *The social and religious life of a Guatemalan village.* Memoirs of the American Anthropological Association 71. Menasha, Wisc.
Willey, Gordon R.
1966 *An introduction to American archaeology,* vol. 1: *North and middle America.* Englewood Cliffs: Prentice-Hall.
Wilson, Carter
1966 *Crazy February.* Philadelphia and New York: J. B. Lippincott Company.
1972 *A green tree and a dry tree.* New York: Macmillan.
Wisdom, Charles
1940 *The Chorti Indians of Guatemala.* Chicago: University of Chicago Press.
Zabala, Manuel T.
n.d. Fieldnotes on Zinacantan.
1961 Instituciones políticas y religiosas de Zinacantan. *Estudios de Cultura Maya* 1:147–158.

INDEX